MEXICAN GOVERNMENT

AND INDUSTRIAL DEVELOPMENT

IN THE EARLY REPUBLIC

MEXICAN GOVERNMENT

AND INDUSTRIAL DEVELOPMENT

IN THE EARLY REPUBLIC

THE BANCO DE AVIO

ROBERT A. POTASH

The University of Massachusetts Press
Amherst, 1983

This is a revised and expanded English-language edition of a book
first published by Fondo de Cultura Economica under the title
El Banco de Avío de México: El fomento de la industria 1821 – 1846.
Copyright © 1959 by Fondo de Cultura Económica
Bibliographical postscript and other additions to the English-language
edition © 1983 by The University of Massachusetts Press
Printed in the United States of America   ISBN 0 – 87023 – 382 – 3
Library of Congress Cataloging in Publication Data
Potash, Robert A., 1921 –
Mexican government and industrial development in the early republic.
Revised translation of: El Banco de Avío de México.
Bibliography: p.
Includes index.
1. Banco de Avío—History. 2. Mexico—Industries—
History. I. Title.
HG2718.P6713   1983   332.2   82 – 15969
ISBN 0 – 87023 – 382 – 3

FOR CHARLES GIBSON
SCHOLAR AND FRIEND

CONTENTS

PREFACE TO THE ENGLISH EDITION

This work is a reedition of a volume that appeared initially in Spanish under the title *El Banco de Avío de México: El fomento de la industria 1821–1846* (México: Fondo de Cultura Económica, 1959). For over a decade, until the last copies disappeared from the publisher's inventory, scholars and students in Mexico and selected readers in the United States turned to it for information about the political economy of Mexico's Early Republic. The decision to issue an English edition of this work is premised on the belief that new generations of readers, especially those interested in the developing world, might profit from a volume that was not written to prove or disprove a particular theory of development or underdevelopment, but rather to find out, on the basis of archival research, why and how a newly independent state, born into an era of international and domestic tensions, made the economic policy choices it did. An examination of the factors that shaped policy making in independent Mexico, and of the obstacles that confronted its attempts to translate policy into practice might provide insights into the postindependence problems that have confronted recently emancipated states, no matter what the century or the continent.

This English-language edition differs only in minor respects from the earlier Spanish edition. The principal changes occur in chapter 12, where certain observations about the cotton textile industry have been adjusted to embody the results of newer research. However, in order to enable the reader to place this book in the context of what has been published on the Early Republic since the Spanish edition, a postscript has been added in the form of a historiographical essay that examines writings that have appeared since 1960 on the economic history of that period.

Amherst, Massachusetts
February 1982

FOREWORD

Since about 1940, Mexico has been the scene of an intensive effort to build an industrial economy, an effort in which public agencies and public capital have played leading roles. Through such institutions as the Nacional Financiera, the government has sought to encourage once-reluctant private capital to invest in the industrial field, while through other entities like Petróleos Mexicanos and the Comisión Federal de Electricidad, it directly operates important sectors of the economy. To some, the Mexican government's active promotion of industrial development may seem to be a twentieth-century phenomenon without precedent in that nation's history. Actually, the present century is witnessing a new phase of an effort that began shortly after the country gained its independence.

Before the Mexican Republic was ten years old, its governors had decided that the new manufacturing technology developed in Europe and elsewhere in the eighteenth and early nineteenth centuries should be introduced into the country; they had also concluded that action by the state was necessary if the desired changes were to be realized.

The purpose of the present study is to examine why those decisions were reached, and to explore the steps that were taken in consequence. Essentially, this has meant studying the agency established to implement the government's industrial plans, an agency known as the Banco de Avío. References to the Banco de Avío may be found in a variety of works, but no full-scale study of its origin, operations, and accomplishments has ever been made. Such a study will constitute the primary theme of the following pages. But because the impact of the state on industrial development was not limited to the activities of the Banco de Avío, consideration will also be given to other aspects of government policy, especially the role of the tariff.

It might be pointed out at the start that the industry with which this study will be chiefly concerned is the textile industry, which had reached the highest stage of development in the colonial era, and which was the industry around which most of the government's efforts centered.

I wish to acknowledge here my intellectual indebtedness to two former teachers and friends, both now dead, who first aroused my interest in Latin America and who provided staunch support for the project that became this book: Clarence H. Haring and Howard F. Cline. I would also like to express my appreciation to Lewis Hanke, who, as director of the Hispanic Foundation of the Library of Congress at the time I undertook the original research, was very sensitive to the needs of an aspiring scholar for both practical advice and words of encouragement. Even though we are now colleagues at the University of Massachusetts, and are both chronologically older, I still profit from his wisdom and experience.

To all those in Mexico who contributed their time and knowledge to the completion of this study I would like to express my thanks, in particular to the staffs of the Archivo General de la Nación, Archivo Histórico de Hacienda, and Biblioteca Histórica de Hacienda, to two pioneer economic historians of the Early Republic, Luis Chávez Orozco and Miguel A. Quintana. Finally, to my wife, Jeanne, who assisted with both the original study and its present reincarnation, belongs my deepest gratitude.

R. A. P.

1

THE COLONIAL HERITAGE

The achievement of independence in 1821 confronted Mexico with an economic crisis. The decade of internecine war had destroyed property, interrupted normal communications, and uprooted men from their traditional occupations. This in itself would have presented a new government with tasks of overwhelming gravity; but a further factor contributing to economic dislocation was the wrenching of political ties with an empire in which Mexico had long been an integral part, and the consequent breakdown of well-established patterns of trade.

The plight of the mining industry and the steps taken to remedy it are fairly well known to students of Mexican history, if only because this was the industry in which foreigners and foreign capital were most interested. Generally disregarded, however, but certainly essential to an understanding of the country and its people in the troubled years after independence, was the situation in other sectors of the economy. Agriculture no less than mining had suffered from the events of the disastrous decade; and what was true of these fields was also true to an equal, if not greater, extent of the handicraft industries. In order to understand the significance of these handicrafts in the general economy, and to comprehend the full extent of their predicament in 1821, it is well to examine their growth and organization in the preceding two decades.

Artisan labor employing hand methods was responsible for a considerable variety of manufactured articles used personally and in homes; but by far the most important handicraft, both in terms of the number of individuals participating and in terms of the value of the goods produced, was the fabrication of textiles. It is therefore to the manufacture of textiles that attention will be directed.

In using the term *textile industry*, a distinction should be made between the production of goods for immediate consumption and the production of goods for sale. A large part of the Indian population produced cloth for household use, but this industry was an adjunct of other activities, and was not engaged in specifically as a means of obtaining a livelihood. Here we are interested only in the manufacture of textiles that entered into trade.[1]

It is well known that the Spanish imperial government was not anxious to have colonial manufacturing industries develop that might compete with those of the peninsula. What is sometimes overlooked, however, is that the commercial and fiscal policies of the mother country, whether intentionally or not, actually did encourage the growth of textile manufacturing in New Spain. The monopoly of colonial trade, exercised with government support by a small group of Andalusian merchants, had served to maintain the price of textiles legally introduced into New Spain at levels far beyond the reach of all but the top ranks of society. Moreover, the officially approved system of freight charges, which were based on bulk instead of value, induced merchants to prefer articles of high cost and low volume. The result was that imported textiles tended to be the finer material that appealed to the few, rather than the ordinary stuffs needed by the many. It is true that the goods so imported were not the only ones introduced into the country. A brisk trade in smuggled textiles had grown up in the shadow of the law. But even the articles imported furtively had to conform in class and quality to the legal entries if they were to escape detection at the frequent inspection points in the interior of the country.[2] The upshot was that the vast majority of the inhabitants were prevented by price from utilizing imported goods, and were thus compelled, save for those who lived in self-sufficient households, to depend on the cloth woven in the shops and factories of New Spain. These coarse-quality cotton and woolen stuffs consequently enjoyed what was tantamount to a protective tariff in the considerable market constituted by the lower classes.

Even the extension to New Spain of the provisions of the so-called free-trade ordinance of 1778 does not appear to have injured the domestic textile industry. The duties on foreign textiles imported into the colony via the ports of the mother country were still so high as to continue limiting their consumption to the upper classes.[3] Moreover, under the provisions of the ordinance, cotton goods of foreign make were completely forbidden to enter the colony; and cotton, as we shall see presently, was one of the principal materials worked up on the looms of New Spain.[4]

The ordinance did, it is true, reduce the duties on Spanish fabrics exported to the colony,[5] and this, together with the liberalization of shipping regulations, should have facilitated the sale of those products. However, the cloth industry of the colony still prospered, partially because of the continued profiteering of the merchants who handled the imported fabrics, but especially because of the effects of the *alcabala* or sales tax.[6] This duty, at the rate of 3 percent, was first collected at the port of entry, regardless of the actual sale of the goods; moreover, at each subsequent transfer into the interior, again regardless of actual sale, a further alcabala of 6 percent was collected on the articles. The result of this repetitious exaction was to create, in the words of the younger Revillagigedo, "a kind of premium or encouragement to domestic goods which are not subject to such burdens."[7] To this tax the viceroy specifically ascribed the growth of the woolen factories in the interior towns of Querétaro and San Miguel el Grande.[8]

Although the trade and tax measures of the mother country helped insure a market for the textiles made in New Spain, factors indigenous to the colony also played their part in encouraging cloth manufacture. One of these was the need that workers had for employment. Despite the notorious scarcity of labor in tropical agricultural regions or in some mining areas, the situation was quite the reverse around the cities and towns of the central plateau.[9] The redundancy of labor there made it only natural for individuals who were unable to work in the mines or in the fields to turn to handicrafts as a means of supporting themselves. Viceroy Revillagigedo was quick to notice this and to realize that no law could ever prevent such people from engaging in manufacturing.[10]

Another factor contributing to the growth of cloth making was the availability of raw materials. The wool and cotton raised in New Spain required an outlet, and the authorities in Spain had been quite anxious to have these materials shipped to the factories in the mother country.[11] But the high cost of transporting such bulky items from the interior to Veracruz served effectively to limit their export. In the case of wool, the relatively poor quality of the domestic clip was an added deterrent to sale overseas. The consequent necessity of finding a market for the wool and cotton further induced the development of a local textile industry.[12]

At the close of the eighteenth century, the handicraft textile industry of New Spain was devoted primarily to the production of cotton and woolen cloth. Silk manufacture, once an important industry in the sixteenth century, had all but vanished, and only a handful of looms were still devoted to that material.[13] In fact, in Mexico City silk weavers were reduced to making cotton fabrics mixed with a few silk threads, despite the fact that their own guild ordinances, proudly formulated in more prosperous times, still forbade the mixture of silk with lesser materials.[14]

The manufacture of cottons and woolens was carried out in producing units that varied in size from the single home-operated loom to the factory, or *obraje*, with its scores of workers. The obrajes were more characteristic of woolen manufacture than of cotton, and appear to have specialized in the volume production of solid-color cloth *(paño)*, leaving the multi-color outer garments worn in the higher altitudes, the *serapes* and *frezadas*, to the smaller shops. The typical producing unit in the manufacture of cotton was the craft shop, or *obrador*, and its most important products were the plainly woven coarse cloth known as *manta*, and the special shawl worn by Mexican women of every class, the *rebozo*.

The obrajes, as befitted an institution that had grown up on the margin of the law, were subject to special viceregal regulations, but these regulations had less to do with the techniques of production than with the selection and treatment of workers. The regulations, periodically reissued, set forth an ideal from which the practice often diverged quite sharply. Despite prohibitions against the enclosure of workers within the obrajes, the assignment to them of criminals, and the arbitrary administration of punishments by their owners or foremen,[15] such practices continued openly according to the testimony of Baron von Humboldt, who visited the Querétaro factories at the turn of the century.[16] Yet in the interests of a balanced judgment, it should be pointed out that the European scientist saw the obraje at its worst. The owners of the Querétaro factories, for some reason, had long been able to avoid the enforcement of the protective regulations.[17] But in other communities, notably Puebla and Valladolid, it is clear that the regulations were better enforced. There it was the employers who were complaining about the liberties taken by the workers, charging them with engaging in such practices as taking long week ends, accepting monetary advances from two prospective employers at the same time, and stealing wool from the obraje to weave at home and sell in competition with the factory.[18]

In contrast to the obrajes, the craft shops, where most of the cotton cloth was produced, were subject to rigid production requirements. Guild ordinances issued on a municipal basis, but with the approval of the viceroy and the monarch, regulated the output of these shops, specifying such details as the length, breadth, and number of threads for each of the basic types and grades of cotton cloth they offered to the public. Even the size of the loom that might be used for each grade of cloth was subject to strict regulation, narrower looms being used for the cheapest quality.

Guild ordinances were especially precise on the matter of loom ownership. Only qualified master weavers were allowed to possess looms, and in Mexico City the number permitted to any one master was no more than four.[19] It was not always possible to enforce this rule, however, as is indicated by a survey made in the capital in 1796 which revealed that several individuals, including some who were rank outsiders to the guild, had as many as twelve and fourteen looms.[20]

The restrictive features of guild regulations, in regard to both loom ownership and nature of output, could not fail to arouse objections. In Mexico City starting in 1791 a campaign got underway within the cotton guild to reform its ordinances in order to curtail those provisions that restricted production. Periodically over the next two decades, proposals for reform were put forth by guild members, but not until 1810 was anything substantial achieved.[21] In that year, the advisers to the viceroy —pointing out that the guild as it was then constituted stood in the way of expanding and perfecting industry—urged him to approve a revision of the ordinances that would restrict the guild's function principally to the training of apprentices.[22] Viceroy Venegas agreed, and ordered the drawing up of new regulations that eliminated all reference to production techniques, allowed Indians and women to engage in weaving without interference from the guild, and dropped the former limitation on loom ownership by guild members.[23] This radical change in the spirit of the guild ordinances came, however, on the very eve of the revolution, and had no observable effect on the progress of cotton manufacture. It is significant, nevertheless, in demonstrating that the highest authorities of the colony had become aware of the defects of the guild system and that finally, if belatedly, they tried to remedy them.

The volume and variety of textiles produced in New Spain were far from static in the twenty years prior to the outbreak of the revolution. This was the period of the Napoleonic Wars in Europe, and the effects of the conflict were felt in the colony in the form of economic isolation from the motherland. The cutting off of communications between New and Old Spain served to encourage the expansion of textile manufacture, though much of the progress achieved in the industry was subsequently lost in the intervals of peace.[24]

In 1793, the principal wool-weaving centers were Querétaro, Valladolid, San Miguel, and Acámbaro. Querétaro, with its score of obrajes, which alone employed 1,500 people, and its several hundred moderate-sized shops, was by far the most important. In the manufacture of cottons, Puebla held the principal place with over eleven hundred looms in use within its limits. The cities of Oaxaca and México stood next in importance, but with only about half as many looms as those in Puebla.[25]

The surprising thing about the distribution of the handicraft textile industry at this time is the relative insignificance of the Guadalajara intendancy. Despite the fact that it was one of the most populous areas and that it raised both cotton and wool, this western province had traditionally sent these raw materials to places like Querétaro and Puebla, and had obtained from them the finished goods it needed.[26]

The decade after 1793, however, saw a transformation in the position of Guadalajara as a textile center. In 1803, it was reported that 20,000 individuals were engaged in full or part-time employment in the manufacture of textiles. The value of cotton-goods output for that year was fixed at $1,386,591 (the symbol $ stands for Mexican pesos; at this time they were equivalent in value to U.S. dollars), an amount practically equal to the normal product of Puebla, the principal cotton center of New Spain.[27]

Guadalajara was not the only area to enjoy an expansion in the fabrication of textiles. Certain of the older centers also benefited from the demand created by international wars. Valladolid, for example, in the four years between 1796 and 1800 saw almost three hundred new shops, including five obrajes, come into existence.[28] Querétaro, the woolen leader, also prospered. The steady growth of the industry there may be measured in the statistics for wool consumption, which rose from 46,000 *arrobas* (units of twenty-five pounds) in 1793 to 64,000 a decade later, and to 83,000 in 1808. At that time, 6,000 people were employed in the manufacture of textiles.[29]

Exactly how many were occupied in the entire country in the manufacture of textiles it is impossible to state. Spinning and weaving were practiced in varying degrees throughout the colony. But in the places mentioned above, textile manufacture constituted one of the principal, if not the chief, source of livelihood. In Puebla, for example, it was reported in 1803 that half the municipal population was devoted to cleaning and spinning cotton for the use of the city's 1,200 weavers.[30] In the light of this information, and what is known of textile employment in Guadalajara and Querétaro, it is not at all unlikely that the total number of people deriving a livelihood from the manufacture of textiles was in the vicinity of 60,000.[31]

The total value of textile output in New Spain prior to the outbreak of the revolution in 1810 is also a matter open to conjecture. Humboldt believed that the value of all manufactures, of which textiles constituted the largest single component, was only $7 to 8 million.[32] On the other hand, the secretary of the Veracruz *consulado*, José María Quirós, was of the opinion that the value of cotton and woolen textiles alone was in excess of $10 million.[33] His method in arriving at this figure, however, reveals it to be little more than a guess based on certain assumptions about the purchase of textiles rather than on knowledge of actual production.[34] Nevertheless, Quirós was not alone in believing that Humboldt's figure was too low. A modern writer has suggested that the value of the cloth manufactured within the colony amounted to $23 million, though he offers this figure as little more than an educated guess.[35] With present information, it is not possible to determine which of the cited figures most approximates the truth. It is not at all unlikely, however, that Humboldt's figures err on the conservative side, and that New Spain's cloth industry was much more important in terms of the value of its output than has generally been recognized.

In order to understand the predicament in which this industry found itself in 1821, it is well to examine the nature of its organization during the years of comparative prosperity prior to 1810. As mentioned earlier, the production of textiles was the work of units of varying size, ranging from single looms to large factories. However, in the cotton industry, which overshadowed that of wool in both output and number employed, practically all the producing units were small shops owned and operated by individual craftsmen. Nevertheless, despite the artisan character of this industry, merchant capital played a critical role in the development of the principal cotton-textile centers. This can be demonstrated by examining the organization of the cotton industry where it had reached the highest stage of development, in the intendancy of Puebla.

The intervention of Spanish merchants in the production of cotton cloth began at the raw-material level. The bulk of the cotton that kept the looms of Puebla artisans busy was drawn from the lowlands of Veracruz and Oaxaca. There the volume of cotton produced depended to great extent on the activities of the so-called *capitalista habilitador*, the merchant who advanced supplies to the farmer at the beginning of the growing season, and who normally took over his crop at harvest.[36] In some cases, Spanish merchants living in Puebla or Veracruz actually owned the land on which the cotton was raised, and absorbed the output of their own tenants.[37]

In either case, the cotton had to be transported long distances on muleback to the place of manufacture. Here again the merchant who had the capital or credit to finance the shipment and await the ultimate sale of the cotton played a vital role. The transportation alone required considerable funds because under the rates that prevailed prior to 1810 and even long after independence, the price for packing just one quintal (100 pounds) of cotton the ninety leagues from the port of Veracruz to the city of Puebla was about four pesos.[38] With cotton selling at the port city in 1810 at six to seven pesos,[39] one quintal of cotton deposited at Puebla was worth at least ten pesos. At such prices few artisans had any alternative but to obtain their cotton from the Spanish merchants who controlled the local supply.

It should be pointed out that the cotton that was transported up the mountain paths to Puebla was not ginned, but contained the seeds and miscellaneous matter of just-picked fibers. Because the extraneous matter, which ordinarily constituted about two-thirds of the weight, was eventually discarded as useless, it is clear that the freight cost borne by the useable fibers was three times what it should have been.[40] The price of these fibers at Puebla was thus needlessly inflated, and the amount of capital required to maintain an inventory of cotton was correspondingly increased.

The reason for this uneconomic system of shipping seed cotton from farm to city was the scarcity of labor in the regions where it was grown and the ignorance there of labor-saving devices. The mechanical cotton gin was completely unknown at the time of Humboldt's visit, but though one was subsequently set up on the Veracruz coast, it had little effect on the established system.[41] The apparent impossibility of finding the necessary labor in the hot and frequently unhealthy growing areas led to the transfer of the cleaning process to the manufacturing site.

In fact it was the cleaning of cotton, together with the various operations for preparing yarn, that accounted for the large numbers who gained their living in the cotton industry. The city of Puebla and its environs readily supplied the necessary workers for the processes preliminary to weaving, and, as mentioned earlier, more than half of the city's population was so engaged. Twelve hundred weavers absorbed the product of their labors.

The specialization of so large a number of people in the multiple activities connected with cloth manufacture obviously would have been impossible if the consumption of the finished goods, the mantas and rebozos, had been restricted to the needs of the local population, or even of those of the surrounding towns. Additional markets had to be found in other parts of the country to absorb the annual output. But the ordinary artisan weaver did not have the resources to engage in the risks and delays involved in sending goods for sale to distant regions. Unable to tie up his meager capital for long periods in unsold goods, he was forced to turn his output over to those merchant firms with the funds and facilities to engage in such trade.

As of 1803, there were twenty-eight such firms in the city of Puebla. *Almacenes de ropa de la tierra* they were called, specializing, as their name indicated, in the handling of domestic textiles. To these houses went not only much of the output of the cities' 1,200 looms, but also the cloth produced by the several hundred weavers who lived in the adjacent districts of Cholula, Huejotzingo, and Tlaxcala, and who turned their output over to commission agents acting for the Puebla firms.[42] The goods that were thus accumulated in small quantities went to make up the burden of the thousands of mules which annually plodded out of Puebla to all parts of the realm. To Mexico City alone, for sale there or for reshipment to other destinations, the annual volume of textiles shipped from Puebla in the period from 1790 to 1805 averaged 6,300 *tercios*, or in excess of 1,100,000 pounds.[43]

The role of the Spanish merchant in the cotton industry of Puebla was not restricted to the distribution of woven goods or to the procuring of raw materials; it even extended, though how far is not known, into the fields of actual production. Although guild ordinances forbade the ownership of looms by any but qualified master weavers, there is evidence that merchants directly financed journeymen to operate looms in their own homes free of the supervision of a master weaver.[44] The journeymen in such cases became little more than employees of the merchants, and their output, not infrequently substandard in quality, served to swell the volume of textiles annually dispatched to the *tierra adentro*.

From this examination of the manufacture of cottons in Puebla (and what was true there was in all likelihood typical of other large centers), it is clear that the cotton industry of New Spain, though artisan in form, was essentially a capitalistic enterprise. The fact that the characteristic unit of production was the small, owner-operated craft shop is put into proper perspective by noting that merchant capital organized the production and distribution of the raw materials and the sale of the finished product.

Thus it may be said that the prosperity of the handicraft textile industry of New Spain depended on two conditions: the first was the availability of Spanish mercantile capital; the other, which was discussed earlier in the chapter, was the persistence of a market from which foreign competition was excluded. Should either of these conditions change, the domestic industry would inevitably be faced with serious difficulties. But in the momentous decade that began in 1810, not one but both of the favoring factors disappeared.

The first hint of the impending collapse of the protected market enjoyed by Mexican textiles came during the Napoleonic Wars, even before the outbreak of the independence movement. In December 1804, the Spanish government, unable to maintain normal commercial contact with the colony in the face of British naval superiority, authorized neutral merchants in the United States to transport any kind of goods to the port of Veracruz.[45] For the next four years, non-Spanish vessels openly entered that port, unloading cargoes of which the largest single component was textiles. Though these goods tended to substitute for those normally supplied by Spanish merchants, the way was also thrown open for the introduction of types of cloth that could compete directly with locally made articles. The record of importations through Veracruz shows that of the textiles unloaded from 1806 to 1808, cotton goods were predominant, exceeding in value the more expensive linens, silks, and woolens. These cotton goods, moreover, included not only the finer qualities that would appeal to the wealthy few, but also cheap Asiatic fabrics that could substitute for the domestic product in meeting the needs of the lower classes.[46]

The cessation of the neutral permits in 1809 seemed to augur the restoration of the protective wall that had enabled the handicraft industry to subsist, but the eruption of violent revolution the following year led rather to the complete destruction of that wall. Over the course of the next decade, machine-made fabrics from Europe and cheap cloths from the Orient were able to enter New Spain in substantial quantities without the heavy duties established under Spanish trade regulations. The ports of San Blas on the Pacific and Tampico on the Atlantic became highways for foreign merchandise emanating from British possessions in the Caribbean or from Asia. Such goods passed into New Spain with the blessing of insurgent leaders, and even on occasion with that of royal officials.[47] By the time independence was finally achieved, little was left of the traditional trade monopoly, and with the destruction of that monopoly went the protected market that the textile crafts of New Spain had long enjoyed.

The struggle for independence affected the textile industry in other ways. Cloth manufacture, no less than the rest of the economy, was exposed to the destructive consequences of military operations. The uprooting of workers from farm and city, with consequent shortages of labor and materials, and the interruption of normal transportation and communications all contributed to the paralysis of shops and factories.[48]

Of more vital significance, however, was the flight of Spanish merchants from New Spain with funds they had formerly invested in its economy. Estimates of the amount of capital withdrawn after 1810 vary from $36.5 to 140 million, but whatever the figure there can be no doubt that its removal dealt a severe blow to the trade and industry of the country.[49] The production of textiles, to be sure, had absorbed only a small proportion of those funds, but their loss was nonetheless disastrous.

The close of the revolutionary decade thus found the domestic textile industry in dire straits. Thousands of individuals who once gained some sort of livelihood raising raw materials or converting them into cloth were now left largely unemployed.[50] Their methods of production were obsolescent by the standards of Europe and the United States; their products could only sell if protected by a heavy tariff barrier. But since a fundamental aim of independence had been to establish free trade, how could such protection be justified in 1821? Even if this contradiction could be reconciled, there still remained the difficulty of securing capital. To revive the industry to its former state required considerable funds; to modernize it further required an even larger investment. Where could the necessary capital be found? To the ambitious individuals who grasped the reins of power in 1821, and to those who succeeded them in the political arena, was bequeathed the perplexing task of discovering an answer to this problem.

TARIFFS AND TAXES, 1821 – 1828

The achievement of Mexico's independence in 1821 promised a new era in the economic life of the former colony. Coincident with the establishment of the new government was its assumption of responsibility for national economic policy. The extent to which official agencies might intervene in the economy, the direction such intervention might take, and the means that might be employed were now matters to be determined within the country and not in distant Spain. It could no longer be charged that selfish interests in the peninsula were obstructing the progress of the Mexican people. The development of their resources, to the extent that this could be influenced by government action, was at last in the hands of their own authorities. It is the purpose of the present chapter to inquire how that power was exercised, in as far as manufacturing industries, and especially textiles, were concerned in the periods of the regency and the empire of Iturbide, of the triumvirate that followed, and of the federal administration of Guadalupe Victoria.

An examination of the legislation enacted during the eight months when a regency ruled the newly created empire (September 1821 – May 1822) reveals that a primary concern of the men in authority was to revive the mining industry from the decadence into which it had been thrust by the recent war. The attitude taken toward this industry by the temporary legislative committee appointed in September 1821, the so-called *Soberana junta provisional,* is reflected in the laws they adopted to relieve it of much of the tax burden weighing upon it. "From the first moments of its installation," reads the preamble to one of their decrees, "the Soberana junta provisional . . . took into consideration the deplorable and decadent state of mining and the necessity of granting this activity the means within its power to contribute to its greatest prosperity upon which the prosperity of the empire depends. . . ."[1] The means resorted to consisted of the elimination of all the taxes imposed on the precious metals during the revolution, the reduction to a single 3-percent duty of the long-standing exactions known as the *diezmo, uno por ciento*, and *real de señoraje*, and the freeing of much-needed mercury, regardless of origin, foreign or domestic, from the duties formerly imposed on its sale or production.[2]

This preoccupation with the precious metals is understandable in view of the industry's traditional importance as a source of government revenue; it is also explicable because of the view dogmatically advanced in the latter years of the colony by men like Fausto de Elhuyar, late director-general of the mining guild, that this industry was the principal agent of economic progress in Mexico, and that the population depended on its development for support and growth.[3] The sublime confidence in the future of Mexico that characterized many of its leaders at the time of independence was in a great part founded on the belief that mineral wealth would become the basis for general prosperity and power.

Despite the emphasis given to the development of the mines, the governing authorities during the regency could not be completely indifferent to the desirability of promoting, or at least protecting, other sectors of the economy. A formal manifestation of their interest was the creation of a patriotic society devoted to the advancement of the general welfare. This society, patterned after those established in Spain in the eighteenth century, and called after them the *Sociedad económica mexicana de amigos del país*, had special committees named to promote manufacturing, agriculture, commerce, and mining, as well as various cultural activities.[4]

Far more important than this *sociedad* as an indication of the attitude of the authorities was the tariff law adopted by the government on December 15, 1821. The first law to regulate the foreign trade of the new Mexican empire, it opened the ports to the ships of all nations, thus fulfilling the long-held desire for direct trade with the world at large. A simple ad valorem of 25 percent was imposed on all imports, regardless of their nature, while small lists of prohibited items and of those to be admitted duty-free were also established.[5]

Of the nine articles, or groups of articles, on the duty-free list, four were of purely cultural or educational value.[6] The others, however, did include one of potentially great significance to artisan industries. This provided for the unrestricted entry of every kind of useful machine for manufacturing and farming as well as for mining. It seems reasonable to infer from this that the officials were anxious to eliminate whatever obstruction import taxes might offer to the improvement of productive processes in all branches of the economy, and not merely in mining.[7]

That the prohibitory list contained only nine classifications is evidence of the new government's reluctance to resort to the wholesale exclusions that had characterized commercial regulations of the colonial era. In fact, when the provisions of the tariff were up for debate in the Soberana junta, there was some sentiment for doing away with prohibitions altogether, and the final result was thus in the nature of a compromise.[8]

Of the nine categories of excluded items, three, it should be noted, were related to the growth or manufacture of cotton.[9] Raw cotton, cotton yarn up to weight number sixty, and cotton ribbon were barred from importation. At first glance, the presence of these three in the limited prohibitory list would seem to suggest that the government had decided to give the cotton industry the benefit of a closed market. But it should be realized that ribbon making was relatively unimportant in the total textile picture, and that the protection of domestic cotton and yarn was of limited significance unless the finished goods into which they were converted could survive the competition of foreign cloth still allowed to enter on payment of duties.

Perhaps it was expected that these duties would serve to protect the coarse fabrics woven on domestic looms. Foreign cloth, as other merchandise, paid the 25-percent duty on valuations stipulated in the tariff act, or determined by customs appraisers at the ports of entry. These valuations frequently exceeded the actual cost of the goods, and in the case of fabrics resembling domestic manta, they were two to three times the delivered cost at Veracruz.[10] Nevertheless, the original cost of such cloth was so low as to enable it to be sold there at from twenty-two to twenty-five centavos per vara (thirty-three inches) even after payment of nine centavos in duties.[11] Domestic manta, which was only twenty-two inches wide compared to the thirty-six inches of the imported varieties, cost at least twenty-five centavos, and sometimes sold for much more.[12]

The tariff act thus fell far short of guaranteeing the domestic market to locally made cloth. Such cloth continued to be sold, but apparently not in the volume enjoyed before independence. From the results of the tariff act, it would almost appear that the provisions affecting cotton textiles were designed more to increase government revenues than to protect the domestic industry.

What was true of cotton manufacturing appears equally applicable to other artisan industries. Despite what seemed to foreign eyes as artificial valuations and excessively high duties,[13] the tariff law was not a protective one in the light of Mexican realities. It is not surprising, then, that it became the object of immediate and bitter attack from interested groups. One writer who hailed from Guadalajara, a leading cotton-weaving center in the prerevolutionary years, likened the tariff to an order prohibiting the sale of all domestic manufactures. This law, he asserted, was the root cause of the unemployment of 2 million people, and the only remedy lay in imposing duties on foreign merchandise of from 400 to 1,000 percent.[14] Other suggestions submitted to the government by other groups or individuals varied from prohibiting specific items to completely excluding everything of foreign manufacture that competed with something made in Mexico.[15]

Neither the temporary Soberana junta nor the elected Constituent Congress which replaced it in February 1822 was disposed to accept any of these radical proposals. Still, the authorities could not be wholly indifferent to the plight of their artisan countrymen. Accordingly, when it was decided to raise the rate of the alcabala from 8 to 12 percent, domestic cotton and woolen textiles were specifically exempted from the 4-percent increase, thus gaining that much of an advantage in competition with imported goods.[16]

The policy of minimizing the use of prohibitions that characterized both the Soberana junta and the elected Constituent Congress was abruptly, if temporarily, reversed early in 1823. This change was one of the by-products of the coup d'état by which the newly proclaimed emperor, Iturbide, sought to impose his will against the wishes of a hostile congressional majority. As is well known, he dissolved that elected assembly by force, and created in its place a smaller legislative body hand-picked from among his adherents in each province. It was this select body, known as the *Junta nacional instituyente*, that voted for the absolute exclusion of all foreign textiles similar to domestic cotton and woolen fabrics, and to the prohibition of a variety of other foreign manufactures.[17]

The passage of this measure raises the intriguing question of whether the partisans of Iturbide had economic as well as political interests in common. It seems more than a coincidence that an important measure like the prohibition of textiles failed to be adopted in both the Soberana junta and the Constituent Congress—where Iturbide's adherents were a minority[18]—yet was approved by the Junta nacional, which his partisans dominated. Still, one must not make the mistake of identifying all the followers of the creole emperor as proponents of the use of tariff prohibitions to protect domestic industry. The measure was adopted in the junta only over the opposition of an articulate minority well versed in the reasoning of the free-trade school of European economists.[19]

The final victory, as it developed, rested with this minority, for it was shortly thereafter that armed uprisings forced Iturbide first to recall the Constituent Congress, and then to abdicate his throne. With the fall of the empire, the prohibitory measure, together with others adopted by the Junta nacional, was deprived of legal force.[20] Once again, the importation of merchandise was governed by the provisions of the original tariff act of 1821.

The overthrow of Iturbide in March 1823 inaugurated a period of political transition for Mexico. For the next eighteen months the executive power was exercised provisionally by a triumvirate, while the Constituent Congress debated the establishment of a federal republic, and took steps to draw up an appropriate constitution. In this period the government gave even more explicit recognition than in the past to the thesis that the prosperity of the mines was the cornerstone of general wealth. To encourage foreign capital to invest in them, the legal restrictions incorporated in the Laws of the Indies, which had traditionally forbidden non-Catholic foreigners from owning mining properties, were eliminated by legislative action.[21] This sharp break with the past was followed by other measures designed to facilitate the revival of mining. Internal taxes on the circulation of money, for example, were waived for monies sent to the mines. Moreover, the importation of Spanish mercury, so essential to the refining of silver, was continued even when, as a result of the bombardment of Veracruz, an embargo was placed on all other imports from the former mother country.[22]

The individual chiefly responsible for these measures was the minister of *relaciones*, Lucas Alamán. It was he who had helped organize an Anglo-Mexican mining company during his travels in Europe and who, on his entry into the cabinet, had taken the initiative in recommending to Congress the suspension of the laws against foreign ownership.[23] It was Alamán, moreover, who set forth most cogently the philosophy that underlay official policy:

> The mines are the source of the true wealth of this nation and everything that speculative economists have said against this principle has been victoriously refuted by experience. We have seen agriculture, trade, and industry constantly follow the course of the mines, flourishing and declining with them in the same propor-

tion. The reason for the close connection among these economic activities essential to national prosperity is the nature of the majority of our mines—poor in quality but exceedingly abundant in quantity. From this has followed the necessity of utilizing great numbers of workers, machines, and animals in both the extracting and the refining phases. This has given rise to an immense demand for goods which is equivalent to a considerable exportation and which in turn promotes all industries and especially agriculture. Thus it is that the encouragement given to mining is given also to the others; the recovery and prosperity of all, and consequently of the nation, is simultaneous.[24]

Committed though he was, both as a private individual and as a government official, to the goal of developing the mines, Alamán, unlike some of his contemporaries, was not doctrinaire to the point of completely excluding manufacturing from a place in the national economy. In his view, the basic need was to mechanize existing manufacturing processes. To this end, his official recommendations were for the use of tax exemptions to encourage the import of machinery, already a part of existing tariff laws, and for the enactment not of prohibitions, but of protective duties that would bridge the gap in price between imported and domestic merchandise until the time when the latter, produced by mechanical means, could be sold more cheaply.[25]

The importance of reducing manufacturing costs was also recognized by Alamán's colleague in the cabinet, the finance minister, Francisco Arrillaga. As a resident of Veracruz, the latter was especially concerned with lowering the cost of cotton textiles by eliminating the wasteful practice described in the previous chapter—that of transporting unginned cotton from the coastal farms to the highland manufacturing centers. The obvious solution was to use mechanical gins; but Arrillaga was convinced that the species of cotton raised in Mexico were less suited to such devices than those grown in the United States. Accordingly, to encourage farmers to acquire and plant foreign cotton seed, he persuaded Congress to vote a ten-year exemption of all domestic taxes, including the oppressive tithe and alcabala, on cotton that was raised from improved foreign seed. At the same time, similar exemptions were voted to encourage the production of a variety of other staples including wool, flax, hemp, and silk.[26]

As measures to effect the mechanization of manufacturing procedures, thus enabling domestic industries to survive, the proposals of Alamán and Arrillaga suffered from at least one serious weakness. Their success depended on the willingness and the ability of private individuals to take advantage of the tax incentives. But under the conditions that existed in the early twenties, it was hardly to be expected that private capital would interest itself in the acquisition of machinery for manufacturing, or even in obtaining cotton gins and new types of seed.

The economy as a whole was still staggering from the effects of the recent war, especially from the withdrawal of merchant capital. The exodus of Old Spaniards, first begun in 1810, renewed itself once independence became a reality, and, from 1821 on, the extraction of capital continued with paralyzing effects on every branch of trade. The loss of what a contemporary British observer estimated in 1824 to be 20 millions sterling in the previous three years[27] left the Church and foreigners as the principal nongovernment sources of investment capital. But in view of the known preference of religious corporations for mortgages on real property, and of the superior attractions that mining and commerce offered to the foreigner, the prospect of private investment in manufacturing industry on the scale necessary to mechanize production procedures was small indeed.

While the cabinet of the triumvirate seemed satisfied to limit the assistance given to manufacturing to the measures described above, pressure for stronger restrictions on foreign trade continued unabated in the manufacturing centers. The reason is not hard to find. Two years of independence had done nothing to dispel the depression that had befallen the handicraft industries. The value of manufactures, according to an American diplomatic agent, was only half of what it had been at the turn of the century,[28] and in the textile field, the decline was even more catastrophic. In these circumstances, it is quite understandable that artisans identified the relative prosperity of the prerevolutionary days with the prohibitions that had existed then, and that they believed, somewhat naively to be sure, that the "good old days" could be restored merely by imposing similar tariff restrictions. That the distress of the artisans was also due to the very factors underlying the general economic paralysis did not deter them from single-minded concentration on the tariff as the panacea for their ills. Through their provincial representatives in the national Congress they called the government's attention to their plight, and demanded action against the flow of foreign merchandise.[29]

Partially as a response to this pressure and to kindred demands made by agricultural groups, but also out of awareness that the existing tariff law needed revision, the finance minister early in 1824 recommended to the Congress the adoption of extensive reforms. To reduce the opportunity for inconsistency and arbitrariness in the valuations given to foreign merchandise, Arrillaga proposed that a number of items formerly appraised at the individual ports of entry should be given fixed valuations. He also suggested that valuations already established in the act of 1821 be revised in a number of cases; he justified increases for some of these on the grounds that they would promote domestic production, but defended reductions in others with the argument that the articles in question were not being produced in Mexico, and that high duties merely encouraged smuggling.[30]

More important than either of these recommendations was his proposal of a substantial list of products, agricultural and manufactured, which were to be banned completely from importation. The list included a wide variety of foodstuffs, leather goods, articles of clothing, and even cheap-quality woolen cloth. But no mention was made of cotton textiles, whose exclusion was the overriding concern of the artisans in the cotton centers. The argument presented by the finance minister to justify his selection of items for exclusion was that these were the ones that were abundantly produced within the country. This condition, he insisted, was not met in the case of cotton cloth, and its exclusion "would only do grave injury to consumers who came from the neediest class and therefore deserve consideration, and [also] it would be an incentive to smuggling because of the high price of [domestic cloth]."[31]

The anxiety voiced by Arrillaga over the harm done to the unfortunate classes of Mexico by excluding cotton textiles was probably matched by an unstated concern for its effects on the public treasury. The revenues of the government had already proved inadequate to sustain the burden of expenditures and, as minister of finance, Arrillaga could hardly have been indifferent to a sharp reduction in those revenues. Cotton textiles had become an increasingly important source of customs duties in the two years since independence, constituting in 1823 almost 30 percent of the value of all merchandise imported through the principal port of Veracruz.[32] That Arrillaga for purely fiscal reasons would not have been prepared to yield to artisan pressure for the exclusion of the tejidos ordinarios is readily understood.

The Congress reacted to Arrillaga's proposed list of prohibitions by adopting it almost without change. On May 20, 1824, the 1821 tariff act was officially amended to raise from the original 9 to the formidable number of 116 the articles whose entry into Mexico was forbidden.[33]

This step, however, should not be taken as evidence that the government was now fully committed to a policy of promoting manufacturing industry. Of the items excluded, over one-third were in the category of foodstuffs. With the exception of cheap-quality woolen cloth, no textiles as such were on the list. It was the tailoring professions, rather than the basic cloth producers, that saw their products protected.

If further proof were needed that the attitude of the government toward manufacturing industry had not undergone a basic change, it can be found in the words of the congressional committee that recommended the adoption of the prohibition measure. The members of this committee expressed the hope that the bill, while preventing those already occupied in craft industries from perishing, would discourage further capital and labor from entering the field of manufacturing.[34] Certainly the enactment of May 20, 1824, offered no incentive to invest in the country's most important manufacturing industry, that of the cotton textiles. Neither did it offer any assurance that this industry could be preserved from further deterioration or even complete collapse.

The provisional executive, who had governed since the fall of Iturbide, was succeeded in October 1824 by General Guadalupe Victoria, the first constitutional president of a federated Mexico. Before examining the economic policies of the Victoria administration, note should be taken of the changes made by the Constituent Congress in the internal duty system, changes that were of some benefit to domestic industries. As far as can be told, these steps did not originate in a conscious effort to foster industry, but were concomitant to the fiscal reorganization necessitated by the establishment of a federal system.

The chief innovation in the duty system was the transfer of the alcabala from the control of the central government to that of individual states. Foreign merchandise, which had been subject to this duty since 1822 at the rate of 12 percent, was now wholly exempted from it; but in its place, a new federal impost known as the *derecho de internación* was established. Nominally 15 percent, but actually 18 3/4 percent of the value of imported articles, this duty was levied when they left the port of entry for any interior destination.[35] However, if such goods were consumed within the limits of the port city, they were not subject to the duty, a provision that hardly seems equitable to the purchasers elsewhere, who had to sustain not only this duty, but also additional freight costs. Nevertheless, from the viewpoint of farmers and artisans trying to compete with imported products, the new tax gave them an added measure of protection in all but a few parts of the country.

This was not the only tax change that redounded to the benefit of domestic producers. In the allocation of revenues between federal and state governments, the Constituent Congress allowed the latter to impose a 3-percent consumer tax *(derecho de consumo)* on foreign goods sold within their respective jurisdictions.[36] Imported merchandise thus paid a series of duties, state and federal, which totaled 51 3/8 percent of their appraised value.[37] Domestic textiles, in contrast, were subject only to the state alcabala of 8 percent.[38] Even so, the producers of cotton goods did not regard these tax advantages as an adequate substitute for the complete embargo on foreign textiles, the enactment of which they now hoped to obtain from the Victoria administration.

The inauguration of Guadalupe Victoria as Mexico's first constitutional president did little to alter the basic direction of government economic policy that had been followed since independence. Open concern over the development of the silver mines, coupled with considerable reluctance to take active measures in behalf of manufacturing industries, continued to characterize the outlook of both executive and legislative branches of government.

This negative attitude toward the development of manufacturing was, in part at least, a reflection of the influence that the works of recent European economists, especially Jean Baptiste Say, were exercising over the Mexican mind. The years since 1810 had seen the rapid dissemination of liberal economic theories, and it became highly fashionable in the halls of Congress, in the press, and in the schools to cite them against the use of tariff prohibitions and against government intervention in economic life.[39] Under President Victoria, it became official doctrine that the proper role of the state was to limit itself to the construction of public works, and to the elimination of hindrances that stood in the way of private enterprise. As the president himself phrased it at the closing session of the first bicameral legislature elected under the federal Constitution:

> The spirit of regulation, the desire for minute control . . . is the best means to diminish or destroy abundance and wealth perhaps forever; on the other hand, to create and foster them, an enlightened and well-meaning government need only remove the great obstacles, leaving the rest to the action and interest of private individuals.[40]

The actual steps taken to promote industry during the four years of Victoria's administration were fully consistent with this concept of restricted government activity. The chief executive, in his periodic messages, laid principal stress on road building as the most practical way of aiding industry, agriculture, and commerce; and when Congress finally adopted a measure authorizing the executive to make contracts for the opening of roads, Victoria lauded the action as a "step which ought to have eternal influence on the promotion of the wealth and prosperity of the Republic,"[41] a prediction that time did little to sustain.

The Victoria administration, to be sure, did give some assistance to Mexican industries, but this was done in ways that did not violate the principle of nonintervention. The purchase, for example, of quantities of woolen cloth to equip the military gave a powerful stimulant to the Querétaro woolen industry.[42] But the effects were only temporary, for a permanent expansion of production depended on private demand, which still preferred imported cloth to the high-cost domestic fabrics. As in the cotton industry, the wool weavers suffered from archaic methods and were at a disadvantage in competition with Europe's machine industry.

Another gesture of the Victoria government in the direction of assisting agriculture and industry was its acquisition from France of a breeding herd of merino sheep and Kashmir goats. The introduction of such animals by private parties was already encouraged by the duty-free status given animals in the 1821 tariff act; but even liberal writers had urged the government to assume responsibility for importing useful species.[43] In bringing these animals into the country, the government was able to demonstrate that they could sustain the vicissitudes of the Mexican climate,[44] but as far as obtaining any practical advantage from the finer wools, the experiment was less successful. Mexican weavers, accustomed to making coarse fabrics on their crude looms, had no need for the merino fibers, and there were as yet no factories with machinery that could process them.[45]

The clearest instance in which the Victoria government offered encouragement to industry involved the paper manufacturing industry, but here, too, public action was restricted to removing obstacles to private initiative. The manufacture of paper had been unknown before independence, but in 1823 the retiring minister to the United States, José Manuel Zozaya, had brought with him on his return to Mexico a full complement of paper-making equipment. Zozaya and his associates sought to erect their mill in San Angel, a suburb of the capital, but the temporary exhaustion of their own funds, and their unsuccessful attempt to obtain a direct loan from the Treasury in 1824, delayed until the following year the production of their first paper.[46]

This achievement of private enterprise was recognized by the Victoria administration in their ordering the government ministries to print their *memorias* on the paper of the San Angel plant.[47] But the entrepreneurs wanted something more substantial in the way of public assistance, and appealed to Congress for a specific exemption from all internal duties on the sale of their paper, and at the same time, a waiver of import and alcabala duties on the rags they used as raw materials.[48] It was this request that underlay the action of Congress in granting, not just to Zozaya but to all who within the next two years engaged in paper manufacturing, a seven-year exemption from the alcabala on their paper, and a permanent exemption from such duties on their rags.[49]

The enactment of this measure constituted the first instance in which a Mexican government took steps to encourage directly the development of a specific manufacturing industry. The concessions of tariff protection or tax relief given in the past had been aimed primarily at aiding those already engaged in existing and often outmoded crafts, not at promoting the establishment of new industries, nor at introducing new techniques of production. The measure granting tax exemptions to paper manufacturers was thus a new departure, but one, it should be observed, that did not conflict with Victoria's concept of the proper role of government in economic life. However, as a device to encourage private investment in paper production, the law remained largely without effect, for, aside from the already constructed San Angel mill, no new plants came into existence to take advantage of its provisions.

It is interesting to note that at the very time the federal government was acting to foster paper manufacturing, the authorities of two important states were engaged in a similar task, though with means that differed sharply from those adopted by the federal administration. The legislatures of Jalisco and Puebla, apparently uninhibited by notions of nonintervention, voted to loan or invest public funds in private enterprises that would erect paper mills within their respective borders.[50] For reasons that are not clear, these undertakings failed to materialize. But the attempts themselves are significant in indicating the belief of these officials that private initiative without public financing would be inadequate to do the job; that private investors would be unwilling to shoulder alone the heavy expense of purchasing, transporting, and installing the necessary machinery to set up paper mills. The plans of these state officials miscarried, but the day was not too far distant when men of similar views would control the federal government and would seek to devote its funds to a more ambitious program of industrial change.

The reluctance of the Victoria administration to take energetic measures to develop manufacturing industry is well revealed in its tariff policies. Revenue, not protection, is the first concern of a finance minister, and each of the eight men who assumed the burdens of that position during Victoria's four-year term had to face the fact that the duties collected on the import and sale of foreign merchandise constituted the principal financial support of the government. Protecting the income obtained from this source was, accordingly, the constant preoccupation of these ministers. It was only natural, then, that they should oppose those measures that threatened to reduce their funds, especially the ever-recurring demand to cut down the import of cotton textiles. Cotton-goods imports were far too important a source of income to be treated so casually, for by 1826 they constituted 32 percent of the value of all imports, and more than 46 percent the following year.[51]

Measures that offered a prospect of raising existing revenue did, however, win the support of Victoria's finance ministers. From the first days of his administration, attempts were made to have the various duties affecting imported merchandise reduced, in the conviction that lower rates would inhibit smuggling and consequently increase income. But the legislative process was slow. Not until 1827 did both chambers of Congress agree on a single measure to replace the tariff act of 1821 and other laws affecting foreign trade that had been adopted since that time.[52]

The underlying objectives of the tariff legislation of 1827 may be seen by examining the recommendations drawn up by the Chamber of Deputies' Committee on Finance, recommendations that were the basis of the measure as finally adopted. For this committee, the primary goal was to set a level of duties high enough to produce sufficient revenue, but low enough to discourage smuggling. Because the existing duties collected by the federal government under the three categories, importation, *internación*, and *avería*, exceeded 48 percent, the committee proposed as a single substitute an ad valorem of 40 percent.[53]

In regard to the protection of domestic products, the committee expressed itself as preferring, at least in theory, absolute freedom of trade. But bowing to the necessity of protecting certain industries, it urged that reliance be placed on duties, and that outright prohibitions be kept to a minimum. It suggested specifically that the existing list of 116 excluded articles be cut down to a mere 15. More significant than the actual number is the fact that its proposed list did not include textiles of any sort, nor the earthenware, metal, or leather goods previously prohibited.[54]

As finally enacted, the tariff act of November 16, 1827, did not quite correspond to the committee's intentions. The proposed ad valorem of 40 percent was indeed adopted, together with various technical provisions suggested by that body for enforcing payment.[55] But instead of accepting the committee's brief exclusion list, the Chamber of Deputies adopted the procedure of debating each of the more than five score articles currently under ban, and of voting then on members' proposals for new exclusions.[56] The result was the approval of a list of fifty-six items, less extensive to be sure than the existing one, but still much larger than the committee recommended. Nevertheless, it must be noted that, despite the well-organized efforts of a determined minority to place cotton textiles of ordinary quality on the excluded list, the Chamber of Deputies, by a small margin, refused to do so and was subsequently upheld by the Senate in this critical decision.[57]

Viewed in its entirety, and against the background of the protectionist demands of various interest groups, especially the cotton industry, the tariff reform of 1827 was far from constituting a concession to such demands. Quite the reverse, the law represented a step toward freer trade in textiles as well as other products. Not only could cheap cotton fabrics continue to enter Mexican markets, but even cotton yarns above weight number twenty, and raw cotton—both articles that had been consistently excluded before—now were allowed in the country. The law, moreover, failed to yield to an alternate demand of the cotton industry, which was that if cotton fabrics were not prohibited, they should at least be charged a substantially higher duty. Under previous regulations, imported goods similar to manta paid importation, internación, and avería duties amounting to 48 3/8 percent. On a valuation generally fixed at 37.5 centavos per vara,[58] such goods bore a levy of 18.14 centavos. Now under the tariff act of 1827, it was stipulated that these goods would pay a specific duty of 18.5 centavos, a difference so little as to be meaningless.

It was possibly because it had failed to meet the major demands of the domestic cotton industry that the Congress that adopted the tariff act of 1827 agreed the following year to exempt the principal products of that industry from the internal taxes usually collected in federal territories. A proposal to exempt domestic cotton, wool, and silk textiles from such duties had been made during the tariff debates, but it was not until February 1828 that the proposal became law.[59] Unlike the tax exemption granted previously to paper products, this one applied only in the federal district and territories. However, the governments of several states had already taken similar steps, and others were soon to follow.[60]

The notable feature of much of this state legislation was its discriminatory character. Only the textiles produced within the borders of the legislating state were to enjoy the tax exemption, not those that came from other parts of the country.[61] The underlying intention of such measures obviously was to assist local artisans, not only in meeting foreign competition, but also in withstanding that of artisans in other parts of the federation.

The use of tax concessions in such a manner sheds some light on the economic outlook of state leaders, and incidentally on their concept of federalism. As was natural in a country of poor communications and one with a tradition of internal tariff barriers, the interests of the local community were viewed as the supreme goal, and those of the nation as secondary. Attempts were made periodically to identify the national interest with that of the state or region—one will be described in the following chapter—but economic localism remained the fundamental characteristic of the country throughout the period under study. And, as we shall see before the final chapter, from the relatively harmless use of tax exemptions as a means of favoring local craftsmen, it was an easy and natural step to engage in the more dangerous practice of discriminatory tax impositions to protect factory industries. Economic warfare between the states was an unfortunate accompaniment of the rise of mechanical industries, but it was not, as Pablo Macedo would have us believe, a consequence of their creation;[62] it had its roots before their establishment, and was already resorted to, as shown above, when manual labor alone was utilized.

The close of Victoria's administration found Mexico's manufacturing industries in much the same state that they had been at the beginning of the independent empire seven years before. This interval had witnessed no fundamental transformation of the traditional handicrafts, no extensive introduction of new industries. The basic processes of manufacture were still those that had been followed in the colonial era, and with the exception of a few cotton gins, a paper mill, and apparently some spinning jennies, the utilization of machinery in common use abroad was unknown.[63] The Mexican government, both imperial and republican, had refrained from active intervention in support of industrial change, partially because of the influence of doctrines of laissez-faire, but also because of the practical consideration of cost. The granting of exemptions from internal taxes was the full measure of the assistance given to manufacturing industry by the government.

Official favor shown to the mining industry, to be sure, had involved little more than the waiving of taxes, but here the expectation of huge profits, stimulated by the writings of Baron von Humboldt, had led foreign investors to shoulder willingly the heavy expense of reviving production and modernizing operation.[64] Manufacturing in Mexico, however, offered no such incentive to foreign capital, and what remained of domestic capital after the Spanish exodus preferred to invest in landed property, as in the case of church funds, or sought, through speculation in government paper, a rate of return that untried manufacturing enterprises could not promise.[65]

The tariff measures of the first seven years, despite their protectionist overtones, had not been designed primarily to encourage the flow of new capital and labor into manufacturing enterprises. Their goal had been rather that of protecting agricultural producers, and of preserving the practitioners of outmoded handicrafts from utter destruction. Moreover, where protection meant imposing heavy sacrifices both on the Treasury and on the public, as in the case of the cotton textiles, the policy makers in this period consistently drew a line beyond which they refused to go.

In view of the conflict in interest between consumer and Treasury on the one hand, and producers of cotton goods on the other, the decision not to exclude foreign textiles was certainly logical. But its logic was no substitute for positive measures to alleviate distress in those areas where cotton growing or its fabrication had long constituted the chief occupation. Of the serious effects on such areas of the importation of foreign textiles there can be little doubt. In the capital of Oaxaca, where once 500 looms had clattered in the production of cotton cloth, a mere 50 were working in 1827.[66] In the state of Mexico, the governor reported in 1828 that entire towns had been affected, "especially Texcoco, Tulancingo, and Sultepec, and the first to such a degree that we have all seen a city deserted and ruined by the emigration of families who went to seek a living in more fortunate places."[67] Similar situations existed in other states. Certainly in Jalisco the artisans never ceased to complain of the poverty, idleness, and misery which was their lot. Moreover, some of them warned the authorities that unless something were done, they might well attribute their misery to the system of government.[68]

Such a threat issued in the spring of 1828 suggests an economic basis for the restlessness that accompanied the critical presidential election held in the fall. The role that artisans' discontent played in the electoral victory of the Yorkinos, and in the uprising that put General Guerrero into the presidency, at the cost of violating the Constitution in its first real test, is a subject worthy of detailed study.

Here it can only be suggested that the failure of the government to offer a tangible remedy to the conditions that had generated the recurring demand for prohibitions must have played a significant part. At any rate, the pressure on the government to adopt such extreme tariff measures continued unabated, and the victory of General Guerrero's partisans meant, as shall be shown in the next chapter, that government had fallen into the hands of proponents of an unrestrained protectionist policy.[69]

3

THE YEAR OF TRANSITION, 1829

The twelve-month period that began with December 1828 constituted a particularly violent time for Mexico. The riot of the *Acordada*, which assured General Vicente Guerrero the presidency, the Spanish invasion that followed seven months later, and the rebellion that finally expelled the revolutionary hero from office all make of this period one of the most hectic in the young republic's existence. Yet, amid the violence and confusion, events were taking place in the field of economic policy which in the long run were to exercise more influence than military maneuvers. For in the brief administration of General Guerrero, the decision was made to utilize the power of the government to foster the development of domestic industries; in other words, it was decided to abandon the policy of restraint, if not of indifference, that had characterized previous regimes.

Once made, this decision proved surprisingly permanent. At least it became part of the avowed policy of succeeding governments. To be sure, the specific methods for aiding manufacturing varied in nature and effectiveness. In Guerrero's presidency, as will be shown, tariff measures were relied upon exclusively. But whatever the means, the idea that government shared responsibility with private individuals for promoting industry persisted through changing administrations.

The man who assumed the Mexican presidency on April 1, 1829, had already given evidence of a personal interest in industrial development. Only a year before, Vicente Guerrero had agreed to become chairman of the board of directors of a stock company launched by a group of French and native entrepreneurs for the purpose of establishing various manufacturing and agricultural enterprises. The organizers of the company had hoped to raise a capital of $300,000 by selling shares, but their efforts had been halted prematurely by the very political crisis that catapulted their chairman into the nation's presidency.[1]

As chief executive, Guerrero had some opportunity to promote his ideas on the role of government in economic life. These ideas were clearly, if crudely, revealed in the manifesto he addressed to his fellow citizens on his inaugural day:

> Industry, both agricultural and manufacturing, can not only be improved, but also extended into entirely new fields. The bastard application of liberal economic principles, and the inconsiderate latitude given to foreign trade, aggravated our wants. . . . For the nation to prosper, it is essential that its laborers be in every branch of industry, and particularly that manufactures be protected by wisely calculated prohibitions.[2]

Guerrero was not alone in his confidence that rigorous tariff measures could increase industrial production and employment. A majority of the new Chamber of Deputies that assembled on January 1, 1829, gave evidence of this even before his inauguration. Swept into office in the Yorkino victory of the previous September, these deputies by and large represented the most radical elements of the electorate. But their legislative program, unfolded in the opening weeks of the session, soon demonstrated that economic liberalism played no part in their philosophy.

The first task this Congress faced was to open the votes cast by the state legislatures for the presidency. This accomplished, and Guerrero proclaimed president-elect—through the simple expedient of disqualifying the larger number of votes given to his opponent—the legislature turned its attention to two important matters, the expulsion of Spanish residents and the reform of the tariff. It is the latter that concerns us here.

On January 14, eighteen deputies, practically one-fourth of the membership, joined in presenting a bill to prohibit the entry of coarse cotton and wool textiles.[3] This bill, which was referred to the Finance Committee, was promptly and favorably reported by that body. The measure was recommended as one that deserved enactment, not only because public opinion demanded it, but also because it would rectify the erroneous commercial policy followed in the past eight years, a policy that had resulted in the destruction of industry, farming, and trade.[4]

To suggest, as this committee did, that the various tariff laws enacted since 1821 had established free trade "without limits or restrictions" would have aroused sarcastic comment in the merchant community. But in the Chamber of Deputies there was apparently general agreement on this point, as well as on the desirability of further restricting foreign trade. With but ten dissenting votes to forty-seven in favor, that body on February 10 approved the measure to exclude foreign textiles.[5]

This action proved but the prelude to a wholesale expansion of existing prohibitory legislation. The Chamber of Deputies, yielding with apparently little hesitation to the pressure of special interests, soon produced a bill that extended the prohibition principle to over fifty articles not already proscribed. Most important next to textiles were metal products. Every kind of iron tool used in farming was to be barred.[6] The mania for exclusions had indeed reached a new high.

The Chamber-adopted list of prohibitions, far from meeting opposition in the Senate, was extended even further, and the resulting measure, heartily approved by President Guerrero, was finally signed into law on May 22, 1829.[7] Thus, for the first time since independence, an outright ban was placed on the entry of inexpensive cotton textiles. The industrial and agricultural interests who had consistently opposed anything resembling freedom of trade had finally won out over fiscal considerations and consumer needs.

This law represented a complete surrender to the popular opinion that the solution to the problem of depressed industries was to be found in trade restrictions. The exclusion of competitive goods, it had so often been urged, would not merely revive the handicraft industries, but in time would regenerate agriculture and internal trade.[8]

Such reasoning, of course, was blind to the fact that the continuing crisis in the artisan industries was the reflection of basic ills, which could hardly be cured by treating their symptoms. The technological inferiority of the handicraft system vis-à-vis European factories was a fundamental problem, and it could not be totally solved by commercial restrictions. Such measures could not miraculously produce the considerable investment needed to modernize the industries, or even to restore them to their former state. Furthermore, the uncertainty of political conditions was not encouraging to investment. The attacks on property in the Acordada riot the previous December, and the countrywide persecution of Spanish residents, which culminated in the decree of expulsion enacted by the selfsame Congress, both only served to reduce the volume of capital available for investment purposes.[9]

Even as a measure to protect existing production, the law of May 22, 1829, had its drawbacks. The value of any legislation in the last analysis depends on its enforcement. Yet without the funds obtained from the importation of cotton textiles and other merchandise the government was less capable than ever of building up the honest, efficient bureaucracy needed to administer a policy that conflicted with the immediate interests of broad sectors of the population. Even the colonial authorities with their budgetary surpluses had failed to stamp out smuggling. How could a government already operating at a deficit expect to prevent its underpaid employees from conniving in the entry of illicit goods?

Nevertheless, the enactment of the law of May 22, 1829, was warmly applauded in artisan circles, and nowhere more vigorously than in Puebla. As the center of the country's most extensive cotton-handicraft industry, Puebla had been actively urging the adoption of similar legislation since independence. The local legislature on several occasions had petitioned the national congress to halt the influx of foreign fabrics; Puebla's representatives in Mexico City had introduced motion after motion, all without success.[10] That Congress in 1829 finally adopted the prohibition on cottons may be attributed in no small degree to pressure exerted by citizens of that state. In the Chamber of Deputies it had been the Puebla deputation that had joined solidly in sponsoring the original textile-exclusion bill of January 14; and, by more than a coincidence, two-thirds of the Finance Committee, which had promptly urged its adoption, consisted of Puebla deputies. Perhaps symbolic of their influence in the Chamber's final enactment of the prohibitory measure is the fact that two of their number were selected to carry it triumphantly to the floor of the Senate.[11]

The interest of Puebla's leaders in the prohibitory law of 1829 is readily understood. More than any other state, that area stood to gain from a law that promised to restore the trade conditions of colonial days. When foreign cottons had last been prohibited, Puebla's textiles dominated the domestic market. Even in the midst of foreign competition, some 6,000 looms, it was claimed, were in operation within the state.[12]

That the prohibition of foreign textiles was not likely to result in the spread of modern factories had some advantages for Puebla because if such factories were established, they might well be erected in other states. Locally, the Puebla legislature had already taken steps to introduce new industrial techniques.[13] But nationally, Puebla representatives had shown no enthusiasm for federal measures that would enable other states to establish modern textile enterprises. For all their avowed interest in fostering national industry, the Puebla leaders were primarily concerned with maintaining the industrial ascendancy of their home state. Any plan that would upset that position aroused bitter opposition. Such was the case with the second major industrial measure to come before Congress in 1829, the so-called Godoy project.

Juan Ignacio Godoy, chief minister of the Supreme Court and unsuccessful candidate for the vice-presidency in the recent election, had submitted a petition to Congress on behalf of a textile company which he and two English entrepreneurs had organized. The petitioners sought the exclusive right to import currently prohibited cotton yarns (those under number twenty-one). In return, the company undertook to purchase abroad 1,000 handlooms of recent design for use in the federal district and territories, and to establish 1,300 others in eight states if their local legislatures approved. An alternate proposal was to sell the latter looms at cost to the state governments, or to private individuals, on the condition that the company be allowed to operate 20 looms in each state. In either case, the company pledged itself to import and sell at cost a minimum of 4,000 looms similar in style to the ones it planned to operate itself.[14]

For Godoy and his associates to have sought a yarn-import concession from the very Congress that was engaged in the wholesale extension of prohibitions would seem to have been highly futile. Yet the possibilities inherent in the proposal for replacing crude Mexican looms with more efficient apparatus and for providing employment in the capital and various provincial cities attracted the interest of several deputies, including some who had already voted to exclude coarse textiles.

The members of the Chamber's Industry Committee, led by the historian-deputy C. M. Bustamante, saw merit in Godoy's project, but with his consent rewrote some of its provisions. The basic feature of an exclusive privilege to import currently prohibited yarns was retained; but the period of the concession was reduced to six years, and the types of yarns involved were limited to those above number twelve, thus preserving the existing prohibition on the coarser grades. Moreover, it was provided that the foreign yarns could not be introduced into the seven states where cotton was now raised, except with the consent of the local legislatures.

The loom distribution features were also revised so as to increase the company's obligation to supply apparatus at cost, while restricting it from monopolizing the use of the looms to the disadvantage of independent artisans. Four thousand looms were to be made available to individuals, in addition to a minimum number for each territory and state in the republic. The company would be restricted to operating 90 in the national capital, and from 10 to 20 in each of twelve other states. However, if independent artisans failed to take advantage of the opportunity, the company would have to set up 900 in Mexico City, and from 100 to 200 in each of twelve states, provided that the local legislature approved. The total number of looms to be introduced into Mexico was expected to exceed 8,000.[15]

In recommending adoption of these proposals, the Industry Committee took the position that the advantages outweighed the objections. Modern weaving apparatus would be made available throughout the republic; the resulting increase in the output of textiles would restrain the sharp price rise to be expected from the recently adopted prohibition on foreign fabrics; the duties paid on the imported yarn would nearly compensate for the loss of revenue to be caused by the cessation of cloth imports; the purchase of foreign yarns would ease the reaction to be expected in England and the United States over the loss of a valuable cloth trade. To be sure, the yarn-import concession created a monopoly, but the Constitution gave Congress the power to grant exclusive privileges to promote industry and the entrepreneurs could not undertake to acquire and distribute the looms at cost unless assured of profits. As for domestic spinners, most of their yarn output, being of number ten grade and below, would still be protected, while they would have the stimulus of foreign competition to improve the better grades.[16]

Despite an expression of confidence that all objections had been met, the members of the Industry Committee were not so sanguine as to expect the revised plan to pass without opposition. In particular, they warned against the "two or three states whose private and temporary advantage it might be if the others were not to undertake cotton manufacturing and would purchase [the former's] textiles at exorbitant prices."[17]

This anticipation of hostility proved only too well founded, for it was the state of Puebla that took the initiative in frustrating the Godoy project. The local legislature rang with speeches denouncing it; instructions were sent to the state's representatives in Mexico City to act accordingly, and resolutions were adopted calling on the federal Congress to reject the entire plan.[18]

The reaction of the Puebla legislature to the Godoy project raises a question of interpretation. The Mexican historian Luis Chávez Orozco has emphasized the strength of an artisan class fearful of industrialization. The members of the assembly, he asserts, were themselves mostly artisans, and their actions reflected their concern over the approach of the Industrial Revolution with its fatal implications for the independent craftsman.[19]

One must agree that such concern was voiced in the legislature; but its opposition to the Godoy project was more complex than is suggested by Chávez Orozco's interpretation. This was not simply an issue of artisan versus machine. Local merchants and muleteers were as much concerned in preserving Puebla's primacy in the domestic textile field as the spinner and weaver were. So, for that matter, was the state treasury. It is not without significance that the state legislature's Committees of Finance and Commerce, as well as those of Industry and Agriculture, were called on to formulate the reply to the Godoy project.[20] More than those of a single class, the interests of a region were at stake.

To be sure, the assemblymen constantly referred to the current plight of artisans, and of the even worse fate in store for them if the project were accepted. They also lost no opportunity to condemn it, in view of Godoy's English associates, as a foreign scheme to seize control of the domestic textile industry. But by this industry they seem to have meant chiefly that of their own home state, faced now with the threat of competition from the new centers that would develop.

The idea of distributing looms to other parts of the country was openly attacked:

I agree with the English *proyectistas* [declared one deputy] that Mexico need not be exclusively agricultural; but I will not conclude from this principle that weaving should be undertaken in every part of the American continent in violation, perhaps, of nature, which established commerce. . . . One state produces a thing which it exchanges for another from its neighbor, and the balance of trade remains even. . . . This sumptuous train and apparatus of looms, by embarrassing commerce, will leave the nation in greater misery when the proposed privilege lapses. . . .[21]

The laws of nature, it would seem, had decreed that Puebla be the clothier for the rest of the nation.

Unfortunately for the aspirations of Godoy and his associates, the critical stand taken by the Puebla representatives in Mexico City won the tentative support of a majority of the Chamber of Deputies. A motion to take up the Industry Committee's bill failed of adoption, and it was sent back for additional study.[22]

In a further effort to overcome the opposition, the petitioners offered to make new concessions. They agreed to purchase an amount of domestic cotton equivalent to the yarn they imported to meet the criticism that the latter would ruin the market for domestic cotton. In addition, they pledged themselves to erect at least two spinning mills of European design to forestall the complaint that the project would serve only to make the domestic industry a tributary of foreign yarnmakers.[23]

Meanwhile, Godoy undertook a pamphlet campaign to refute other charges that had been directed against his company. "There is nothing in the present project," he wrote to members of Congress, "that can be objected to as foreign influence; everything is purely national—its author has always been very strict on this point and has never relented."[24] The participation of foreigners, Godoy pointed out, was limited to the purchase of shares, which he defended as useful to the development of national interests as long as his "rich countrymen were reluctant to risk considerable sums in investments beneficial to the majority of citizens, rather than to their personal interests."[25]

In recognition that the principal opposition to his project came from the state of Puebla, Godoy called on members of Congress to view that opposition in proper perspective. It was to be expected that a state which had enjoyed a near monopoly of the textile trade prior to 1810 should wish to restore it. But Congress should place the general interests of the country over the exclusive ones of a single state.[26]

The one argument that Godoy could not refute was that his plan involved increased, rather than lessened, dependence on foreign goods. The very advantages to be obtained from the recently approved measure to exclude textiles would be destroyed if foreign-grown cotton spun by alien hands were to be used on Mexican looms. A congress that had voted to prohibit textiles could hardly welcome the import of yarn. Despite Godoy's determined efforts and those of his supporters, congressional opposition to his project was not to be overcome. The Godoy project was dead.

This outcome was greeted with open relief in the state of Puebla.[27] The shelving of the project and the enactment on May 22 of the prohibitory tariff law seemed to bring closer the day when local textiles would dominate the domestic market. But the prospect that the influx of foreign fabrics would cease at once was rudely destroyed by a government ruling of June 15. Lorenzo de Zavala, Guerrero's finance minister, announced that the recent act could not go into effect for six months, on the grounds that the general tariff law of 1827 required such an interval before the enforcement of any enactment restrictive of trade.[28]

That Minister Zavala might issue such a ruling was not entirely un-foreshadowed. A leading spirit in the Yorkino party and editor of its newspaper, Zavala differed from Guerrero and the rank and file of the party in his opposition to the use of tariff controls to encourage manufacturing. Even before entering the ministry, he had expressed himself emphatically on this point:

> The spirit of regulating everything, and the desire to do directly what can only be the result of time and civilization and of the advances of the social system have made many good patriots believe that manufacturing industry could be advanced among us by avoiding the competition of foreign goods. . . .
>
> Industry will always owe its progress to liberty and to the stimuli of individual interest which utilizes all its resources when it finds profit in its labors and security for the property acquired by them. Restrictions on foreign trade in certain items will increase the nakedness of the working class. . . .[29]

Even though he agreed to become Guerrero's finance minister, Zavala did not abandon his ideas on the evils of trade restrictions. In fact, his official duties made him all the more critical, and, despite the stand taken by the president, he tried to prevent the adoption of the prohibitory legislation. From the columns of the *Correo de la Federación* he called the attention of the legislators to the plight of the Treasury, especially to the smuggling problem, and urged them to ignore popular prejudices. In an argument that may well have seemed strange in a newspaper that had supported the "people" against the "aristocracy" in the last election, Zavala proclaimed that the popular will should not extend to the special sciences understood by the few, and that, just as it would be foolish to have troops select generals, so it would be unwise in matters of finance to have the people determine the policies of a finance minister.[30]

Zavala's views failed to sway the legislature, but through his administrative powers, he was able to forestall the effects of the May enactment at least until November. This step, to be sure, did not enhance his popularity, and eventually served to inspire demands for his resignation,[31] but in view of article 29 of the general tariff act, as well as the state of the federal Treasury, his action was as legitimate as it was necessary.

Even before the expiration of the six-month waiting period, a new crisis threatened to postpone indefinitely the enforcement of the prohibitory law. In August, a small Spanish force under General Barradas landed near Tampico, arousing the fear that a major assault would soon follow. To provide the resources for meeting the invasion, a group of deputies proposed a four-year suspension of the prohibitory law, with the duties on textiles to serve as the guarantee for a $4 million government loan. The necessity for Congress to act, however, was avoided when it granted the president the power to govern by decree.[32]

The invasion crisis, however, did not deter the principal beneficiaries of the prohibition law from making one further effort to preserve it. Only four days after Congress granted the *facultades extraordinarias* to the president, the Puebla deputies in Congress entreated him "in the name of their constituents, as well as of other states and territories of the Federation which grow or manufacture cotton . . . not to adopt the step of suspending the salutary effects produced . . . by the law which prohibited the import of coarse cotton textiles. . . . But in the event that revenues are inadequate to pay for the war, . . . [they asked] that the suspension of the above law be left for last."[33]

The reply to this request was encouraging. The deputies heard from the president that the law, which he regarded as the "soul of industry," would be preserved.[34]

But this promise was not to be fulfilled. The immediate threat of foreign conquest lessened with the defeat of General Barradas; but President Guerrero soon had to confront a new crisis as his domestic enemies, led by his own vice-president, Anastasio Bustamante, unfurled the flag of revolt. The need for funds was as great as ever, and Guerrero, utilizing the extraordinary powers voted him for another purpose, decreed postponement of the prohibitory law to the end of December.[35]

The final months of the year saw the rebel forces gather momentum. Even General Santa Anna, whose assistance had enabled Guerrero to seize the presidency, now stood aside and allowed the hero of independence to be thrust from power. It was only a matter of weeks before Guerrero was forced to abandon the national capital and resume his revolutionary role of fugitive in the mountains of southern Mexico.

The seizure of power by Vice-President Bustamante provided the necessary opportunity for re-examining the economic policies of the fallen president. It was now for the new regime to decide whether to enforce the law adopted the previous May, or to shape other policies for attacking the problems of developing Mexico's industries.

4

THE FOUNDING OF THE BANK

The shift of political fortune that placed General Anastasio Bustamante in power in January 1830 brought with it a significant change of emphasis in government industrial policy. General Guerrero had been more interested in protecting Mexico's artisan industries from foreign competition than in improving their obsolescent techniques. But the new administration was to be primarily concerned with encouraging technological change, especially with introducing factory methods of manufacture. Thus, while the deposed administration had sought its ends exclusively through tariff legislation, its successor was soon to embark on an ambitious program of underwriting with public funds the first stages of industrial rehabilitation.

The idea of devoting funds to such a purpose was by no means original with the Bustamante government. It had been proposed more than once in the past decade.[1] In fact, only the previous year, during the debates over adopting the prohibitory act, Lorenzo de Zavala, then finance minister, had suggested to the artisan supporters of the bill that "instead of eliminating the customhouses . . . [they should] ask the government for a part of the duties to aid them in the establishment of their manufactures."[2]

This proposal went unheeded at the time, but Zavala's concern over the potentially harmful fiscal effects of the prohibitory measure was bequeathed to his successors in the Finance Ministry. Enforcement of the ban on foreign textiles, adopted on May 22, 1829, could only mean a severe cut in public revenues. The law had not been enforced during the year of its enactment, for reasons explained in the previous chapter, but on January 1, 1830, its provisions went into effect. Unless further action were taken, the new administration stood to lose about one million pesos in annual revenue. Such a loss must have seemed all the more painful in view of the extra funds the government required to pacify the country and to deal with the ominous crisis that was now brewing in Texas.

It is not surprising, therefore, that the first suggestion of a new policy to deal with the industrial problem, which would at the same time relieve the Treasury, came from within the Finance Ministry. Its author was Ildefonso Maniau, a permanent official and chief of the *Departamento de Cuenta y Razón*. Entrusted since 1825 with the preparation of the annual general trade balances, Maniau had gained a good understanding of the significance cotton-goods imports had in the overall revenue picture.[3] In fact, in the trade balance he prepared in September 1829, he had warned of the serious consequences to be expected from the exclusion of cotton manufactures.[4]

One month after Bustamante took over, Maniau presented a special report devoted to an analysis of the related problems of industrial need and tariff policy.[5] After indicating that enforcement of the 1829 prohibitory law would mean a loss to the Treasury of around one million pesos, Maniau challenged the very assumptions on which that law had been based. He pointed out that the decline of domestic manufacturing was not solely the result of the competition of foreign goods, but was also produced by the series of events that had led to the diminution of capital within the country. The consolidation decree of 1804, the Napoleonic Wars, and the eleven-year struggle for independence all contributed to the destruction or outflow of capital. The tariff ban on cheap foreign goods, therefore, could not by itself promote the desired expansion of industry, because the artisans lacked funds and apparently there were no capitalists interested in textile manufacturing.

But, Maniau went on, even assuming the availability of capital, the law could not effectively promote artisan industries. The high cost and poor quality of the domestic product would induce the consumers to prefer the superior foreign goods that could still enter legally, or even to rely on smuggled merchandise. The only circumstance in which prohibitions might help, he contended, was if a de facto prohibition existed; that is, if the domestic product was able to compete with the imported one.

How then could domestic industries be developed? Here was Maniau's plan. To improve Mexico's manufactures so as to make them competitive with imported ones, it was necessary for the state to provide Mexican artisans with capital, with modern machinery, and with the necessary technical training. To meet the cost of such a program, and at the same time to relieve the Treasury of the revenue losses produced by the recent prohibitory act, Maniau recommended the suspension of this act where it applied to coarse-quality textile imports, and the adoption instead of a special 10-percent duty on the same goods. The revenues obtained from this duty, which was to be an addition to the normal ad valorem of 40 percent, were to be devoted exclusively to the promotion of industry.[6]

The report containing Maniau's proposals was transmitted to the Chamber of Deputies on February 23 with the warm endorsement of the finance minister, Rafael Mangino.[7] But in the meantime, another prominent member of the cabinet was stating his views on the industrial problem.

Lucas Alamán, once again minister of relaciones, was the outstanding figure, the "alma inspiradora," of the Bustamante government.[8] It is not much of an exaggeration to say that when the chief executive spoke, it was Alamán's words that were heard. As the formulator of administration policy, Alamán's economic views, especially his attitudes toward the proper place of manufacturing in the economy and toward the role government should play in fostering economic development, became a matter of vital importance.

The first thing to note about Alamán's economic philosophy is that it was not static. It is this that has made most generalizations about him untenable. As was discussed in chapter 2, during his first ministry (1823 — 1825), he had championed the view that national prosperity depended directly on mining activity. His enthusiasm at that time for reviving the prostrate mining industry has led one biographer to contend that he did so because "he still believed in the old mercantilist conception that specie constituted the wealth of nations."[9] Nothing could be further from the truth. Although in his later career, Alamán expressed concern over the outflow of specie, it was not because he believed it to be identical with wealth, but rather because of a concern over the decline of the circulating medium. Moreover, at the time in question, when he was actively encouraging foreign investment in the mining industry, it was hardly with the idea that the increased output of silver would be retained in the country. His attitude then was more accurately depicted by a contemporary writer than by his modern biographer:

In short, the precious metals in Mexico are to be regarded in the same light as the great staple commodities of other countries. . . . And such is the aspect in which Alamán and the enlightened statesmen of Mexico, after conquering old prejudices, now

view them. . . . We have given way to these remarks on the labors of
Mr. Alamán because we believe him to have been chiefly instrumental in establishing among his countrymen [a] liberal and sound
policy. . . .[10]

Alamán's firmly expressed belief that the promotion of mining would
of itself produce the revival of agriculture and the arts and lead simultaneously to national prosperity had undergone a transformation by
1830. Although he still regarded the mines as "nuestra industria peculiar,"[11] he had become a more outspoken advocate of the need to
promote manufacturing.

His position is to be distinguished, however, from those who had supported the enactment of the 1829 prohibitory law. In February 1830,
Alamán wrote:

The purely prohibitive system cannot by itself make factories flour-
ish; other elements are needed such as an abundant population,
capital, and adequate machinery. For the very reason that this kind
of industry demands more diligence, men do not devote themselves to it, except when they cannot find a living more easily in
others. Thus it is that agriculture and mining attract them by preference, and certainly anyone who can extract silver directly is not
going to busy himself trying to get it in another way. Our population is not yet so large that there is a surplus of many men for the
factories. . . .[12]

These arguments against the prohibitory act were almost identical
with those used at the same time by liberals like José María Mora.[13] But
where the latter insisted that nature had intended that Mexico be devoted essentially to agriculture and mining, and that it was on these
activities that its prosperity depended, Alamán took the position that
national independence required the development of manufacturing industry. "A people should try not to depend on others for those things
indispensable to its subsistence," he announced in his memoria of February 12, 1830, and proceeded to describe the type of industries that the
government should encourage:

. . . factories which produce articles of widest consumption and
which are also the easiest to establish should be sought. . . . Inexpensive cotton, linen, and wool textiles needed to clothe the most
numerous class of the population are the things which should be
promoted by encouraging Mexican and foreign capitalists to estab-

lish factories with the necessary machinery so that the goods will be available at a moderate price, a thing which will never be obtained without this assistance. . . . Factories to produce articles of greater luxury should wait for the time being; we should not now seek to rival nations which have the industrial means we lack.[14]

Here is the exposition of Alamán's philosophy of industrialization. The goal to be sought is not the revival of handicraft industries; neither is it the indiscriminate development of manufacturing. He seeks the establishment of those industries, particularly the textile industry, that supply goods consumed by the poorest classes. Moreover, to provide such goods at moderate prices, it is essential for the government to encourage private individuals, native or foreign, to set up modern, mechanized factories.

Alamán's memoria foreshadowed the future course of administration policy. But the first legislative step to assist manufacturing was not wholly consistent with his concepts. This was the adoption by Congress early in April of a measure creating an industrial promotion fund, the first in the republic's history.

This measure was not a separate law, but was rather one of the provisions of the famous Texas colonization act of April 6. This was the law designed to forestall the loss of that province to the United States.[15] Alarmed over the preponderance there of United States citizens, on February 8 Alamán had recommended to the Congress various proposals, including the counter-colonization of Texas by Mexican immigrants. Although he suggested that the government supply indigent colonists with loans and agricultural implements, he did not specify how this or other steps were to be financed.[16]

The solution to this problem was provided by the special congressional committee into whose hands the Texas question had been placed. They recommended that the costs of colonizing and garrisoning Texas be met by suspending the prohibition on coarse cotton textiles and utilizing the resulting revenues. However, they specifically proposed that 5 percent of these revenues be set aside to assist the development of the domestic cotton-textile industry.[17] As finally adopted, this provision read:

> The twentieth part of said duties shall be used to promote cotton textiles through the purchase of machines and looms, the assignment of small loans, and everything else that the government considers opportune. It will distribute this assistance to the states

that have this kind of industry. The Ministry of Relaciones will be in charge of this fund in order to implement such important purposes.[18]

The wording of this article suggests that it was designed more to appease anticipated opposition to the suspension of the prohibitory law than to achieve the objectives put forth by Alamán in his memoria. The specific mention of looms and small loans indicates that the intended recipients were artisans rather than potential factory owners; and the qualification that such assistance would go to the states where this class of industry already existed reinforces such an interpretation. These considerations, plus the fact that the suspension of the prohibitory law was to last only nine months, probably explains why representatives from Puebla and other handicraft centers did not offer vociferous opposition to the measure.[19]

In voting to allocate customs duties to assist the cotton industry, Congress made no effort to estimate the total sum that would become available. Yet on the basis of Treasury claims that the annual duties on the imports in question would run about $1 million, the legislators might have anticipated that the sum would be between $50 − 100,000. Such, then, was the amount that was placed at the full disposal of the relaciones minister with no restraint other than requiring an annual accounting to Congress.[20]

Despite the limited sum and the obvious intent of the legislators to assist the small artisan, Alamán acted as if he had been given much larger resources and a specific mandate to carry out the industrialization program laid down in his memoria. Even before the congressional measure was signed into law, he had issued a circular to all state governors urging them to encourage the establishment of stock companies to undertake textile manufacturing. He announced, moreover, that the federal government was already contracting for machinery and foreign technicians, that the equipment would be distributed to the companies at cost, and that the government would aid these enterprises in every way, including the loan of capital. The goal of the program, Alamán announced to the governors, was the production of textiles equal in quality and price to imported ones.[21]

That the administration was embarking on a program much broader in scope than that envisioned in article 16 of the law of April 6 is not open to question. The government's attempt in subsequent months to encourage the formation of textile companies attests to this.[22] Of course, it might be argued that the April legislation provided a legal basis for such activities, for it authorized not only the purchase of looms and the making of small loans, but "everything else that the government considers opportune." Actually, Alamán was well aware of the disparity between the provisions of the law and his administration of it; and he sought to reconcile the inconsistency, not by reducing the scope of his activities, but by asking Congress to adopt a new and broader measure.

When Congress reconvened in special session in the summer of 1830, it found on its hands an administration bill calling for the creation of a national industrial-promotion bank. The proposed establishment, to be known as the *Banco de Avío para Fomento de la Industria Nacional*, was to have a capital of $1 million accumulated from a portion of the customs duties collected on imported cotton goods. The prohibition on the entry of such goods was to continue in suspension until this fund was accumulated. The management of the bank was to be placed in the hands of a junta of three permanent members under the chairmanship of the minister of relaciones. Its operations were to include the granting of loans on interest to companies or individuals, and the purchase and distribution of machinery for use in various branches of industry, particularly the production of textiles.[23]

In transmitting these recommendations to Congress, Alamán boldly called attention to the administration's recent industrial activities as if they were fully consistent with the law of April 6. The favorable results of the steps taken to implement that law, he explained, had induced the government to propose the continued assignment of custom duties to industrial promotion. The experience of recent months, however, had also served to point up certain obstacles. These were, principally, the lack of sufficient capital for use in the various branches of industry, and the need of a wise and suitable management. The solution offered to these obstacles was the proposal to establish the Banco de Avío.[24]

That the Banco de Avío was the brain child of Alamán has generally been assumed. To him have been ascribed whatever merits or defects have been found in the idea. A denial of Alamán's authorship, however, was voiced by the novelist and later liberal statesman, Manuel Payno. Without mentioning names, Payno intimated that his father, an employee of the Finance Ministry, had drawn up a project for a national industrial bank and that Alamán "saw the project, took possession of it, modified it, varied it, and proclaimed himself its owner and author."[25]

Because the younger Payno did not elaborate on this charge, the exact contribution to the bank project claimed for his father is obscure. Certainly the method of financing the bank was not original with either

him or Alamán. Proposals to utilize customs revenues, instead of prohibitions, to foster the domestic textile industry had been made off and on
since 1823, the most recent being in the Maniau report discussed above.
The possibility that this report also reflected the elder Payno's ideas
does exist, however, because he was an associate of Maniau in the *Departamento de Cuenta y Razón*.[26] But, in this report, as in the provisions
of the law of April 6, which first translated the idea into a working reality,
the emphasis was placed on giving assistance to the artisan. The project
for the Banco de Avío, on the other hand, was the first to stipulate that
industrial companies should receive loans and machinery, the first, in
short, that fixed the establishment of the factory system as its goal. Even
if the proposal for a distinct directing agency, or bank, did come from
the elder Payno, it seems more than likely that Alamán was responsible
for the particular orientation given to the project. His personal observations of European factories, his experience with the workings of stock
companies in the mining industry, his known views on the importance
of modernizing Mexico's industries all lead to this conclusion.

Moreover, in this instance, as in the history of a successful invention,
the critical problem was to win acceptance. If the elder Payno conceived the idea of the Banco de Avío, he is entitled to full recognition;
but it cannot be denied that it was Alamán, with his great prestige, who
had it adopted as administration policy, and who, moreover, used his
extensive influence over Congress to secure its enactment into law.

In view of the fact that this was substantially the same Congress that
had adopted the prohibitory law a year before, the bill to establish the
Banco de Avío met surprisingly little opposition. On the crucial vote to
permit the continued entry of cotton goods for the purpose of financing
the bank, only seven members of the Lower Chamber voted "No," as
against thirty-three in favor.[27] In the Senate, also, the bank measure was
easily carried. Accordingly, on October 16, 1830, the bill authorizing the
Banco de Avío became law.

In view of its importance as the authority for the subsequent administration of the bank, it seems advisable to reproduce, with comment on
their significance, those articles of this law that apply to: (1) the acquisition of capital; (2) the internal organization of the bank; and (3) the use of
its funds. The complete text of the law is reproduced as Appendix A.

(1) The acquisition of capital.
Article 1. A Banco de Avío will be established with a capital of one
million pesos.
Article 2. For the time necessary to provide this capital and no

longer, the permission for entry into the ports of the republic is extended for the cotton goods prohibited by the law of May 22, 1829. Article 3. One-fifth of the total duties accrued, or which shall in the future be yielded by the importation of the goods mentioned in the previous article, shall be applied to the funds of the bank.

It should be noted that no specific time limit was fixed for the resumption of the ban on foreign textiles; this was to depend completely on the conditions of trade. Such had been Alamán's original proposal, and Congress left it intact.[28] But the stipulation that one-fifth of the total duties on cotton goods should go to the bank represented an important congressional modification of the minister's ideas. Alamán had suggested that the bank receive only one-twentieth of the revenues in question until such time as the $500,000 appropriated for the security of Texas in the April 6 law was accumulated; thereafter, the allotment to the bank would be raised to one-tenth. Congress, however, omitting any reference to the earlier law, increased at once the bank's share of the total revenues to one-fifth.[29] This had the theoretical effect of hastening the accumulation of the bank's capital, but at the same time of reducing the net amount that would go to the Treasury. Under Alamán's plan, the Treasury would have received at least $9 million before the ban on cotton goods was resumed; under the plan as finally adopted, it would receive only $4 million by the time the bank had obtained its $1 million. Further, by this plan, the volume of imports needed to produce that sum was considerably less, a point that doubtless appealed to advocates of protection in the legislature.

(2) The internal organization.
Article 5. For directing the bank and managing its funds, a junta will be established under the chairmanship of the minister of relaciones composed of a vice-chairman and two members, with a secretary and two clerks if needed. The members of this junta will not enjoy any salary for the present, and will be replaced one each year starting with the junior member. The government may reappoint the outgoing member if it seems convenient. For the secretary and clerks, able-bodied pensioners will be employed, who will serve at the salary established for their former positions. The government will formulate the regulations by which this junta will be ruled in discharging its functions; and, henceforth, when the fund earns profits, Congress will establish the salaries which the members of the junta and other employees of the bank are to receive.

Article 6. The funds of the bank will be deposited for the present in the *casa de moneda* in Mexico City at the disposal of the minister of relaciones, who, in conformity with decisions of the junta, will issue the sums that are necessary. When, through the increase of the funds, an office will be required to manage them, one will be established with the necessary employees, after congressional approval of their number and salary.

A close reading of these articles reveals the truly extensive authority reserved for the relaciones minister. Not only was he to be chairman of the junta and in control of its funds, but, as a cabinet member and adviser to the president, he, in effect, was the one to select the other junta members, and the one to lay down the regulations governing their activities. The future success of the bank would largely depend on the individuals exercising the office of minister of relaciones.

(3) The use of funds.
Article 7. The junta shall arrange for the purchase and distribution of the machinery needed to develop the distinct branches of industry, and shall grant under legal requirements and guarantees, the capital needed by the various companies that are formed, or by the individuals who are engaged in industry in the states, district, and territories. The machinery shall be provided at cost, and the capital at an annual interest of 5 percent, with a fair period fixed for the return of the principal. The capital by remaining in circulation, shall serve as a continuous and permanent stimulant to industry.
Article 10. Although preference shall be shown to the cotton- and wool-textile fields, and to the raising and processing of silk, the junta may likewise devote funds for promoting other branches of industry or agricultural products of importance for the nation.

From these articles, it is clear that the bank had a well-defined mission. It was not to be a commercial bank with depository or note-issuing functions; nor was it to engage directly in the operation of enterprises. Its special function was to encourage private entrepreneurs and private capital into industrial fields by offering the opportunity to obtain machinery on credit, and supplementary funds at costs far below the current market rates.[30]

Although it was stipulated that the loans should be secured, the law was silent on the nature of the collateral or other requirements. The junta was thus given broad powers to determine the acceptability of the guarantees and to fix the length of loans.

Equally broad was the junta's authority to determine the recipients of funds or machines. There was no stipulation, as there had been in the April 6 law, that the states where certain industries already existed be favored; nor was there a requirement that one type of applicant be preferred to another, that individuals, for example, receive preference over companies, or vice versa. Neither was there any reservation that officials of the bank or members of the government be prohibited from receiving grants. The junta thus enjoyed wide discretionary powers, which, as later chapters will show, were not always used in a manner that did credit to either its wisdom or its sense of ethics.

The emphasis on developing the cotton and wool industries requires no comment, but the inclusion of the silk industry on the same level of importance does. This marked a basic departure from the principle laid down earlier by Alamán, that only those industries producing inexpensive goods of wide consumption should be fostered. This, taken together with the blanket authority to promote any industrial or agricultural undertaking whatsoever, offered the junta an opportunity to experiment with a wide range of activities, but served equally as a temptation to disperse the resources of the bank, and thus reduce its effectiveness.

The establishment of the Banco de Avío proclaimed that the Mexican government was moving still further away from the laissez-faire concepts that had characterized the Victoria administration of the mid-twenties. The power to grant financial assistance to selected enterprises gave the government an instrument for influencing the rate and direction of economic development. The special emphasis on manufacturing industries was a deliberate effort to alter the existing pattern of economic activity.

It was only natural, therefore, that the doctrines of economic liberalism should be used to criticize the administration. Opposition writers condemned the government for putting itself in business contrary to such doctrines, or, as one put it, for "erecting itself into an inspector-general of manufactures."[31] Minister Alamán was charged with holding mercantilist views and with harboring the desire to make Mexico self-sufficient of all foreign manufactures.[32]

The criticism directed against the bank project, in reality, transcended the field of economic doctrine, for it was generated in great part by the hatred felt for a regime that had seized power by force, and that had used repressive measures to silence its foes. The liberal leader, Lorenzo de Zavala, writing from exile, labeled the bank as "one more instrument created to increase governmental power in the Republic." The charge was repeatedly made that the creation of the bank was a political measure designed to delude and distract the Mexican people from the loss of their liberty.[33]

As the minister responsible for internal security, Alamán was fully aware of the political potentialities of the bank. The official government newspaper hailed its establishment as an important step toward achieving national prosperity, and one that would give the needy classes an opportunity for steady employment. After the bank was actually organized, the government press played up its activities and the steps taken to establish factories. At the same time, it chided its critics with being indifferent to the economic needs of the nation. But although the government thus sought to derive political advantage from its industrialization program, no proof exists that such was its primary purpose in establishing the bank.[34]

The administration, in all probability, was motivated by two principal considerations. One has already been explained: the need to create a legal framework for the ambitious industrial promotion program undertaken after the adoption of the inadequate April 6 law; the other was related to the needs of the Treasury. The permission for the import of foreign cottons granted in this law was due to expire within six months, and with it would cease an important source of revenue for the Treasury.[35] By linking the capital fund of the bank to the continued import of these goods, the enforcement of the prohibitory law, as we have seen, was postponed indefinitely. Had Alamán's original proposal been adopted to allocate to the bank a maximum of one-tenth of the cotton duties, the flow of such revenues would have continued until $10 million had been paid in, or, at the current rate of collections, for another six years.[36] In all likelihood, the anticipation of these revenues, and of the additional duties that imported textiles would pay in internal sales taxes,[37] weighed heavily in the administration's decision to introduce the bank measure. Even though the law as finally adopted cut down the Treasury's share of the expected receipts, it had the saving virtue, from the fiscal viewpoint, of preventing the suppression of all such income.

The Bustamante administration, in undertaking its industrialization program, had to contend with critical blasts from more than one direction. Mention has already been made of those economic liberals who denounced the government for regarding all imports as harmful, and for seeking to build up a self-sufficient Mexican industry. Yet paradoxically others were accusing the administration of doing the reverse, of subordinating domestic industry to external trade, of sacrificing the native worker to the foreign merchant. Such accusations, as might have been expected, came from the traditional centers of the handicraft industry, from artisans who viewed the import of cotton textiles as an enemy they had fought against for almost a decade, and one they had believed to be finally destroyed in 1829.[38]

Artisan disappointment with the Bustamante administration's tariff measures led quite naturally to new attempts to restore the former ban on foreign textiles. For some craftsmen, the path to this objective may well have taken the form of open rebellion. In Guadalajara, a deliberate attempt was made to utilize the tariff issue to win artisan recruits for the Guerrerista insurrection smouldering in the south.[39] But in other areas, artisans based their hopes on new legislation. Their spokesman was the Puebla deputy, Pedro Azcué y Zalvide.

Elected a member of the new Congress that convened in 1831, Azcué introduced a bill calling for the outright repeal of the law of October 16, 1830; and from his seat in the legislature, as well as through the press, he carried on a determined fight to secure his goal, which was the restoration of the ban on foreign textiles.[40] But despite his demagogic claim that foreign interests had cunningly secured the enactment of the bank law, and despite his description of its harmful effects on the livelihood of farmers and artisans, the opposition to him in Congress was too strong. With his proposals under attack in the official press, and condemned by several state legislatures, Azcué saw his bill die a silent death in committee.[41]

Nevertheless, his attempt to destroy the bank is significant in bringing to the surface the conflict between the needs of the handicraft industry and the goal of the administration's industrial program. To be sure, the administration did its best to minimize this conflict. The official press described the controversy with Azcué as one "between those who would aid industry solely by prohibiting textile imports and those who would do so by means of the bank."[42] But at stake in this dispute was something more than a disagreement over method; there was also a fundamental difference of objective. Azcué's attempt to eliminate the bank reflected the determination of handicraftsmen to preserve their system of production, with all that implied in terms of cost and inefficiency. The administration, on the other hand, had as its goal the replacement of this very system with the modern factory. And in the search for this objective, the Banco de Avío had the vital task of supplying capital, machinery, and technical assistance to the pioneers of Mexican industrialization.

5

PRELIMINARY ACTIVITIES

The transformation of the Banco de Avío from the realm of legislative enactment to that of a working organization took place quickly after the promulgation of the October 30 law. In less than a week, the selection of the bank's directors was completed, and on the morning of November 5, in what was to become its permanent meeting place, the office of relaciones minister, Lucas Alamán, the junta held its initial session.[1]

The three men named to serve on this body under the minister's chairmanship were drawn, perhaps only by coincidence, but more likely with an eye to social realities, from three distinct economic or occupational groups: the great landowners, the military, and the merchants. Representing the first group, and also serving as vice-chairman, was José Mariano Sánchez y Mora, formerly the Count of Peñasco and owner of large estates in San Luis Potosí;[2] the military man was Ramón Rayón, a brigadier general who was well known to his countrymen for his exploits in the early phase of the movement for independence;[3] Santiago Aldazoro, the remaining and youngest member, was a silk merchant of long standing in Mexico City.[4] Notwithstanding the diversity of backgrounds, none of the three was particularly well qualified for the tasks that lay ahead. General Rayón, it is true, had some experience with iron manufacturing, having forged the cannon used in the defense of Zitácuaro back in 1811; and Santiago Aldazoro, to be sure, was familiar with the silk industry; but no member had the detailed knowledge of foreign technological developments so essential to an agency about to embark on a program of revolutionizing industry. However well intentioned they might have been, the directors of the Banco de Avío were essentially amateurs when they assumed the complex task of promoting industry.

As partial compensation, the bank's chief administrative official was a man of broad experience. Licenciado Basilio José Arrillaga, who was named to the post of secretary of the junta, had served some years before as secretary to the powerful Real Consulado, or Merchant Guild of Mexico.[5] Apart from his experience with mercantile matters, his knowledge of law helped supply the need for legal counsel, for which the bank statute had made no provision. Unfortunately, within seven months of his appointment, illness forced him to take leave; and, although he retained the title of secretary for some years, a substitute official, Victoriano Roa, took over his duties.[6]

In its first few sessions, the junta acted to organize the internal administration of the bank. Theoretically, the government was supposed to issue a *reglamento* for the guidance of the directors, but its continued failure to do so forced them to exercise their own discretion. They did so in a variety of matters ranging from the establishment of accounting and auditing procedures to the expansion of their clerical staff. In this latter activity, their action clearly violated the letter, if not the spirit, of the bank statute. The law had explicitly limited the staff to two clerks and required that they be hired from the list of those currently receiving public pensions; no salaries were to be paid them out of bank funds for the present, but the law held out the prospect that when the funds were earning interest, Congress would assign salaries. Secretary Arrillaga found, however, that he could not get along with two clerks, nor could he find suitable pensioners willing to work without extra compensation. The directors thereupon authorized him to use bank funds to hire the clerks he needed.[7] The five-man staff that resulted, while not overly costly, was nevertheless an indication of the junta's readiness to subordinate legalistic considerations to practical needs.[8]

Among the administrative tasks to be faced, perhaps none was more important than obtaining possession of the funds accumulating to the bank's credit at the various customhouses. Finance Ministry regulations had stipulated that these funds were to be placed in separate coffers, and were to be paid out only on the order of the minister of relaciones, who was to receive monthly statements from the customs.[9] But it was the Banco de Avío that had to bear all the costs of transferring its funds from the ports to Mexico City, or to destinations abroad. The complications were no less than those that faced any private firm trying to operate in an era when communication facilities were still primitive, and a nationwide banking system was nonexistent. To transfer funds, it was necessary to negotiate drafts with private merchants, or to pay the costs of specie shipments. If remittance were made to a foreign country, the current 3.5 percent tax on exported coin had to be paid. The junta naturally tried to avoid this loss by using bills of exchange, but the scarcity of such instruments frequently compelled it to rely on specie shipments.[10]

In its domestic transactions, the junta enjoyed the good fortune that most of its funds were accumulating at the Gulf ports of Veracruz and Tampico. Drafts issued on those ports from Mexico City nearly always earned a premium; thus, the junta was able to obtain its funds promptly, and reap a profit of about 4 percent. In sharp contrast, it had to accept losses of as much as 12 percent to get the funds from San Blas and Mazatlán on the west coast. However, the overall balance of its exchange operations during the first year was in its favor. Also encouraging was the fact that by November 30, 1831, $459,394, or almost 46 percent of the bank's total capital, had been collected.[11]

In order to enlighten itself on agricultural and industrial conditions, the junta undertook, as one of its first projects, a nationwide survey of economic resources and potentialities. It drew up a detailed questionnaire embracing the current status and future prospects of the cotton, wool, silk, wax, and ceramic fields primarily.[12] To obtain the widest possible coverage, the junta distributed more than three thousand copies through channels, civil and ecclesiastical, and in addition made a newspaper appeal to members of the general public who might have worthwhile information to contribute.[13] The questionnaire produced a wealth of data, although the anticipated coverage was not realized because many areas failed to reply.[14] Nevertheless, the answers that were received constituted a unique source of information, one that may be compared with the economic survey conducted by Viceroy Revillagigedo in 1793 and that of the Veracruz Consulado in 1802.[15] From the junta's viewpoint, the questionnaire served a dual purpose, for, apart from the specific data it supplied, it advertised the existence of the bank, and initiated what was to become a fruitful correspondence with enlightened individuals in various parts of the country.

That the junta regarded its mission as one of disseminating information, as well as of gathering it, was revealed by its publications program. In cooperation with the editors of the Registro Oficial, it proceeded to distribute a series of technical treatises designed "to provide . . . the instruction needed to develop those branches of domestic agriculture and industry that are most susceptible of expansion, and that can promptly constitute an important element of national wealth."[16] The first three volumes in the series were reprints or translations of older

Spanish and French works;[17] the subsequent ones were manuals written by Mexicans.[18] All of them dealt with agricultural, rather than industrial problems.

Not content with disseminating technical information via the printed word, the junta went one step further in the field of silk culture, and undertook to provide practical training. At an establishment operated in Coyoacán by Santiago Aldazoro, it offered instruction in the techniques of silk extraction to young men invited from various states. The bank underwrote the living expenses of the trainees during their stay, and in some instances their cost of travel. The hope was that the men so trained would be able to impart their knowledge to others in their home states. How many actually took advantage of the training is unclear, though students came from at least the four states of Nuevo León, Guanajuato, Oaxaca, and Tlaxcala. Later reports indicate that the Oaxacan trainees successfully fulfilled the junta's hope by setting up their own schools; little is known of the subsequent careers of the other students, however, beyond the fact that those from Tlaxcala found no opportunity in their home state to apply their knowledge.[19]

The junta's eagerness to improve the production of raw materials, evident in the activities described above, is seen also in its efforts to import exotic species of wool-bearing animals, and to secure useful agricultural plants. To provide fine-grade fibers for the anticipated textile mills, it ordered the purchase of herds of merino sheep and Kashmir goats, and also llamas and vicuñas. At the same time, it sought to obtain improved varieties of silkworms and of hemp and flax seeds.[20]

Paralleling these efforts, but far more important to the over-all bank program, were the purchases of machinery. The first order for equipment had actually been placed prior to the creation of the bank when Alamán, using the authority vested in him by the April 1830 legislation, had directed New Orleans consul, Martínez Pizarro, to arrange for the construction of a cotton mill.[21] Once the junta was organized, it followed up this original order with a series of requests to overseas suppliers. The largest purchase consisted of four additional cotton mills and two paper mills, for which contracts were placed with tool builders in Pennsylvania and New Jersey. The cotton machinery, which was designed to operate from 2,400 to 3,840 spindles in each mill, was larger than the average United States plant operating at that time, and represented a tremendous advance over handicraft methods for Mexico.[22]

This emphasis on large power-driven units did not mean that the junta was indifferent to the possibility of improving the productivity of the small shop during the transitional phase to a fully mechanized industry. On the contrary, it placed orders for several hundred spinning jennies and a hundred handlooms with the idea that some could be distributed while others could serve as models to be reproduced by native craftsmen.[23]

The machine-purchase program was directed also, though on a lesser scale, to the acquisition of agricultural equipment. The junta was particularly interested in purchasing cotton gins, for it was well aware of the savings possible if the traditional practice of transporting seed cotton to the manufacturing centers could be abandoned. The practical problem of whether United States gins would work efficiently on Mexican cotton had to be resolved first, however, because prior experience with mechanical cleaners had not been encouraging.[24] Accordingly, the New Orleans consul, at the request of the bank, conducted experiments with cotton shipped to him from Mexico, and when he reported success, the junta ordered the construction of equipment for two sizeable mills.[25]

It may be worth noting that all the above-mentioned orders were given to tool makers in the United States rather than to ones in Europe. This is partly because it was expected that time and money could be saved by dealing with the neighboring country, but it was largely because the desired articles were not readily available in Europe. British restrictions on textile-machinery exports made it logical for the junta to purchase cotton-manufacturing equipment in the United States. For woolen and silk equipment, however, Mexico turned to France. The tool makers of that country were commissioned to supply machinery for two complete wool mills, plus a score of looms to produce silk cloth and stockings.[26]

In its quest for modern tools, the junta did not overlook the possibility of domestic construction. The presence in Mexico of foreign mechanics suggested this possibility, and the idea was taken up with at least two English mechanics. The most promising project called for the bank to finance one Thomas Lanson in the establishment of a machine shop where native workmen would be trained to make agricultural equipment. The negotiations reached the stage where Lanson was asked to submit detailed sketches of threshers and winnowers, but for some unexplained reason, the project was pursued no further.[27]

Although the purchase of machinery was an important step, it could not of itself create the industrial establishments desired by the Banco de Avío. It was no less vital to secure the cooperation of individual entrepreneurs, men willing to accept the risks of engaging in untried enterprises by investing their own funds alongside those provided by the bank. But where were such individuals to be found? The traditional attractions of real-estate investment on the one hand, and the lucrative opportunities for speculating in government debts on the other, constituted irresistible alternatives to manufacturing investments. What could be done if private capital were reluctant to enter industry?

The answer of Minister Alamán was to ask Congress to broaden the powers of the bank.[28] In a bill submitted in January 1831, authorization was sought for the junta "to establish on behalf of the bank itself those industrial enterprises it considers opportune for the development of fields regarded as important for the nation." Alamán, moreover, asked for power "to provide investment funds under conditions considered as equitable, without the bank having to limit itself to the 5-percent interest, but rather to acquire equity in the enterprises that are formed whenever the entrepreneurs do not put in capital of their own, and ask the bank for the total needed for the projects they are proposing."[29]

Had these recommendations been adopted, they would have effected a basic change in the nature of the bank as originally conceived. From an agency limited to encouraging private initiative through low-interest loans, it would have become a combination state trust and holding company as well as a loan bank. With the power to select the type of assistance most suited to the circumstances, the Banco de Avío would have possessed the attributes of the flexible development agency of the twentieth century, the *financiera*.

Alamán's proposals, it might be argued, prophetically foreshadowed this latter-day institution, but the Chamber of Deputies to which he submitted them found them too radical. While agreeing reluctantly that the bank should be able to operate the machinery it acquired for demonstration purposes whenever private individuals showed no interest in it, the legislators were firmly convinced of the superiority of private over public enterprise. They consequently sought to hedge the grant of operating authority with safeguards that would discourage the junta from retaining possession of the concerns it established. Unfortunately for the bank, the Chamber consumed so much time in rewriting the bill that enactment was postponed to a future session, which meant, as it turned out, that the bill died.[30]

The fate of Alamán's proposals cannot deny them their importance as evidence of his economic philosophy. Nevertheless, a modern view of Alamán has contended:

It does not appear that he has been a partisan of state intervention in the economy. The influence of economic liberalism on his thought is unquestionable. In his opinion, everything that was the work of nature or of private effort in Mexico had progressed, whereas everything in which public authority was involved had decayed.[31]

Certainly, in the light of Alamán's proposals to reform the bank, the above interpretation leaves something to be desired.

The failure to obtain a legislative solution to the problem created by private capital's reluctance to underwrite the proposed factories gave added importance to another solution attempted by the junta. On the assumption that the major deterrent to individuals was the size of the necessary investment, it proposed to spread the risk by encouraging the formation of stock companies.[32] This plan was, in reality, the continuation of a policy that Alamán had initiated in April 1830 when the first industrial assistance measure was enacted. At that time, he had called on the state governors to foster the creation of such companies within their respective districts, while he himself undertook similar action in and around Mexico City.[33] The result of the relaciones minister's personal intervention was the formation of the Compañia Industrial Mexicana with a subscribed capital that eventually exceeded $30,000.[34] Elsewhere in the republic the results were less impressive, for while plans for some half dozen companies were announced, only three were actually organized, and none of these had a pledged capital of even $10,000.[35]

Early in 1831 the junta directed its efforts toward activating these companies, and encouraging the formation of new ones. It sent an appeal to the governors of four states calling on each to "put in exercise his knowledge of local people and his ascendancy over his citizens" so as to organize one or more companies. At the same time, the junta carried the campaign directly to private citizens in various parts of the country by requesting that those who had shown interest by answering the questionnaire now initiate companies in their own areas.[36]

The success of these various appeals was reported by the junta in its first annual report. Fourteen companies, in as many different communities, were listed with a total subscribed capital, for the eleven on which data was available, of $102,603. While conceding the apparent smallness of the sum, the junta nevertheless took great pride in the accomplishment:

It is without doubt a notable step in the movement for industrialization to have succeeded in reviving the spirit of enterprise among
a people who, proud of the mineral wealth of their soil and retaining still to some extent the inactivity to which they had been reduced for so long, never imagined that they would be considered
as a manufacturing nation.[37]

But can one agree with the junta that in the formation of these companies the spirit of enterprise had arisen? An inquiry into their origin
suggests otherwise. Of the fourteen companies reported on, only two
appear to have been purely private; official sponsorship was responsible for all the others.[38]

The techniques by which these companies came into existence may
be illustrated by what took place in Guanajuato. There, at the insistence
of Alamán and his fellow members of the junta, the governor set the
wheels in motion to organize four stock companies, even though he
personally was skeptical about his constituents' enthusiasm.[39] The
actual tasks of organization were entrusted to the *jefes políticos* of the
various districts. These officials, accompanied in some instances by
local clergy, went about urging their fellow citizens to purchase shares.
Enough pledges were thus received to make possible the three companies set up in Celaya, San Miguel, and León.[40]

Now, it might be argued that official action to create the companies
did not necessarily preclude the presence of the entrepreneurial spirit
among the investors; that those who took shares did so from a genuine
belief in the purposes of the company, and out of expectation of profit.
Such, indeed, may have been the motive for some of the investors; but it
seems altogether probable that many others did so for quite different
reasons. When the jefe político and the local priest, the representatives
of civil and ecclesiastical authority, approached someone about purchasing shares, it must have been extremely difficult for the latter to refuse, particularly if he were in any way dependent on the government.
Perhaps this explains why public officeholders were the largest single
group of investors in the Celaya company.[41]

Another factor that raises questions about the nature of the companies was the role played in their creation by members of the clergy. Ecclesiastical bodies subscribed to shares, and, in at least one instance,
made an outright gift to a company.[42] Individual clergymen from the
rank of bishop down to parish priest were active in all stages of organization of the companies, urging parishioners to invest, purchasing
shares themselves, and even serving as chairmen of boards of direc-

tors.[43] Such activities suggest that the participants viewed the companies more as semipublic associations with patriotic and philanthropic
overtones than as business ventures.

The equivocal nature of these companies, the paucity of their capital,
and the fact that many who pledged shares lacked a genuine interest in
their success, were all factors that augured ill for the future. And yet,
even more ominous was the atmosphere of helpless ignorance that accompanied their formation. None of the leading participants in the various communities had any accurate idea of the capital needed to put a
factory into operation; none of them knew how much it would cost to
acquire, transport, and install imported machinery, to secure the services of foreign technicians, or to overcome the obstacles that inevitably
befall new enterprises. Nor was the junta itself able to enlighten them.[44]
Experience alone could supply such data, and no one in Mexico possessed that experience.

6

LOAN POLICIES AND OPERATIONS TO 1832

The law that created the Banco de Avío authorized its directors to supply capital to those individuals and companies who would engage in
desired enterprises, and who could adequately secure the funds advanced. As the details of the law became known throughout the country, particularly the unusually low interest rate on bank loans, a small
but steady stream of applications flowed into the office of the institution. It is the purpose of the present chapter to examine how the junta
responded to these applications, to explore the policies adopted for
handling requests, and the steps it took to safeguard its funds against
loss. Only when it is fully understood why the junta made the loans it
did, can judgment be fairly passed on its managerial competence.

It should be realized that the junta, in developing lending policies for
the bank, had no body of precedent to fall back on; neither did it have
the guidance that the executive power was supposed to provide in a
regulatory decree. It is understandable why, then, with a one million
peso fund to dispense, the directors were initially optimistic about their
prospects for accomplishment. They readily assumed that they could
scatter assistance to a host of small enterprises, and at the same time
finance the major establishments in which they were interested.

This optimistic assumption underlay the junta's lending operations
for the first six months, or until June 1831. During this period, although
it took action on only a handful of loans, it gave indication of a desire to
approve many more. Not only did it refrain from rejecting flatly any application submitted to it, it even went so far as to solicit new requests.[1]
Moreover, it acknowledged its obligation to make its assistance available to every part of the Republic "enabling all the states to experience
the benefits which the government and the Congress of the Union intended through the creation of the Junta."[2]

The expansiveness of its policy, however, did not blind the junta to the fact that it was necessary to define more precisely than the existing law did, the types of enterprises for which loans could be made. The bank statute had authorized assistance for any project, agricultural or industrial, which, in the junta's view, served the national interest. To be sure, it was legally bound to give preference to the textile industries, but it still had the problem of deciding on projects from other fields. The junta's solution was essentially this: to qualify for a bank loan, a project had to involve either the production of an article currently imported in significant quantities, or else the introduction of productive techniques more advanced than any then in use. The junta, in short, was interpreting the phrase "national interest" as used in the bank statute to mean promoting the self-sufficiency and technological progress of the Mexican economy. Only those projects that served these ends had a public utility that warranted assistance from the Banco de Avío.[3]

Table 1 summarizes the lending operations of the bank in its first full year of activity. The fact that only six loans were granted, all of them before June 1831, hardly seems consistent with the junta's original lending philosophy. But sometime after the end of May, a new and more cautious outlook was adopted; this followed a reassessment of its available resources and existing commitments, which by now included machinery purchase orders and promises of assistance to various companies. Aware of the disparity between its ends and its means, the junta began to retrench by tabling various applications, including some it had actively solicited.[4] The result was that from June to November, not a single new loan was granted.

It is interesting, nevertheless, to analyze the six completed loans in the light of the working principles formulated by the junta. Obviously, these few loans could hardly fulfill its announced intention of making resources available to the entire Republic. Even so, the fact that all but one of the six projects were located within fifty miles of Mexico City suggests that the directors of the bank had temporarily succumbed to the traditional myopia of national administrators, for whom the capital and its environs constitute the entire nation.

From the viewpoint of their impact on the economy, the six loans conformed, though in varying degrees, to the two criteria of utility established by the junta. The Zacualpa de Amilpas ironworks, for which the largest loan was advanced, and for which additional sums were promised, fulfilled both conditions. Its goal was the erection of a modern blast furnace near the iron ore deposits recently discovered in the valley of Cuatla, a location admirably suited to supply the major population centers of Mexico and Puebla with the bar and sheet iron currently imported from abroad. Aware of the significance to the economy of a successful iron industry, the junta assigned a high priority to this enterprise.[5] The remaining projects, with the exception of the Lazo de la Vega silkworks, which enjoyed a priority explicitly mentioned in the statute, were justified as serving the public interest either, as in the case of the apiaries, because they would reduce the need for foreign wax, or, as in the case of the sawmill, because it would put into operation a novel board-sawing machine recently acquired from the Netherlands.[6]

In approving the six loans listed in table 1, the junta, of course, had to consider more than the nature of the proposed enterprises. The selection of these projects was, in effect, a decision to favor certain persons seeking low-interest loans, as against certain others equally interested. The inevitable question arises: To what extent did personal favoritism or political pressure influence the decisions?

TABLE 1

Banco de Avío Loans Granted Prior to November 1831

Date[a]	Borrower	Type of project	Location	Term (yrs)	Amount
Dec. 7, 1830	Vicente Casarín	Sawmill	Mexico City	1	$ 3,000[b]
Dec. 21, 1830	D. Lazo de la Vega	Silk works	Celaya, Gto.	9	5,200[c]
Jan. 13, 1831	Agustín Vallarta	Apiary	Xochimilco	6	3,000[d]
Jan. 31, 1831	Pascual Sánchez	Apiary	Cuernavaca	5	5,000
Feb. 7, 1831	Tlalnepantla Ind. Co.	Bees, flax, mulberries	Tlalnepantla, Méx.	6	3,330
May 27, 1831	Zacualpa de Amilpas Co	Ironworks	Cuatla, Méx.	6	12,000
Total					$31,530[e]

a. Refers to junta session when decision was made.
b. Includes initial loan of $1,000 and two additional sums of like amount voted in Feb. 1831.
c. This was first of a series of annual installments; for subsequent ones, see table 2 below.
d. Only $600 was paid over to borrower before this loan was suspended.
e. Net total paid out was $29,130 (see n. d.).
Source: Libro de Actas.

Such factors appear to have played little or no part in the four smaller loans, those under $5,000. The individual borrowers, Casarín, Vallarta, and Sánchez, were not personal friends of the directors, and enjoyed no special influence. The relationship of the Tlalnepantla Company to the members of the junta was similar, save for the fact that as a company organized in response to official encouragement, it probably enjoyed some advantage over individual applicants.

It is easier to argue the presence of favoritism in the two larger loans, for in both cases the recipients were well known to the bank directors. Domingo Lazo de la Vega was a friend and fellow Guanajuatensen of the chairman, Lucas Alamán. Lazo's project called for the bank to supply all the capital needed for the establishment of an integrated silkworks, while he invested nothing except his time, and pledged no assets of his own to secure the loan. The junta committed the bank to supply annual sums to the enterprise with the probability that the full investment would eventually amount to $40,000.[7] Such an arrangement, with its unequal distribution of risk, is evidence that the borrower enjoyed the junta's confidence to an extraordinary degree, and strongly suggests that had it not been for the personal recommendation of his friend and neighbor, Alamán, Lazo's application would not have prospered.

The relationship of the Zacualpa de Amilpas Company to the directors of the bank was even more intimate, although in this case the loan had greater justification. The Zacualpa de Amilpas Company was a partnership composed of Frederick von Geroldt, the Prussian consul general and discoverer of the Cuatla iron deposits, Richard Francis, apparently an Englishman but of whom little is known, Tomás Ramón de Moral, professor at the School of Mines, and, last but not least, General Ramón Rayón, senior director of the Banco de Avío. Rayón was not only an interested party, but the guarantor for his associates in the proposed loan.[8]

It is curious that not a single note of concern over the propriety of the loan was voiced by any member of the junta. Quite the contrary, Rayón's voluntary offer to withdraw from the conference room during the discussions of the matter was regarded as adequate solution to the ethical problem, and the remaining members gave their approval to what they called "an undertaking of such great public importance that the Bank ought to promote it in preference to others."[9] It can not be categorically affirmed whether the decision would have been the same had the personal relationships been different. What is clear, however, is that the bank directors, as officials entrusted with public funds, should have acted so as to leave no doubts about their integrity. The proper thing would have been to insist that Rayón disassociate himself completely from either the bank or the company.

Although the element of personal influence was present in junta decisions, as indicated above, external political pressures did not play so significant a role as might be imagined. To be sure, the procedure for handling loan requests from distant applicants did permit a kind of negative pressure to operate. The junta, in order to clarify the character and credit status of the prospective borrower, would request information from the governor of his state. While the data sought was only what a credit agency would normally supply in a developed society, this dependence upon a state official paved the way for local prejudices and political partisanship to color the reports. The junta's files show several cases in which the adverse comment of the state leader contributed to the shelving of the request.[10] To what extent such comment was politically motivated, or, indeed, represented an objective review of an applicant's character and standing, cannot be determined; nonetheless, the opportunity for the former was certainly provided. But if the animosity of a public official could thus hurt an applicant's chances, a favorable recommendation did not automatically assure him of success. Several instances might be cited, but the outstanding one involved a federal employee whose request for $10,000 to establish a paper mill bore the recommendation of Vice-President Bustamante.[11] The junta notified General Bustamante of its desire to "please him in every way possible" but when it discovered that the applicant could not provide adequate security for the loan, it refused to grant it.[12] Of course, had Bustamante chosen to make an issue of it, the result might have been different; but the episode demonstrates that the junta under Alamán's chairmanship was no mere puppet of the executive power; rather, it was administering its funds in accordance with its own best judgment.

The exercise of that judgment produced, in the bank's second year, a pattern of lending that differed in several respects from that of the previous year. Most obvious, as table 2 reveals, was the increase in the overall volume of lending, and in the size of individual grants. In several instances, a single loan practically equaled the total of the first year's operations. But more important is the fact that the textile industry was now the principal beneficiary of the bank. Nearly 70 percent of the second year's loans went to the five establishments that proposed to engage in the manufacture of cotton or wool. The balance went to enterprises to which the bank had already extended funds the previous year.[13]

Of the five approved textile projects, four were major undertakings that called for the construction of power-driven factories, each capable of performing all the processes for converting raw materials into finished goods. The fifth involved the expansion of a small already existent woolen factory. To the former went not only the funds listed in the table, but consignments of machinery from the units under construction abroad.

The identity of the four firms that received these major grants deserves scrutiny. The promoter of the Puebla cotton mill, Estevan de Antuñano and Company, was an established merchant house that enjoyed no special connections with the bank or the government. In sharp contrast, the three other firms were all government-promoted stock companies, created for the specific purpose of undertaking industrial enterprises. The previous chapter related the manner in which these and other companies had been organized. Now, by granting to the Mexico, Querétaro, and Celaya Industrial companies the loans listed in table 2, the junta was fulfilling its earlier promises made as a means of encouraging the respective shareholders to invest.

It is not hard to explain why these three companies, of the fourteen that had been organized, should have been the first to receive capital loans and machinery allocations. In the case of the Mexican Industrial Company, subsequently known as the Tlalpam Company, because of the location of its factory, the principal reason is to be found in the intense interest which bank officials had in its success. Alamán had personally initiated its formation even before the bank was created; and, with its factory planned for the outskirts of Mexico City, its development inevitably became a barometer of progress for the entire industrial promotion program. The ties between company and bank, which had been intimate from the beginning, became even tighter when the stockholders selected, as chairman of their managerial board, junta member Santiago Aldazoro.[14]

The Celaya Industrial Company enjoyed a similar status for somewhat the same reasons. Alamán and his associates on the junta had been very active in promoting the formation of this company, more so than in any other. Here, however, the underlying motivation seems to have been Alamán's personal familiarity with the people and conditions of the city of Celaya, and his desire to develop its industrial potential.

TABLE 2
Loans Granted November 1, 1831 — October 31, 1832[a]

Date	Borrower	Type of project	Location	Term (yrs)	Amount
Nov. 11, 1831	D. Lazo de la Vega	Silkworks	Celaya, Gto.	9	$ 6,450[b]
Dec. 5, 1831	Zacualpa de Amilpas Co.	Ironworks	Cuatla, Méx.	6	28,000
Dec. 16, 1831	Vicente Casarín	Building orna-ments mfg.	Mexico City	5	1,500
Dec. 20, 1831	E. Antuñano and Co.	Cotton mill	Puebla, Pue.	5	30,000
Jan. 10, 1832	Mexico Indus-trial Co.	Cotton mill	Tlalpam, Méx.	9	25,000
Jan. 26, 1832	Francisco Puig	Woolen textiles	Puebla, Pue.	5	10,000
Jan. 26, 1832	Celaya Indus-trial Co.	Cotton mill	Celaya, Gto.	9	15,000
Jan. 26, 1832	D. Lazo de la Vega	(see above)	(see above)	9	12,940
Feb. 21, 1832	Querétaro In-dustrial Co.	Woolen mill	Querétaro, Qro.	9	30,000
Jun. 1, 1832	Mexico Indus-trial Co.	(see above)	(see above)	9	25,000
Sep. 12, 1832	Zacualpa de Amilpas Co.	(see above)	(see above)	6	10,000
Total					$193,890

a. Not listed is a $20,000 loan approved on Jun. 1, 1832, but not taken up by the applicant.
b. Includes $1,000 approved on Dec. 5, 1831.
Source: Libro de Actas.

Indeed, some five years before he had made an unsuccessful attempt to set up a cotton factory of his own.[15] Now from his official position he had a chance to aid the economy of this city to which he was bound by ties of property and sentiment. Accordingly, while the first set of for-eign-built cotton machinery went to the Tlalpam Company, the second was assigned to the Celaya Company.[16]

The success of the Querétaro Industrial Company in obtaining ear-ly junta consideration is attributable to a series of fortuitous cir-cumstances. In November 1830 the junta had ordered from France the complete equipment for a woolen factory, at the request of an Aguascalientes woolen manufacturer.[17] Some time after February 1831, the arrangements between the bank and this manufacturer, Sr. López Pimental, fell through, and the junta was confronted with the problem of reassigning the equipment. The formation in August of the Querétaro Industrial Company seemed to provide the logical solution. Not only was this the sole company seriously interested in acquiring the wool machinery, but Querétaro, as the traditional center of the woolen industry, seemed to offer an ideal location for a modernizing venture. Accordingly, the junta was prompt to encourage the company and to accede to its loan request.[18]

Mention has been made of the fact that the private firm of Antuñano and Company was one of the first factory operators to be aided by the bank. In view of the junta's standing offer to supply loans and equipment to a number of industrial companies, many of which wanted to establish cotton factories, its decision to give priority to the Antuñano works requires explanation. As of November 1831, the junta had decided not to order additional cotton machinery from abroad "until it saw the results of those already commissioned."[19] These included the cotton mill for the Tlalpam Company already in the country, the mill for Celaya which was to be ready by January 1832, and three others in various stages of construction. The junta fully anticipated that these latter would eventually go to industrial companies, and, indeed, in the November 11 session, it tentatively designated the Puebla, Tlaxcala, and Morelia associations as the future recipients.[20] In December, however, it decided to reassign the Puebla Industrial Company's mill to Estevan de Antuñano, who was proposing to erect a cotton factory along the Atoyac River.[21] This decision was undoubtedly influenced by the purposive energy displayed by Antuñano in contrast to the paralysis that had lately possessed the industrial company.[22] The two were not unrelated, for Antuñano, curiously enough, had been its treasurer and a leading shareholder; but then he began to devote himself to his own plans, and the company sank into lethargy.[23] The junta, primarily concerned with getting the mill into operation, had no qualms about abandoning the moribund industrial company and placing its faith in the private entrepreneur.

In the two years of lending operations that ended in November 1832, the Banco de Avío distributed $223,020 in loans, or almost one-fourth of its legally assigned capital. None of this money, however, passed into the hands of a borrower until he had agreed to the terms of a contract approved by the bank's directors.[24] Through such contracts, the latter sought to achieve three principal objectives: first, to prevent, or at least discourage, the misuse of bank funds; second, to determine the conditions of interest payments and the periods for which loans would run; and last, to provide safeguards against non-repayment of the principal.

The junta's determination to prevent misuse of its funds was reflected in the standard contract provision that established its right to inspect the borrower's books at any time, and to cancel the loan immediately if circumstances warranted. As an additional guarantee of honest behavior, the junta frequently insisted on disbursing a loan in several installments. Most borrowers agreed to these provisions without hesitation; the sole exception was the Querétaro Company, which vainly objected that the inspection clause "degrades the company so that no one will want to risk his money, or offer his services, while subject to an inspection of this sort."[25] Such extreme sensitivity did not deter the junta from standing its ground. Experience was soon to demonstrate the value of the installment procedure when, in the case of the Vallarta loan, the junta found cause to suspend the transaction after only one-fifth of the $3,000 approved had been disbursed.[26]

The conditions governing interest payments were set down in detail in the various contracts. Each borrower had to promise to satisfy his obligations in quarterly installments, and to make the payments "en moneda doble de plata del cuño mejicano." This latter requirement was intended to protect the bank from the copper and other depreciated coinage circulating in the country. The payments had to be made in Mexico City, and for this reason distant borrowers had to name a resident agent to handle their obligations. Interest began either from the date of the contract, or, in the case of those loans issued in installments, from the date of each one.

The rate of interest was of course established by law, and the bank directors had no authority to alter it; they did, however, have discretionary power over the length of loans inasmuch as the statute had merely stipulated that they should fix "a normal period for repayment." In practice, although the maximum period allowed was nine years, most borrowers were given either five or six to return their loans. Indeed, only $3,000 out of the total of $223,020 had to be repaid in less than five years; and in none of the contracts was there any provision for systematic amortization.[27] It is clear, then, that the directors were committing themselves to a policy of slow turnover in the use of their capital, a policy that inevitably limited the bank's potential impact on the economy.

In establishing security requirements for loans, the directors were

under few statutory restraints. Apart from requiring that all loans be secured, the bank law was completely silent on such matters as the nature
of the guarantees, the definition of acceptable collateral, or the amounts
that could be loaned against such collateral. The result of the interpretation that the directors gave to the security requirement was to demand that each borrower supply as his principal guarantee a mortgage
of certain assets. This insistence on mortgages, adopted possibly in imi-
tation of the traditionally conservative lending practices of the clergy,
gives the Banco de Avío a superficial resemblance to the *bancos hipote-
carios* of a later era; but unlike them, it was prepared to accept mortgages on assets other than real property.

Undoubtedly, the junta would have preferred to lend its money on
the guarantee of *bienes raíces* (real estate) and whenever possible it did.
Indeed, on such security it advanced $61,930, or over 27 percent of its
loan portfolio.[28] But to have insisted in every case on a mortgage of *fin-
cas urbanas ó rústicas* (rural or urban properties) would have meant reducing the possibility of providing investment credit, particularly to the
industrial companies and other sponsors of major enterprises. Faced
with the choice of taking risks to advance the fundamental purposes of
the bank, or of playing it safe for minor gains, the junta preferred to gam-
ble. Accordingly, it accepted mortgages on a variety of assets: machinery, as in the Casarín and Puig loans; mines and equipment, as in the advances to the ironworks; and, in the case of the industrial companies,
the equity of the stockholders, and whatever of value was added to their
enterprises such as the factory site, water rights, buildings under construction, tools, and so forth. In two instances where the pledged assets
seemed least adequate, the junta claimed the "privilegio que las Leyes
conceden a los acreedores refaccionarios," which gave at least the assurance that in any future bankruptcy proceedings the claims of the
Banco de Avío on the unpledged assets would take precedence over
those of all other creditors, save tax collectors.[29]

The junta's willingness to provide sums on what it knew to be sketchy
collateral was related to its confidence that the assisted enterprises
would soon become working realities. It particularly believed that the
year 1832 would find one or more textile factories in operation. Such
confidence was not without basis, for the last few months of 1831 had
borne noisy witness to the industrial changes in preparation. At Tlalpam, and in the outskirts of Puebla, construction had begun on the
buildings that were to house cotton mills; in Celaya and Querétaro, a beginning had been made with the selection of sites for their respective

factories. Meanwhile at Veracruz, port workers had already unloaded the first of the foreign-built plants to arrive: the cotton mill for the Tlalpam factory and the woolen mill for Querétaro. And coincident with the arrival of this equipment came the teams of foreign technicians hired to supervise the assembly of the factories and to teach native workmen the intricacies of their operation.[30] The only obvious source of delay that the junta could foresee, and this did not seem too serious, derived from the difficulties of domestic transport. The movement of heavy crates from Veracruz to the various factory sites required the use of wagons, but few freight handlers were equipped to do the job, and indeed only one made a serious bid for it.[31] The junta consequently had to allow four months from October 1831 for the delivery of the Tlalpam factory's equipment, and only in February 1832 could a beginning be made to move the Querétaro Company's machinery. Other equipment arriving at the port would have to wait its turn.[32] But in spite of such delays, the dawn of a new industrial era for Mexico seemed close at hand.

THE STRUGGLE FOR SURVIVAL,

1832 — 1835

The officers of the Banco de Avío overlooked one vital consideration in anticipating that 1832 would find Mexican factories producing their first cotton and wool textiles. In this as in any economic development program, the minimum condition for success is the maintenance of public order. Here the critical factor was the inability of the Bustamante regime either to gain voluntary acceptance for itself, or to crush its enemies beyond the point of revolt. After rising to power through a revolt of its own, this administration had to devote 1830 to pacifying the country. Its policy of executing the leaders of insurrections and curbing all expressions of criticism finally won it a breathing spell in 1831. But it was only a respite, not a permanent peace. The execution of General Guerrero, from whom Bustamante had wrested control, was a moral and political blunder; it merely numbed the opposition, it did not destroy it. Moreover, the national conscience was shocked that a Mexican government would resort to treachery to destroy this great patriot of independence.

Violence burst out again on January 2, 1832, when the strategically located Veracruz garrison rose in revolt. The stated objective of this movement, whose leadership General Santa Anna assumed, was the removal of the cabinet, especially the relaciones and war ministers, Alamán and Facio, who were accused of responsibility for Guerrero's death. Government forces dispatched to Veracruz were successful in restricting Santa Anna's forces to the port, but failed to destroy them. Meanwhile, the movement spread as the liberal governor of Zacatecas, Francisco García, joined in demanding the removal of the cabinet; and the authorities of Jalisco and Tamaulipas soon followed suit.

In May, Vice-President Bustamante yielded to circumstances and accepted the resignations of his ministers; but this was not enough to appease the opposition. For the revolutionaries now were seeking another goal: the return of Manuel Gómez Pedraza to serve out the presidential term for which he had been elected in 1828. Bustamante took to the field himself in an effort to put down the rebels, but finally, convinced of his inability to suppress his opponents, he came to terms with them.

The agreements signed at Zavaleta on December 23, 1832, provided, apart from promotions for troops on both sides, that the federal and state administrations should be wholly renovated; and that Gómez Pedraza should exercise the presidency until April 1, 1833, when a newly elected executive would assume the office. The agreements were carried out. On December 24, Gómez Pedraza took up his duties; and in the elections that followed, General Santa Anna was declared the victor, while Valentín Gómez Farías, a liberal and a civilian, was named vicepresident.

When the civil war first broke out in Veracruz in January 1832, it had an immediate and disastrous impact on the industrial development program. With the port city in hostile hands, normal communications to the interior ceased, and the transfer of bank-purchased machinery came to an abrupt halt. Even the wagons used to freight this equipment were pressed into military service. The timing of the revolt, from the viewpoint of the textile companies, could not have been worse, for it immobilized at the port the woolen mill intended for Querétaro plus some forty crates of equipment awaiting transfer to the Tlalpam factory. The succeeding weeks, moreover, saw other equipment, including the silk textile machinery designated for the León company, arrive from abroad only to pile up uselessly at the port.[1]

Most serious was the fate of the woolen mill. The other equipment had been stored in warehouses, but because of the huge size and weight of its twenty-five crates, this mill was allowed to remain on the open docks. For a year this valuable equipment lay exposed to sun, rain, and salt spray, all with ruinous effect. Moreover, during the confusion of military operations, unknown individuals broke into several of the crates and made off with essential pieces. Meanwhile, the junta, seated in the opposing camp, was powerless to protect the mill from the destructive forces of man or nature.[2]

The impossibility of delivering the mill to its Querétaro factory site brought with it other inconveniences. The foreign technicians hired to assemble it were already in the country, drawing salaries in accordance with contracts signed the year before. Under the circumstances, the bank had the unhappy obligation of paying these technicians even though they remained in idleness. A similar situation developed with the silk experts who arrived at Veracruz with the machinery intended for León only to be caught in the siege of the port city.[3]

The effects of the civil war were not limited to the cessation of machinery transfers and the losses entailed thereby. Graver still was the direct impact on the resources of the bank. At Veracruz the revolutionaries had felt no compunction at seizing the monies set aside for it in the local customhouse. This disregard for the sanctity of bank funds was duplicated elsewhere, and not only by rebel forces. Loyal troops also were utilizing monies possessed by the bank at various depositories. At Tampico in particular, the bank lost the $60,000 it was planning to send to the United States to pay for machinery under construction. Such seizures, costly in themselves, were all the more serious because the spread of military operations to the major ports cut off the possibility of new income from customs duties.[4]

With the disappearance of its funds, the junta not only saw its hopes for the early completion of various factories destroyed, it also faced the loss of much of the capital already invested. Abroad, the inability to forward payments for equipment under construction led irate tool builders to threaten with attachment other equipment already paid for but awaiting shipment.[5] At home, the junta found itself unable to respond to loan requests from several textile companies that had already used up their own funds and those previously advanced by the bank. The paralysis of these companies before the completion of their factories meant almost certain loss for the monies previously invested in them both by the bank and their own shareholders.

In these circumstances, the junta resorted to extraordinary measures to enable the textile companies to continue. To help them conserve their liquid funds, the junta voted to waive interest payments due on monies previously loaned until such time as their factories were actually in operation. And to obtain immediate funds with which it might assist the companies in achieving that goal, it resolved to float a public loan at whatever interest rate might be necessary. It was the junta's belief that the burden of such a loan would be "incomparably less than the damage which the enterprises would otherwise suffer."[6]

Both the waiving of interest and the floating of a loan were steps that required legislative sanction; but the junta experienced little difficulty in getting the necessary approval. Congress authorized the government to raise up to $100,000 for the bank at the lowest cost possible, and to pledge as security for such a loan the duties assigned to the agency under the law of October 16, 1830.[7]

This authorization, however, proved utterly useless. The attempt to raise the $100,000 coincided with the floating of a $4 million Treasury loan which offered to the moneylenders advantages greater than the bank could ever provide.[8]

With the failure of this expedient, every remaining source of funds, however small, became vitally important to the junta. In the past, the bank had been receiving a small income from *comisos*, goods confiscated for violation of tariff regulations. The law governing the sale of such goods had stipulated that one-half of their proceeds should be deposited at the *Casa de Moneda* "for use in the development of industry ... as may be provided by a law."[9] Since no other legislation was adopted on the use of these funds, it had been the practice hitherto to turn them over to the bank.

Such sums had not loomed large to the junta before, but in the summer of 1832 they seemed quite significant. And, in fact, the sale of contraband did produce substantial amounts. In June, word was received that the Sinaloa commissary was holding $25,759 in an account marked *fomento de industria*. To obtain immediate use of these funds, the junta promptly sold a draft at a 14-percent discount, and from the $21,578 realized in this case, it advanced sums on two loans previously voted but not fulfilled.[10]

However, the finance minister, Rafael Mangino, had also come to regard the comisos in a different light. In a new ruling, he announced that the bank had no right to the funds; and in a communication to its officers, he requested the return of the $25,759.[11] The junta proposed that the sum be deducted from the monies seized from the bank to pay government troops, but when Minister Mangino, in Vice-President Bustamante's name, insisted on the immediate return of the sum, the junta had no recourse but to comply.[12] The resignation of Alamán had left it without a champion in the cabinet.

Thus, for the directors of the Banco de Avío, 1832 closed in gloomy contrast to their optimistic expectations of twelve months before. They had witnessed the disappearance of their sources of revenue, the useless accumulation of equipment, and the paralysis of enterprises they had sought to help. And while their records indicated that $478,000 had been spent since the bank's inception, they could not show to the Mexican people a single textile factory in operation. The experiences of the past year, moreover, served to shatter their earlier illusions. They now realized the heavy outlays needed to establish just a single factory, and the vanity of their earlier promises to assist the numerous industrial companies of whose existence they had been so proud. Accordingly, they now announced that their present intention was to limit assistance to a few chosen enterprises, conceding that "if one or two cotton factories are successfully established as the final result, that is all that could be desired even in less calamitous circumstances."[13]

The revolution that swept out the vestiges of the Alamán-Bustamante regime and installed Gómez Pedraza as a caretaker president created an air of uncertainty over the future of the Banco de Avío and its directors. Those gentlemen could not help but wonder about the new chief executive's attitude. Would he be sympathetic to the purposes of the bank? And even if he were, would he retain its present officers, all of whom owed their appointment to the fallen regime?

The first two months of the new administration appeared to offer the answers. President Gómez Pedraza showed no intention either of closing the bank, or of firing its directors. It is true that one member of the junta, Santiago Aldazoro, was relieved, and José María Icaza appointed to his post. But the bank law authorized the annual replacement of one member, and no other changes in personnel took place.[14]

Encouraged by the return of peaceful conditions and the indications of presidential confidence, the junta once more sought to revive activities that had been at a standstill the previous year. Orders were issued for the resumption of freight transfers, and soon wagon trains, straining under the weight of gears and looms, were making their way up from Veracruz. The junta also approved the issuance of new loans of $52,000 and $40,000 respectively, to Estevan de Antuñano and the Tlalpam company in line with the decision to give aid to only those enterprises that showed the greatest promise.[15]

Funds for these loans were not immediately available, but the junta gave the borrowers bills of exchange drawn on the Veracruz and Tampico customhouses in the hope that sufficient revenues from cotton duties would soon accumulate there in its accounts. The junta was aware that the practice of diverting bank revenues to alien purposes, which Treasury officials had engaged in during the civil war, had not ended with the return of peace. But in mid-February the president, responding to junta complaints, ordered Finance Minister Gómez Farías to have his subordinates respect the bank's funds.[16]

The junta also undertook to pay off debts to United States tool builders, and here again the president's cooperation was necessary. Word had been received from the bank's agent that immediate action was needed to save various machines from the auctioneer's block. The junta had no funds available, but Gómez Pedraza agreed to its proposal to send $45,000 from the Treasury and deduct it from amounts owed to the bank for past seizures.[17]

In view of such manifestations of presidential good will, it seemed as if the junta were finally recovering its former autonomy. But then, without warning, the administration took a step that entirely changed the junta's status. On March 1, Finance Minister Gómez Farías ordered that none of the duties collected at Veracruz be paid over to the bank, and that the income it was entitled to from cotton-goods imports should remain in the Treasury's general fund. One week later, the same order was extended to all other customhouses.[18]

This arbitrary suspension of the revenues assigned to the Banco de Avío by the October 16, 1830, law had its explanation in the desperate financial straits of the Gómez Pedraza government. The recently concluded civil war had bequeathed it a near-empty treasury and a heavy burden of debt. This debt included the short-term obligations that had been issued at ruinous rates by both sides in the conflict to secure funds from the money merchants, or *agiotistas*.[19] The new government was at first indisposed to recognize the debt incurred by the ousted Bustamante regime, but the pressure exerted by creditors (some of whom, being foreigners, were able to enlist the support of their legations), produced a change of heart. An agreement was thereupon worked out whereby 40 percent of the customs revenues was allocated to the liquidation of this debt.[20]

It was this agreement that led to the suspension of the duties assigned to the Banco de Avío. The government, compelled to subsist on only 60 percent of the usual custom revenues, needed to economize. The bank's financial independence was sacrificed to this need.[21]

The Finance Ministry directives of March 1833, however, did not mean the end of the Banco de Avío, nor of all public expenditure in its behalf. Though payments were subject to exasperating delays, the Treasury met the claims that rose from existing commitments to overseas machine builders, domestic freight handlers, and foreign technicians.[22] Moreover, it even found money for a few new loans, though here, too, the disbursement to the borrowers was subject to painful delays.

What the directives did signify above all else was the demotion of the junta from being managers of a semi-independent agency to a mere consultative body. They could no longer make decisions that involved funds; and, in fact, the exercise of all but routine decisions gravitated into the hands of the chief executive. For the next two years, the president and his minister of relaciones were the real directors of the Banco de Avío.

This era of executive control in the bank's history coincided with a period of confusion in the national government itself. It was the time of the ill-fated attempt of Vice-President Gómez Farías and his liberal advisers to reform Mexican society; these were the years when Gómez Farías and President Santa Anna alternated frequently in the exercise of executive authority until the vice-president's exile. This was also a time of frequent ministerial changes; from April 1833 until March 1835, when the junta recovered its powers, ten men served as minister of finance, four as minister of relaciones.[23]

With the highest executive authorities exercising direct control over the bank activities in this period, it is pertinent to inquire whether significant changes were introduced into previously established junta policies. In the past, one notorious ethical failing had been the financing of enterprises in which bank officials were personally interested. The government's attention was specifically called to this matter in June 1833 by an official report on previous bank management. José Antonio de Unzueta, appointed to investigate financial dealings under the Bustamante government, wrote in criticism:

> If the previous government has been remiss . . . in the distribution of public funds, it has been no more circumspect with those belonging to the Banco de Avío, an establishment which would have been an inexhaustible source of happiness to the nation in pure and truly patriotic hands. . . . It seems that it has been more a matter of favoring friends and financing themselves than of fulfilling the purposes of the bank.[24]

Whether such condemnation would influence future practice could only be revealed as instances involving loan requests from bank officials arose. In November 1833, the government had to make a decision on a request from Victoriano Roa, the secretary of the junta. Roa had applied to the junta for part of the textile mill once assigned to the defunct Celaya company, but now in storage in the bank's warehouse. The secretary pointed out that the machinery had been idle for over a year, and insisted that if it were advanced to him on the usual credit terms, he would have it in operation in a matter of months with funds supplied by a private source. Roa was aware that an ethical question was involved, but countered it with the argument that the bank law did not specify who should be eligible for aid, and hence this meant that no one was excluded.[25] The junta, impressed by the prospect of seeing the machinery in operation without further outlay of public funds, ignored the issue of propriety, and approvingly referred the request to higher authority.[26] President Santa Anna, on whom the final decision rested, saw no objection either, and Roa received the equipment.[27]

A few months later when Gómez Farías held the executive powers, he was confronted with a similar problem. Junta member General Rayón made a direct appeal to the vice-president to approve a $10,000 loan for the Zacualpa de Amilpas iron foundry, of which he was part owner. And here, again, the request was granted.[28] The assumption of executive control over loan decisions had certainly done little to eliminate the practice that had given rise to Unzueta's criticism.

In other ways too, the junta's loss of the power of decision brought surprisingly little change. It might have been expected that with Gómez Pedraza, Gómez Farías, and Santa Anna succeeding one another as chief executive within the space of three months, and with the latter two alternating in the office even more frequently, inconsistency in loan policy would have resulted. Actually, all three men, insofar as the state of the Treasury permitted, respected the basic decision made by the junta to concentrate monetary assistance on a few enterprises. Estevan de Antuñano, whose $52,000 loan voted by the junta in February 1833 had been voided by the suspension of the bank's funds, received $36,000 on it from Gómez Pedraza and Gómez Farías before the year was out. In March 1834, Gómez Farías approved a new loan to Antuñano for $60,000, and Santa Anna supplemented that with a $30,000 grant early in 1835. The Tlalpam Company, whose $40,000 loan voted by the junta had also been interrupted, was less fortunate; it obtained only $1,000 on account during 1833; but late in 1834, Santa Anna approved a transaction whereby the $40,000 was finally received.[29]

The outstanding instance of a difference of opinion between Gómez Farías and Santa Anna involved, not surprisingly, a member of the clergy; at stake in this case was not the granting of a new loan, but collection of monies due on an old one. The Puebla presbyter Antonio González Cruz had signed an agreement with the junta in January 1832 whereby he would repay $2,000 in 1833 and $3,000 in 1834 on a $5,000 claim held against property he had purchased.[30] The first payment was

made according to schedule, but in January 1834, González Cruz petitioned for a three-year stay before paying the balance. His explanation
of crop losses, suffered in connection with the internal disturbances
and the recent cholera epidemic, persuaded the junta to recommend
approval.[31] Gómez Farías, however, ordered the junta to collect the
$3,000 as soon as due.[32] González Cruz's second petition, this time for
a two-year extension, was also refused by the vice-president, who directed that, if necessary, legal steps should be taken to collect the
sum.[33] But the sudden return to the presidency of Santa Anna, now the
avowed champion of clerical interests against the liberal reformers,
changed the situation for González Cruz. By order of the general, the
cleric was granted an additional eighteen months to pay off his debt.[34]

With the reduction of the junta to a subordinate role, its relations
with the relaciones minister underwent a change. During Alamán's
ministry, the association of the junta with its chairman had been very
close; and apparently Alamán never made any decisions affecting the
bank's assets without consulting his fellow members. But after March
1833, it is clear that the successive occupants of the relaciones ministry
had less regard for their duties as junta chairmen than for their powers
as cabinet members. Bernardo González Angulo, for example, who occupied the dual post until April 26, 1833, turned over looms and other
bank equipment to the Federal District poorhouse and jail, without
even notifying the junta, and without any legal formalities whatsoever.
Later, when this body tried to have the officials of those institutions assume legal responsibility for the equipment, endless complications
arose.[35] Carlos García, González's successor, was guilty of a similar dis-
dain for the junta when he arbitrarily took some $10,000, which the bank
had in a London deposit, to finance the legation in Prussia. The junta,
uninformed of this, later issued a draft on the deposit, only to be embar-
rassed by having its paper protested.[36]

The frequent resignation of ministers introduced an element of instability that had not been known before in the administration of the bank.
To be sure, ministerial changes would have taken place even if the junta
had been permitted to exercise full power of decision, but their effects
on bank administration would have been diminished. This was one reason why a separate agency had been set up in the first place. As Alamán
had explained back in 1831:

> In order to give uniform and consistent management to the efforts
> to promote domestic industry, the government proposed, and the
> chambers agreed, to establish the junta which administers the

Banco de Avío. . . . If the activities were entrusted to the respective government ministries, many forces would work to their neglect. The minister is frequently distracted by immediate concerns, especially in times of unrest; he can spend only a moment on each matter, and when he is familiar with the details through knowledge acquired over a matter of months, it frequently happens that the minister is changed. The new occupant needs time to familiarize himself with the affairs; meanwhile everything slows down, or at least remains static, and this at times is enough to produce a new change; and so on from one to another, while the business remains forgotten.[37]

Alamán's prediction of administrative confusion if the industrial promotion program were left in ministerial hands was to some extent confirmed by the conditions that developed after 1833. During the last month of Carlos García's tenure as relaciones minister, arrangements were made for the sale on credit of various bank-owned machines. Mention has been made already of the disposal to Victoriano Roa of part of one textile mill; the balance of this mill, twenty looms plus spinning equipment, was turned over shortly thereafter to ex-junta member Santiago Aldazoro. The arrival at this time of two paper mills ordered from the United States three years before also led to an understanding whereby the state of Puebla would assume ownership and operation of one of them.[38]

The terms of the agreements concluded with the purchasers were extremely lenient. Some responsibility for this must be placed on the junta, which worked out the wording of the contracts, but even more must be assigned Minister García. It was he who recommended their approval to the chief executives—both Santa Anna and Gómez Farías were in and out of office at this time—and who in effect exercised the power of final decision.[39]

But then a change of ministers produced an unanticipated result. On December 16, Francisco Lombardo replaced García.[40] Lombardo was much more assertive than his predecessor in protecting the bank's interests. After examining the contracts that had already been signed with Roa and Aldazoro, he bluntly informed these individuals that changes would have to be made. The two would-be entrepreneurs had no choice but to accept.[41] In the case of the paper mill granted to Puebla, a written agreement had yet to be signed. Lombardo notified the state governor that the contract would have to embody the new requirements, and he brushed aside the latter's subsequent protests.[42] The entire episode revealed not only the administrative fluctuations that Alamán had foreseen, but also something of the danger of doing business with an unstable government.

From the viewpoint of promoting the bank's industrial objectives, Francisco Lombardo was the most effective relaciones minister since Alamán. It was during his tenure that Gómez Farías and Santa Anna agreed to the new loans previously mentioned. He was also successful in wrangling money from the Treasury to pay off a considerable amount of overdue debt.[43]

Lombardo, moreover, displayed greater concern than several of his predecessors in watching over the bank's investments. Shortly after taking office, he ordered all companies that had received funds in the past to render an accounting of their expenditures, and he notified those currently receiving loans to provide monthly statements of their outlays.[44] His determination to renegotiate contracts that failed, in his view, to protect bank interests has already been noted. He was also circumspect in granting new loans. Before approving Antuñano's request for $60,000 to continue construction on his cotton mill, Lombardo had experts survey the structure and examine the prospects for its completion. In addition, since the loan was to be made in Treasury drafts to be paid when funds were available, the minister carefully stipulated that any loss resulting from the discount of the paper would be at the borrower's risk.[45]

Lombardo's relations with the members of the junta appear to have been cordial. On several occasions, when individuals made direct application to him for grants of equipment owned by the bank, he did not, as some of his predecessors, take unilateral action, but asked the junta to vote on the requests. He followed this procedure also in connection with the Antuñano loan request.[46]

Nevertheless, the members of the junta were not content with their secondary role. They had warned the Finance Ministry, when the flow of bank funds was first cut off in March 1833, that this was a direct violation of the law. Their warnings at that time had produced little effect beyond encouraging that ministry to refer the matter to Congress. The issue of the legality of the action, however, had aroused little interest there.[47] In June 1834, the members of the junta renewed their appeal for the return of the bank's legal revenues, and for the restoration of their own authority.[48] When written requests to the chief executive were without effect, they even journeyed out to Tacubaya to appeal in person to Santa Anna. But apart from a promise to refer the matter to the next legislature, the president offered no encouragement.[49]

The close of the year thus found the officers of the bank discouraged and disillusioned. In their annual report, they could add little to what had been said before. It was now four years since the bank was founded, and the industrial changes anticipated then had not materialized. Of the major enterprises that had been aided in the intervening years, the Querétaro and the Celaya textile companies were now completely defunct, while the silk works of Domingo Lazo de la Vega was in similar straits. At Zacualpa de Amilpas, the iron foundry, beset by a variety of difficulties, was still not operating. The Tlalpam cotton mill and the smaller ones undertaken by Aldazoro and Roa in Mexico City had yet to produce their first skein of yarn. Meanwhile, the thousands spent to obtain foreign technicians for the Querétaro and León companies had been a total loss.[50]

The public explanation for this dismal situation which the junta offered was a simple one: the Finance Ministry directive of March 1833 was responsible for the total lack of achievement; it was that order which had "dealt the mortal blow to Mexican industry."[51] Nowhere in its report of January 1, 1835, did the junta admit what it had once conceded earlier, that it had undertaken to finance too many projects. In underestimating the costs of establishing new industries, the junta had become the victim of its own mistaken judgment, as well as of the civil disturbances of the past two years.

Nevertheless, in the midst of the gloom that pervaded this annual report, there was one encouraging note—the news that Antuñano and Company's textile mill was all but finished. And, indeed, on January 7, 1835, with a notary present to record this momentous event, the Puebla firm proudly began production in its cotton factory. It had taken almost four years to construct and had absorbed, apart from its owners' capital, $164,000 provided by the government.[52] The name given to the mill, *La Constancia Mexicana*, fittingly commemorated its owners' patience. But it was the constancy of public officials in supporting the project throughout the previous years of political uncertainty that made the mill possible. Under the aegis of the Banco de Avío, the first water-driven cotton mill in the nation's history had come into existence, and the first significant victory in the struggle to modernize Mexican industry had been won.

8

THE BANK REVIVED—FUNDS AND LOANS,

1835 — 1837

From what has been seen in the previous chapter, it is clear that the fate of the Banco de Avío was inevitably linked to political circumstances and to the demands these made on public finances. Indeed, in the years 1835 — 1837, Treasury requirements were to hold the key to bank activities.

In the early months of 1835, the officers of the bank were encouraged once again to seek the return of their authority and the restoration of the bank's rightful revenues. The occasion was a sudden change in the presidency brought on by General Santa Anna's differences with Congress. The newly assembled legislature, dominated by ultraconservatives who were bent on abolishing the federal constitution, had found the president too unresponsive to their wishes. Santa Anna, who never enjoyed dealing with a critical Congress, resorted to his earlier practice of retiring to the sidelines, while a substitute, in the person of General Miguel Barragán, was named.[1] It was to General Barragán that the junta now appealed, using the same petition that had been submitted in vain to his predecessor.[2]

But the time had passed when the chief executive could restore the funds of the bank by a simple executive order assigning to it its share of the cotton duties. For a movement had arisen in the country, and in the new Congress as well, to halt the flow of the foreign textiles on which these revenues depended.

Ever since the October 16, 1830, law was adopted, discontent with it had existed in artisan circles. In a previous chapter, it was related how a Puebla deputy, acting on behalf of artisan constituents, had tried to have the law repealed. The failure of this attempt in 1831 had neither stifled artisan fears of foreign competition, nor softened their antipathy to a bank that was trying to introduce factory methods. Indeed, in the

city of Puebla during 1833, feeling was so high among weavers and spinners that Estevan de Antuñano, who was constructing a factory with
bank assistance, felt impelled to become a pamphleteer to sing the
praises of the bank, and the virtues of factories.[3]

Nevertheless, in the following year in Puebla and several other states,
the pressure to exclude foreign textiles increased.[4] In Puebla, the state
legislature adopted a resolution calling for the repeal of the bank law insofar as it permitted the entry of foreign cottons.[5] Once again Antuñano
rushed to his pen to condemn such action, and to persuade his fellow
citizens that there was much to be gained if a few modern factories were
established before prohibition of foreign textiles went into effect.[6]

In the national Congress, the efforts to establish such prohibitions
only became serious in 1835. Between January and April of that year,
with at least four major states submitting resolutions calling for their
adoption, specific bills were introduced and referred for study to congressional committees. The most vociferous proponents of such legislation came from Puebla, Jalisco, México, Oaxaca, and Veracruz, the states
where the handicraft cotton industry had once prospered, or where the
raw material was raised extensively.[7] But the artisans and farmers in the
present struggle had a new ally. For the first time, the owners of cotton
factories, including some who had been aided by the bank, joined in the
clamor for prohibitions. Foremost among these was Antuñano, whose
pen was now devoted to proving that the time to exclude foreign yarns
had arrived.[8]

The increasing pressure for prohibiting the import of cotton textiles
confronted the executive with a grave situation. Ever since 1830, it had
been relying on the considerable duties produced by such imports. To
be sure, 20 percent of the cotton duties belonged legally to the Banco de
Avío, but after March 1, 1833, this percentage had been absorbed directly by the Treasury. The proposed exclusion threatened to destroy a
principal source of its already inadequate revenues.

Faced with this threat, the executive devised a political strategy that
directly impinged on the status of the Banco de Avío. It decided to exploit, as a major argument against prohibiting cotton goods, the negative impact this would have on the Banco de Avío and its industrial program. However, the executive could hardly take such a position while
continuing to deprive the junta of its legally assigned authority. Accordingly, it permitted that body once again to exercise the power of independent decision,[9] and called on the legislature to adopt the following bill: "The fund of the Banco de Avío shall consist of one million five

hundred thousand pesos instead of the million that was assigned to it by article 1 of the law of October 16, 1830. This law shall remain in effect and shall be enforced until the bank actually receives the sum mentioned."[10]

On the surface, this bill was equivalent to an announcement by the executive of its intention to respect the bank's funds. But its real significance lay in the proposal to increase its capital to $1.5 million. This required the continued entry of foreign cottons until the bank obtained the entire sum; and, of course, for each peso that the bank received from its share of the cotton duties, the Treasury would receive four.

Apart from introducing this bill, the executive sought in various ways to discourage the adoption of prohibitory legislation. The official press, for example, attacked the efforts to enact such measures. When the Industry Committee of the Lower Chamber in March 1835 presented a report that favored the exclusion of cotton goods, the editors of the *Diario del Gobierno* devoted four successive days to destroying the committee's case.[11]

With each passing week, the debate between the executive and the supporters of the exclusions grew more intense. It was the latter's contention that the requirement established by article 2 of the law of October 16, 1830, for restoring the 1829 prohibitory law had been met. That article had limited the suspension of the earlier law to the time needed to provide the bank with $1 million. This amount, it was contended, had already been collected at the customs, and even if the bank itself had not received the entire sum, this was the Treasury's responsibility, and should not delay the restoration of the earlier law.[12]

This view was accepted by the Committee on Industry and incorporated in a bill, the initial paragraph of which read: "Since the term granted by article 2 of the October 16, 1830 law has passed, the law of May 22, 1829 is now in full force and effect."[13]

The presentation of this bill aroused government spokesmen to new vigor. They denied emphatically that the requirement of article 2 had been met, for the bank had received only $617,243 of the $1 million assigned to it. Even granting, they argued, that the full sum had been collected at the customs, the Treasury was in no position to make up the difference. The basic purpose of the law, which was to provide the bank with $1 million, was therefore still unfulfilled.[14]

Apart from such legal arguments, the executive sought to discourage adoption of the measure by attacking its proponents, especially the new industrialists. From the columns of the official gazette, it was asserted that

> the motive of this whole story is private interest, which is neither patriotic nor honorable. . . . Why, who are the enemies of the bank? Who are the seekers of prohibitions? The people who want to consolidate their position without fear of competition; and among them are some who were already financed by this bank, or who have utilized its imported machinery, and who now wish to stop the source so others cannot enjoy its benefits.[15]

But despite all the protests of the executive, and despite veiled warnings of political reprisal,[16] a majority of the Chamber of Deputies voted to adopt the committee's measure.[17] The proponents of excluding foreign textiles had thus won a major victory—in the Lower House; but the Senate had still to be heard from. This body had in the meantime been giving favorable attention to the executive's proposal for increasing to $1.5 million the funds assigned to the bank. A bill to this effect was adopted by an overwhelming vote on May 21 and sent to the Lower Chamber.[18]

The situation, therefore, toward the end of May 1835 was this: the Senate had under consideration the Chamber bill to restore the 1829 prohibitory act; the Chamber, in turn, had the Senate measure to increase the funds assigned to the bank. The Chamber was the first to act. Even though a majority wanted to see the prohibitory law restored, they were not averse to allowing the bank to receive currently collected duties until the new regulation went into effect at the ports. In fact, on the day following the adoption of the prohibitory measure, six of its leading supporters introduced a resolution calling on the executive to respect the duties assigned to the bank, and expressly permitting it to receive funds in excess of the million peso limit set in 1830, until such time as other regulations went into effect.[19] When the Senate measure for increasing the bank's capital was received, the Chamber substituted in its place the resolution described above. Forwarded to the Upper Chamber, it was promptly adopted there, and became law on May 23, 1835.[20]

But then, to the dismay of the protectionists, the unintended happened. The Senate made no move to act on the Chamber's prohibitory measure, and the legislative session came to an end. Instead of putting a definite ban on the entry of foreign textiles, and, consequently, on the revenues assigned to the bank, Congress had put on the books a measure that forbade the government to seize the bank's funds, and fixed no limit to their total. For the balance of the year, or at least until the next session, the financial prospects of the Banco de Avío seemed brighter than ever.

The officers of the bank, even before the May 23 enactment, had been exercising their newly recovered powers to resume the issuance of loans. Between April and June, they made six grants totaling $152,000 to four individuals for the following enterprises:[21]

J. R. Pacheco	wax-bleaching factory	$10,000
J. R. Pacheco	paper mill	$20,000
Santiago Aldazoro	cotton factory	$40,000
Victoriano Roa	cotton factory	$50,000
Lucas Alamán	paper mill	$20,000
Lucas Alamán	cotton factory	$12,000

With the exception of the first one, each of these loans was intended either to further an enterprise in which the bank already had an investment, or to facilitate the erection of idle machinery. The two paper-mill loans fall into the latter category, for they supplemented the assignment of machines that had been sitting in the bank's warehouse since 1833. The three cotton factories, on the other hand, were older enterprises that had reached various stages of development.

The factories of Aldazoro and Roa had been started in 1834 with equipment provided at the close of the previous year. At that time, the bank had been in no position to supply funds, but the two borrowers had been confident that they could put their plants into operation with capital raised from private sources. Aldazoro actually achieved that goal in May 1835, thus gaining for himself the distinction of being the "primer fabricante de hilaza en la Capital."[22] But both he and Roa had gone into debt, and they saw in a bank loan, with its modest interest, a way of reducing the burden of their private debts and, in Roa's case, of acquiring additional capital to complete his mill.[23] The junta, revealing once again its indifference to propriety, acceded to the requests of its secretary and its former colleague.

The third cotton factory listed above was none other than the ill-fated Celaya Industrial Company enterprise. That company had collapsed in 1833 when it learned that the bank could not supply additional funds. Up to that time, the bank had provided it with a steam engine and with $10,000 of the $15,000 originally promised. With these funds and the first installment paid in by its stockholders on their shares, the company had purchased a site and completed all but the roof of a factory building. But when the prospect of further bank aid disappeared, the stockholders refused to risk more of their money, even though it meant leaving a roofless structure to the mercy of the elements.[24] The bank had subsequently assigned the textile machinery intended for this factory to other entrepreneurs. In June 1835, however, former minister Lucas Alamán, who had already obtained the paper-mill loan, proposed to buy out the Celaya stockholders and carry through the original project, provided that the bank supply $12,000 and a new set of machines. The junta was only too happy to revive the defunct enterprise on the terms its former chairman proposed.[25]

In none of the loans discussed above was the junta able to supply the borrowers with cash, since the bank had no ready funds on deposit, and even after the May 23 enactment, time was needed for customs revenues to accumulate. Consequently, the loans were issued in the form of credits, some in Treasury orders acceptable for customs payments, others in bank drafts payable from its future balances. And to allow these to accumulate, the junta refrained from approving further loans for several months thereafter.

It was during this time that work was completed on a set of regulations governing the administration of the bank. The 1830 law had prescribed the issuance of such regulations, but little had been done about it heretofore. In February 1835, with the agency involved in the tariff controversy, the junta felt the necessity of "organizing the management of the bank on fixed and definite bases."[26] The result was the *Reglamento para el régimen y gobierno interior de la dirección del Banco de Avío.*[27]

This lengthy document described in full the positions and duties of each member of the staff from the chairman of the junta to the custodian of the warehouse. But more important, it set forth the conditions under which loans were to be made, and laid down procedures for the junta to follow.

In this regard, the reglamento was largely a summary of practices adopted since the bank's inception. For this reason, the purpose of the document seems to have been to clothe with a mantle of respectability the junta's earlier policy decisions, including even those of dubious value.[28] In fact, the junta seemed unwilling to profit from past experience. The reglamento ignored the valuable procedures introduced by Minister Lombardo in 1834. No mention was made of requiring machinery purchasers to repay the cost within a fixed period instead of from a percentage of hypothetical profits; nor was there any express stipulation that borrowers who received loans in drafts would be obligated for the full face value, a step that might have prevented later controversies.

Nevertheless, in one significant respect, the reglamento did reveal that the junta had taken cognizance of public criticism. The last article of the section devoted to describing its own powers read: "The junta shall not by itself direct nor take charge of any industrial establishment for whose development bank funds are needed; and, in the future, neither the individuals who compose the junta nor the employees in its offices shall be allowed to do so."[29]

In other words, the reglamento admitted the inappropriateness of allowing bank officials to receive loans for their own enterprises. However, the sense of the article was carefully qualified by the phrase "in the future," and there was no disposition to take immediate action on the two individuals who fell into this category. General Rayón, it is true, left the junta at the close of the year, after five years' service, but Victoriano Roa continued to enjoy his dual role of secretary to the junta and debtor to the bank.

Whatever its inadequacies, the reglamento did establish a fixed procedure for handling loan applications. Final action on such requests was to be made only at the regular weekly meeting of the junta, or at a special session called by its chairman. The presence of three members in addition to the secretary was necessary for a quorum, and decisions were to be made by majority vote. But before any application for money or machinery could be considered, it was to be referred to a committee for study and recommendation.[30]

The committee itself was to observe certain rules, of which the very first seemed highly significant. It read:

> [The committee] will examine the last monthly financial statement indicating the state of the bank's funds. If the current balance, or the sum total of the fund, is, in its opinion, only sufficient to promote undertakings already begun and to fulfill other previously contracted obligations, the application in question, regardless of its utility, will be tabled.[31]

In other words, the reglamento was committing the bank to a policy of prudence in its future lending.

Unfortunately, the value of this and other commendable rules of procedure was wholly negated by the failure to observe them. For shortly after adopting the reglamento, the officials of the bank went on a lend-

TABLE 3
Loans Granted in Drafts in Lieu of Specie
September 1835 — January 20, 1836

Date of Junta Approval	Date of Draft Issuance	Borrower	Type of Project	Amount
Sept.—	Oct. 26, Nov. 4	Ramón Pardo	Cotton weaving	$ 50,000
Oct.—	Oct. 19	Puebla Hospicio	Paper mill	40,000
Oct.—	Oct. 19, 26, Dec. 2	Juan Icaza	Sawmill	50,000
Oct.—	Oct. 22	Tlalpam Co.	Cotton factory	40,000
Oct. 16	Oct. 20	Luis Ruiz	Cotton gin and sawmill	30,000
Oct. 22	Dec. 20	Mariano Domínguez	Cotton weaving	8,000
Oct. 22	Unknown	Ignacio Leal	Cotton weaving	8,000
Oct. 22	Unknown	Antonio Prieto	Flax and silk raising	15,000
See n. a.	Oct. 26	Luis Bracho	Sawmill	40,000
	Oct. 26	Carlos Sodi	Cotton gin	32,000
	Oct. 27	M. Miranda and A. Padilla	Cotton factory	25,000
	Oct. 27	Gen. J. Tornel and M. Escandón	Paper mill	20,000
Dec. 16	Unknown	Gen. Guadalupe Victoria	Agricultural enterprises	100,000
Jan. 2	Jan. 2	Gen. M. Arista	Agricultural tools	2,000
Jan.—	Jan. 18	Gen. M. Barrera	Woolen factory	16,000
Total				$476,000

a. The junta apparently did not approve the four following loans; the drafts were issued without the usual formalities by its chairman, relaciones minister, Manuel Díaz de Bonilla.

Sources: "Relación circunstanciada," Memoria del ministerio de lo interior (México, 1838); DG, Dec. 13, 1838; Oct. 31, 1843; MSS in AGN, B/A, 3.

ing spree that had no parallel in its history. Within a period of four months, as table 3 reveals, they granted fifteen loans totaling $476,000, a sum almost equivalent to the bank's entire expenditures in its first two years. Eleven of these loans were for entirely new undertakings; only four could be rationalized as assistance to enterprises in which the bank already had an investment.[32]

Moreover, there is little question that its current balances were inadequate to meet prior obligations. A debt of $91,000 was still owed for machinery purchases in the United States; and the junta did not even have the cash to pay its own office expenses.[33] Accordingly, the bank had to issue drafts against future revenues in order to provide these loans.

But it is hard to believe that the officials did not foresee the inevitable results of such a procedure. Sufficient income from customs duties to cover the drafts could not possibly accumulate in only a few months. In the past under the best of conditions, it had taken over a year to produce a lesser sum.[34] The holders of drafts, consequently, unable to cash them at once, would naturally be tempted to sell them to speculators. But the circulation of so much paper would inevitably depress their value. This is exactly what the borrowers found, and the losses in some instances reached 30 and 40 percent of the original loans.[35]

One can only speculate why the bank officials, in contravention of their own regulations, engaged in this wholesale lending operation. The complete answer lies hidden in the files of the individual loans and in the record books of junta proceedings, most of which have disappeared. Yet from the available data, one conclusion seems inescapable. Although some of the loans were justified on their merits, several were the product of personal favoritism and political pressure.

A glance at table 3 reveals that most of the loans were issued in a relatively brief period, the fortnight prior to October 27. This period coincided with Manuel Díaz de Bonilla's final weeks as minister of relaciones and, hence, as chairman of the junta.[36] Moreover, on the last two days before he left office, he issued drafts to four borrowers, apparently without even the junta's consent, and without the signing of formal contracts. In each of these cases, the junta later suspended payment on the drafts because of the borrower's refusal to provide adequate guarantees.[37]

The borrowers listed in table 3 include several men prominent in political and military circles. But just because a borrower was an army general or a member of Congress it would be unfair to assume that a loan granted him was a simple instance of political pressure. The projects themselves may have merited favor, as in the case of General Barrera, who was proposing to rehabilitate the partly ruined woolen mill originally purchased at great cost for the Querétaro Company.[38] Nevertheless, apart from the utility of an undertaking, the junta might not have decided to grant a loan at this particular time were it not for the weight of external pressure.

Evidence exists to show that this is exactly what happened in the case of the largest single loan, the $100,000 grant to ex-President Guadalupe

Victoria. When General Victoria first applied to the bank in June 1835, his application bore the strong personal recommendation of the interim president, Miguel Barragán. Even so, the junta at that time decided it could not comply in view of its limited resources and its other obligations. But after the chief executive insisted that the junta reconsider, that body reversed itself and voted the loan.[39]

However, neither the junta nor its clients could foresee the wholly disastrous course these loans would take. For once again, as in 1832, a major political crisis confronted the nation to shatter the hopes of lender and borrower alike. The outbreak in October 1835 of a revolt in Texas, ostensibly in behalf of the recently abolished federal Constitution, placed an extraordinary burden on national finances. In such an emergency, the income of the bank was no more sacred than it had been in the past; and Congress, on January 20, 1836, voted to cut off its assignment of duties "while the present war provoked by the Texan colonists lasts."[40] With this step the bank's financial autonomy was once more suspended.

The legislature, however, did make some gesture to the bank's frustrated clients. Apparently in response to the lobbying efforts of two of them, the same enactment promised that those bank drafts issued in the past would be paid.[41] But it was not until March that this statement was clarified by a separate decree that ordered the Finance Ministry to provide a minimum monthly sum of $15,000 for their redemption. A further clarification issued in June placed in the junta's hands the delicate task of determining the priority in which the drafts could be presented for payment.[42]

From the viewpoint of the holders of drafts, the suspension of the bank's customs revenue would not have been so painful had the Finance Ministry complied with the new arrangement. But pressed by a host of other obligations, that ministry more often than not was unwilling or unable to do so. In the forty-four months after January 20, 1836, it redeemed only $195,000 worth of drafts, or the equivalent of thirteen monthly installments.[43] This figure, moreover, represents the face value of the credits, not the amount received in cash. For, in order to obtain payment, bank clients first had to exchange their drafts for Treasury orders, a process that sometimes involved the client in unorthodox expenses; then the orders had to be presented to customhouses, or commissaries for acceptance. Before payment in cash was finally received, the value of the original loan usually depreciated considerably.[44]

From the viewpoint of the junta, the new dispensation was equally discouraging. Additional loans now seemed out of the question; and to obtain funds even for operating expenses, it had to scramble with the other creditors of the Finance Ministry. In this situation, as in 1832, minor sources of income took on new importance. One of these was the interest accruing on previous loans.

Income from this source had not been significant in the past because, under the law, no interest could be collected until an establishment was in operation. However, for several enterprises, the exemption period had either just ended, or was drawing to a close. In 1835, both Antuñano's cotton factory in Puebla and Aldazoro's in México had gone into production; by 1836, the Tlalpam factory and that of Victoriano Roa were also nearing that stage; and of the recently aided enterprises, Luis Ruiz's ginning establishment and Ramón Pardo's weaving shop had both been in production prior to the granting of the loans.

The bank's prospect for substantial interest collections was clouded, however, by the actions of Congress. When the junta pressed Antuñano early in 1836 to pay the first year's interest on his $146,000 debt, the Puebla entrepreneur appealed to Congress for a further exemption. That body obliged by granting a five-year waiver on payments, to be figured from the time his factory had opened.[45]

Antuñano's success started a veritable chain reaction among the bank's other industrial debtors. The Tlalpam company and Aldazoro immediately applied for similar waivers; a few weeks later, Luis Ruiz and Victoriano Roa followed suit.[46] The Congress was willing to extend the same grace to the others, but the executive vetoed the bill granting exemptions to Aldazoro and the Tlalpam Company. These debtors, nevertheless, reapplied to Congress, and in the meantime obstinately refused to make interest payments.[47]

It was in such discouraging circumstances that the junta found itself when its former chairman, Lucas Alamán, confronted it with a unique proposal. For the past year or so, Alamán had been unable to cash the $32,000 in drafts granted him in June 1835 to develop both a paper mill and the defunct Celaya textile factory. Meanwhile he had become interested in a plan to set up a large spinning mill at Cocolapam near the city of Orizaba. Two French merchants, the brothers Legrand, were considering investing in such a mill if Alamán would come in as a silent partner with $50,000. In December 1836, the former minister turned to the junta to provide him with this sum.[48]

Alamán was well aware that the bank had no liquid funds. The junta, to be sure, could ask the Finance Ministry to issue Treasury orders up to

$15,000 per month, but such orders, when paid at all, suffered tremendous discounts because they were issued on the major ports, most of whose revenues were constantly mortgaged to agiotistas. Alamán, however, had a scheme for circumventing this difficulty.

The port of Alvarado, south of Veracruz, was little used, and its revenues were not involved in any transaction with the moneylenders. If the junta would request the Finance Ministry to issue to Alamán Treasury orders acceptable for payment of duties at that port, the Legrand brothers, in their capacity as commission agents, would see to it that several cargoes consigned to them would be unloaded there. Then, on behalf of the owners of the cargoes, they would purchase the Treasury orders to defray the duties. Alamán, in this way, could dispose of the orders with the least possible discount.[49]

To persuade the junta to grant the loan, Alamán painted a glowing picture of the contribution the bank would be making to Mexican industry. The loan to the Orizaba spinning mill would increase the national production of cotton yarn, and also stimulate cotton agriculture. Moreover, from the profits he derived from the factory, Alamán planned to develop the Celaya factory, converting it into a weaving outlet for Orizaba yarn. Finally, when that factory became operative, part of its profits would be devoted to establishing the paper mill. Meanwhile, from the very beginning, a part of the Orizaba profits would also be applied to liquidating the debt, and the same would be done with the earnings of the other plants. Thus the bank would recover funds that had long been frozen unproductively, and three new enterprises would be spreading benefits to various parts of the country.[50]

To the members of the junta, the picture that Alamán drew seemed very attractive. But it was not only the prospect of facilitating new enterprises that intrigued them; for, in his plan to discount Treasury orders with minimum loss, they saw an opportunity to obtain additional funds for the bank itself. Accordingly, among the conditions that the junta laid down in approving the loan was one that Alamán should undertake to discount, in the same terms as the $60,000 in credits extended to him, an additional $30,000 for the account of the bank.[51]

On the day following the junta's decision to grant the loan, Alamán entered into his contract of partnership with the Legrand brothers;[52] a few weeks later, he received from the Finance Ministry the orders for $90,000. But the original scheme for negotiating the documents ran into unexpected snags. Suspicious customs authorities forced the Legrands to divert some of the cargoes from Alvarado to Tampico. Moreover, a subsequent Finance Ministry directive reassigning government revenues made no provision whatsoever for the 15,000-peso monthly allotment against which the documents had been issued. These changes occurred after Alamán had placed some of his own drafts, but before he had negotiated any in behalf of the bank. The upshot was that, while he eventually obtained the sum he needed to enter the partnership, the junta was forced to take back its drafts without receiving a centavo of the $30,000.[53] Nevertheless, that body could take some satisfaction from the results of the loan. On March 3, 1837, the first stone of the Cocolapam spinning mill was laid, and, a little over a year later, the factory entered production, an important addition to the expanding domestic textile industry.[54]

EFFORTS AT REFORM, 1838 – 1840

The directors of the Banco de Avío had enjoyed what appears to have been complete immunity from public comment or criticism, in the two years following the spring of 1835, when they had resumed full control of the bank's management. For reasons not altogether clear, the major periodicals in the capital hardly, if ever, mentioned the name of the bank, and never discussed the way in which it was being managed.[1] Neither did members of the national legislature pay attention to it. Public indifference seems to have been the order of the day. But suddenly, in the spring of 1837, this curious silence was broken. Voices arose in the newly elected legislature, as well as in certain quarters of the press, voices that questioned the integrity of those who were managing the bank.

Two circumstances tended to arouse suspicions that the public monies entrusted to the bank were not being properly handled. One was the continued presence of Victoriano Roa on the staff of the agency. It was public knowledge that Roa was the proprietor of a textile establishment that owed money to the bank, though it may not have been generally known that this debt amounted to over $70,000.[2] That the secretary of the bank was at the same time one of its principal borrowers was not an encouraging sign. The second factor that gave a dubious aspect to the situation was the continued failure of the junta to give a public accounting of the funds it was handling. Under the act creating the bank, the junta had been charged with the responsibility of presenting annual accounts; and from 1832 to 1835 such accounts had been periodically submitted to the legislature.[3] But ever since the presentation of those for the calendar year 1834, the officers of the bank had failed to render a public statement of its income and expenditures. This in itself aroused speculation hardly flattering to the reputation of the bank.

This reputation, moreover, was not helped by the fact that among its clients was the highly unpopular Ignacio Loperena. Loperena, a former deputy, was one of several moneylenders, or agiotistas, who were under attack for making usurious loans to the government during the recently concluded administration of President Justo Corro.[4] In Loperena's case, the special charge was made that "having obtained $30,000 from the Banco de Avío, with this same money he made loans to the government . . . so that just through this scandalous traffic of lending the nation its *own* money, Loperena became powerful. . . ."[5]

The truth of this accusation, unfortunately, cannot be conclusively determined on the basis of the available evidence. It is known that Loperena and another agiotista, Felipe Neri del Barrio, had formed a textile company with Victoriano Roa early in 1835 to operate the machinery which Roa had previously acquired on credit from the Banco de Avío. The partners had subsequently obtained the approval of the junta to a $50,000 loan, which was to be distributed to them in three equal parts. President Barragán had given final approval to the loan, which was issued, not in cash, but in the form of customs bills. Shortly thereafter the company was dissolved, and Victoriano Roa, according to the notarized statement of dissolution, received from his former partners the full assets of the firm, including the sums they had received from the bank. Roa, in turn, with the approval of the junta, assumed complete responsibility for the $50,000 loan. Two years later, Roa reported that the money derived from the loan had been spent for various purposes incidental to the establishment of his factory.[6] The accusation against Loperena would thus seem to be without foundation, but the possibility cannot be ruled out that the funds were used temporarily for speculative activity, and then applied to their legitimate end. Regardless of the real facts, however, the very identification of the Banco de Avío with the unpopular agiotistas must have strengthened the suspicion that the junta was failing in its duty to safeguard the public's funds.

The first indication of congressional concern over possible irregularities within the bank came in June 1837 shortly after the newly elected assembly met in regular session.[7] The Committee on Industry of the Lower Chamber presented the officers of the lending agency with a request for a detailed report on its operations. The type of information requested included such data as the guarantees taken by the bank in each of its loans, the possible instances in which borrowers misused the funds they received, and the remedies taken in such instances by the bank's officers.[8] The latter undertook to assemble the necessary information. They prepared a report by the end of September, but apparently not until the following January was it submitted to Congress.[9] Until that time, then, the details of the bank's operations were unknown to the public.

Even as the junta moved to comply with the Industry Committee's request, the legislature acted to eliminate the questionable practice of allowing borrowers to serve on the staff of the agency. While no names were mentioned, it was evidently the case of the secretary, Victoriano Roa, that inspired the action. A member of the Industry Committee, Tomás Illanes, who had once been a close collaborator of the bank, introduced a bill to forbid any individual in its debt to serve as a member of the junta or in its secretariat. The mood of the Chamber may well be inferred from the fact that it took only three days for the proposal to clear the legislative hurdles and be sent to the Senate. There it was subsequently approved, and became law on July 29, 1837.[10]

The intervention of Congress into the affairs of the Banco de Avío did not, however, put an end to press criticism of the agency. Quite the contrary; the bank proved to be too good a whipping boy to be ignored by the opposition papers. The leading federalist organ, *El Cosmopolita*, maintained a constant barrage against the management of the bank as a means of discrediting centralism and the current centralist government. Its favorite target was Lucas Alamán, now a member of the *Consejo de Gobierno*, and a stalwart supporter of the regime. Again and again from August until the following spring, the editors of *El Cosmopolita* needled the conservative leader, and hammered away at the government's seeming unwillingness to publish the names of those who had received loans from the bank. On January 10, 1838, for example, the federalist paper asserted:

The investment of the funds belonging to that establishment is a mystery to the nation. All that is known is that centralist persons of the rank of a Lucas Alamán have been aided with very fat sums. The writers for the government haven't had the courage to present the list of those who have been financed by the bank; but this silence is eloquent enough.

A few weeks later, the newspaper again returned to the attack:

The nation is condemned to ignorance as to what the Banco de Avío has done with the very large sums it has received. Sr. Alamán was the creator of this establishment. How much has His Excellency profited from the work of his hands? It isn't known because ... everything must be centralized.[11]

While the opposition press was thus crusading to unmask the clients of the bank, the government of President Bustamante was itself making changes of considerable significance in bank personnel. Although the agency's regulations prescribed that its directors' terms should run to the end of a calendar year, the rising tide of hostile criticism in the summer and fall of 1837 made earlier action desirable. Before the end of October, the vice-chairman, José Delmotte, and his two colleagues on the junta were dismissed. Moreover, in a move to eliminate another target of unfavorable comment, Victoriano Roa was relieved of the secretaryship he had held for six years. This position was then entrusted to Ignacio Leal, a former client of the bank, while posts on the junta were given to Miguel Cervantes, a former governor of the Federal District, and to Luis Vieyra, the then-governor of the state of Mexico.[12]

To the most responsible administrative position in the bank, that of the junta vice-chairmanship, President Bustamante appointed the distinguished savant, José Gómez de la Cortina. Cortina, who was subsequently to found the still-existing *Sociedad Mexicana de Geografía e Estadística,* served the Banco de Avío until illness forced his resignation in May 1839.[13] He was then succeeded by a member of the Consejo de Gobierno, José Mariano Marín, who held the position until his entry into the cabinet in September 1840.

During the three-year period when Gómez de la Cortina and Mariano Marín occupied the principal post on the junta, the affairs of the Banco de Avío were managed in a way that contrasted sharply with the loose practices of the past. The junta, in this period, made a conscientious effort to increase the efficiency of the organization, and to place its relations with clients on a safe and businesslike basis.

For at least part of this period, the junta was fortunate in having the cooperation of cabinet ministers who were genuinely concerned with protecting the interests of the bank. From March to December 1838, the poet-statesman, José Joaquín Pesado, served as minister of the interior, and hence ex-officio head of the bank.[14] Pesado proved to be a vigorous defender of the agency's rights vis-à-vis its delinquent clients. Moreover, he showed himself to be equally concerned with establishing good public relations for the bank. It was he who started the practice of publishing the minutes of junta sessions in the official gazette.[15] This practice did not survive Pesado's departure from the ministry; nevertheless, for a period of six months, the reading public had the opportunity to follow the deliberations of the junta, and to become informed on various aspects of its work.

Though Pesado was responsible for the decision to publicize the proceedings of the junta, the real credit for this step might well be taken by the opposition newspaper, *El Cosmopolita*, which, as mentioned earlier, kept hammering away at the government to reveal the names of the bank's clients. On March 10, 1838, this newspaper published its own list of borrowers, challenging the government to publish an official one if this were incorrect.[16] This action appears to have inspired Pesado to give full publicity to bank operations, for it was shortly thereafter that the decision was made to publish not only an official statement of the enterprises financed by the bank, but also the minutes of the meetings in which loan applications were discussed.[17]

Under Minister Pesado's leadership, Gómez de la Cortina and the other officers of the bank set to work to introduce order and efficiency into its administration. Regular working hours from 9 A.M. to 3 P.M. were established for the staff, and all salaried personnel were required to be present under penalty of fines. To economize on expenses, the staff was reduced from the level established in the 1835 table of organization. This effort to save money was not wholly successful, for one of the dismissed employees was later able to recover his post through the personal intervention of General Santa Anna, when the latter was temporary president of the republic in May 1840.[18]

Problems of personnel, however, were on the whole less vexing than the difficulties that the newly organized junta encountered in straightening out the records of the bank. The first time Cortina and his associates sought to determine the status of the bank-owned machinery stored in the Dominican convent in Mexico City, they discovered that their predecessors had failed to maintain a formal inventory of the equipment, and had not even safeguarded it from possible theft. The new junta attempted to rectify the situation by calling on Mexican artisans to survey the machinery with a view to its sale. However, to make a comprehensive inventory that would reveal the purpose of each piece, and indicate whether any parts were missing, it was necessary to have the services of a foreign mechanic who could assemble each machine. For reasons that are not clear, but probably shortage of funds, the junta was unable to have this done.[19]

The disorder encountered in the status of machinery holdings was paralleled by the near chaos that the junta found in the *contaduría*, the accounting department of the bank. Many important files were missing. Some, it was learned, had been turned over to other government offices and never returned; others had been taken by former officials of the bank. A former junta member still had in his possession the record of interest collections, while ex-Secretary Roa had the important *libro de carga y data*, the record of income and outgo. The lack of such records prevented the preparation of an annual statement, as requested by the Finance Ministry for inclusion in its memoria for the previous fiscal year; it also made it impossible for the junta to determine accurately the status of debts owed the bank. The junta did make an effort to recover the missing papers, but the strained relations existing with the former officials appear to have prevented complete success.[20]

The disorder in the contaduría outlasted Cortina's term as vice-chairman. Under Mariano Marín, a new effort was made to bring the office up to date; but lack of progress finally led the junta to suspend the *contador*, Ignacio Madrid, and in February 1840, to appeal to the congressional auditing agency, the *Tribunal de Revisión de Cuentas* to make an inspection of the office.[21]

Members of the Chamber of Deputies had been requesting such an investigation since 1838, but apparently a jurisdictional issue had prevented the audit.[22] This obstacle was now eliminated, however, with the junta voluntarily requesting the services of the tribunal, and thus the way was paved for the first independent examination of the bank's accounts in the ten years of its existence.

The findings of the examiner were hardly flattering to those who had been responsible for the lending agency's administration from the very beginning. He found the contaduría in what he called "frightful disorder," with vouchers filed haphazardly and essential books not even kept. All this led him to conclude that the office "had never been staffed by employees even modestly trained in the principles of bookkeeping." The double-entry bookkeeping system that had been started in 1830, he contended, was obscure and enigmatic, and even this had been interrupted suddenly in 1832. Since then, he asserted, "one can be certain that there disappeared from the contaduría of the bank even the idea of arithmetic and of a simple book or notebook in which just a chronological listing of what came in and went out of its coffers could have been kept."[23]

This sweeping generalization is hard to reconcile with the fact that the bank officials had prepared annual accounts for each calendar year through 1834.[24] Obviously some kind of books had been kept, which, even if incomplete, would hardly justify the contentions of the examiner. His accuracy in discussing conditions in the bank in its first five years can, moreover, be challenged on one other score. In his report, he maintained that Ignacio Madrid, the recently suspended contador, could not be held responsible for the disorder in the accounting department, partly because the bank's regulations for keeping records were inadequate, and also because Madrid "found the disorder in the books deeply rooted when he took charge of the accounting department in December of 1835." Now, while it is true that he became head of the separate accounting section that was established at that time, the files of the bank reveal very plainly that this same Madrid was in charge of its books almost from the day the bank opened in October 1830.[25] It would appear, then, that the examiner was either not well informed about the facts of the bank's history in the early years, or was, for some reason, giving an unduly black picture of conditions then.

Be this as it may, the examiner did more than criticize existing shortcomings in the contaduría; he tried by various means to rectify them. In place of what he called the "reprobado sistema de partida doble" he introduced a simpler system of bookkeeping more suited to the needs of the bank; he assigned one man to the task of drawing up reports on the status of every loan granted by the bank since its inception; and he set the rest of the staff to work preparing financial statements for all previous fiscal years. The fruit of this labor began to appear in following years. In January 1841, the junta was able to present a detailed analysis of all loans granted to date; in the following January it was able to submit promptly the accounts of the bank for the recently ended fiscal period.[26] Thus, in at least one aspect of its operations, the Banco de Avío had become a considerably more efficient agency that it had been for several years in the past.

As the various steps described in the preceding pages were taken to improve the internal administration of the bank, the junta was simultaneously engaged in an effort to clarify the exact status of the various assets belonging to the agency. These assets consisted, on the one hand, of directly owned property such as livestock and machinery in storage; and, on the other hand, of the notes or obligations of various enterprises for the loans and/or machinery they had received. The junta was primarily concerned, in regard to the latter category of assets, in making certain that every loan was properly guaranteed, and that the money granted was used only for the purposes designated in the loan agreement. Moreover, in those cases where payments of interest or principal were due, the junta was anxious to make prompt collections.

In its efforts to review the status of the various accounts, the newly reconstructed junta was considerably hampered at first by the confused state of the contaduría, and by its lack of reliable information on enterprises remote from Mexico City. Nevertheless, Vice-Chairman Cortina and his associates worked methodically to overcome these difficulties. An examination was made of all the *escrituras*, or loan contracts, found in the files, and bills were sent out wherever it appeared that a client was delinquent. In some instances, it was discovered that escrituras had not even been drawn up and in these cases the files were turned over to the prosecuting attorney of the local Treasury Court *(promotor fiscal del Juzgado de Hacienda)* for his opinion on the possibility of legal action. To secure reliable information on the use made of loans by distant enterprises, the junta, through its chairman, the minister of the interior, called on the governors of the various states to make inspections of the factories and other works aided by the bank.[27]

The inadequacy of the bank's records proved a formidable stumbling block when the junta sought to determine the interest due the bank on its various loans. This was especially true in the case of loans that had been made in customs bills or other paper. Where clients had received such documents instead of cash, it had been understood that their obligation to pay interest was to begin when they discounted their paper. But it had frequently happened that recipients of paper had been unable to negotiate all or even part of it. Thus, while the records of the bank indicated the face value of the original loan, the amount that was subject to interest might be considerably less, or even nothing at all, if the client still held his drafts intact and unused. Moreover, in the instances where the clients disposed of the paper in a private transaction, and not at a Treasury office, the junta was forced to depend, at least temporarily, on the client's statement as to the date of the transaction and the amount involved. This was an obviously unsatisfactory situation from the viewpoint of protecting the bank's rights.

To overcome its ignorance of the current status of Banco de Avío paper, the junta took steps to call in all uncashed drafts for listing and reissuance. An announcement was made through advertisements in the official gazette that holders of such documents should present them within forty days to the contaduría. In order to encourage compliance, the junta obtained the cooperation of the Finance Ministry, which agreed not to accept bank-issued paper that lacked the special signature indicating it had been duly registered.[28]

The registration operation revealed to the junta that upwards of $300,000 of drafts issued in previous years was still uncashed. Of this sum, paper worth $130,800 had been re-endorsed to the bank by the original recipients, who had found themselves unable to cash it. Much of the remainder, however, was held by clients who had acquired it without legal formalities three years before, and who had persistently refused to provide acceptable security for it. In these cases, the junta directed that the drafts be seized on presentation. Thus, within a short period, the junta was able to recover $90,000 worth of drafts that had been carelessly handed out in 1835.[29]

The junta, moreover, sought to root out the practice that had been largely responsible for the existence of these drafts: unilateral action by the ex-officio chairman of the junta without consultation with its regular members. Upon Gómez de la Cortina's recommendation, the junta laid down the policy that all drafts, orders, or endorsements involving funds would thenceforth require the signature of two members and the secretary, as well as that of the minister of the interior. This decision was communicated to the Finance Ministry so that all its offices would refuse to recognize such documents unless they bore the necessary signatures.[30]

The various steps taken by the officers of the Banco de Avío to safeguard its rights in the funds already invested in loans met with moderate success from 1838 through 1840. Agreements were made in the latter year with two borrowers, Santiago Aldazoro and Luis Ruiz, to begin interest payments on loans whose combined principal exceeded $60,000. Both clients had previously pressed Congress to exempt them from such payments. The junta also came to terms in 1840 with the Zacualpa de Amilpas Iron Works to start interest payments on its borrowed capital of $68,000, the first payment to be made in 1843. On the negative side, however, was the continued refusal of the Tlalpam Textile Company to pay interest on its debt, for it was still seeking an exemption from Congress. This company alone, at the end of 1840, owed $18,200 in unpaid interest.[31]

In the two years after 1836, the junta also succeeded in recovering part of the cost of the machines that had been distributed on credit to various enterprises. Estevan de Antuñano repaid the full cost of the textile plant that he had received in 1833 and had placed into production two years later. Moreover, the Puebla Hospicio commenced a series of installment payments on the paper mill that it had finally begun to operate after several years of difficulty. A similar arrangement for installment payments was worked out with Santiago Aldazoro for the textile machinery he had acquired.[32]

Of equal, if not greater, importance than interest collections or the repayment of machinery costs, was the junta's progress in recovering capital invested in loans. Eight loans, representing a total of $343,650, were liquidated. To be sure, a considerable part of this sum—$196,000 —was repaid in the very medium in which it had been advanced: in unused bank drafts; but the balance of $147,650 was repaid in cash or commercial paper, thus liquidating, incidentally, the largest single loan carried on the books, that made to Estevan de Antuñano.[33]

Undoubtedly, much more could have been accomplished in the direction of recovering capital and collecting interest if the junta had been able to rely on the courts to mete out speedy justice in their suits against defaulting clients. Unfortunately, as the officials of the bank gradually learned to their sorrow, court actions involved costly and exasperating delays. The junta's first attempt to recover debts through the courts was made late in 1837 against Victoriano Roa, the ex-secretary of the bank. Roa was already involved in financial difficulties with other creditors when the junta filed suit in the *Juzgado de Hacienda* to recover two years' interest and one-third the cost of his machinery, the payment for which was long overdue. The only tangible result, however, was a court attachment of Roa's factory, and the complete cessation of its operations. Although the junta was besieged by individuals who offered to lease the establishment, thus keeping it in operation, the court could not be persuaded to agree. For four years, the factory remained under attachment, its machinery idle, while the capital invested in it by Roa and the bank wasted uselessly away.[34]

A further effort of the bank to assert its rights in a court of law involved one Ramón Pardo, the owner of a cotton weaving establishment in Mexico City. The principal issue in the dispute was Pardo's refusal to sign an escritura for the $50,000 in drafts which he had received without that requirement in 1835. Pardo, like many other borrowers, had been unable to cash his drafts at the authorized customshouse after Congress had suspended the allocation of duties to the bank in January 1836. However, he did subsequently succeed in exchanging the drafts for Treasury orders drawn against the $15,000 monthly sum which Congress had granted to the bank. But even then he was unable to cash them at the designated Treasury offices and, finally, on his own responsibility, sold the orders to speculators at considerable loss. When pressed by the officials of the bank in 1838 to sign an escritura for the original amount, Pardo refused, and after lengthy and heated negotiations, the issue was taken to court. But just as in the Roa case, no early decision was forthcoming. As of January 1841, the case was still to be decided, though Pardo himself was dead, and his factory silent.[35]

The failure of the Juzgado de Hacienda to act promptly on these cases, at least during 1838, need not have reflected a deliberate attempt to frustrate the bank's officials, though the latter may well have thought so. It is known that the judge before whom the actions were brought was ill for a good part of the year, and that matters in his court were so tied up that special measures had to be taken to transfer cases to other courts.[36] But procrastination in deciding the suits in which the bank was a party continued to be the rule in 1839, by which time the number of cases brought against recalcitrant debtors had risen to four, although none had yet been acted upon. The junta, in desperation, finally appealed to the president of the Republic in June 1839 to take note of the "scandalous delays" suffered by the bank, and to issue a "directive strong enough to eliminate the dilatoriness of the Treasury Court."[37]

As if the bank did not have sufficient troubles with the judiciary, the junta learned that two other debtors with whom it was having difficulties had been nominated as associates of the circuit judge of the Department of Mexico to form a tribunal to hear appeals from the Treasury Court. The junta promptly delivered a vigorous protest to the government against their appointment on the grounds that the bank was planning to bring suit against these men, and they might well be put in a position where they could pass judgment on their own cases. The protest, for once, seems to have fallen on sympathetic ears, for the nominations were dropped.[38]

The junta was still unsuccessful, however, in obtaining a decision on its suits, and in November 1839, it made a second appeal to the president to urge the judge to expedite the cases. The failure to get prompt action on the original suits was encouraging other debtors to disregard their obligations, and to challenge the junta to take them to court.[39] But the appeals to the president had little effect on the administration of justice in this particular court, for 1840 also passed without any improvement. As a consequence, the officers of the bank were reluctantly drawn to the conclusion that the agency's interest could just as well be served by making concessions and reaching agreements out of court as by taking legal action. But they remained convinced that the indifference of the courts was responsible for heavy losses to the bank. "Oh, how much capital would have been recovered," they wrote in their annual report, "how much would not be in immediate danger of loss, and how many obligations would have been lived up to if this beneficent establishment had received support!"[40]

Although from 1838 through 1840 the bank's officers devoted considerable time to securing its investments in loans and allocated machinery, they did not neglect the directly owned assets of the agency. These, as mentioned earlier, included machinery in storage and livestock. The animals owned by the bank were the descendants of the merino sheep and Tibetan goats imported in 1831 to supply high-grade wool to the modern textile plant then being planned for Querétaro. The revolution of 1832 had prevented the establishment of the factory, and at the same time had eliminated the principal outlet for the wool, since the existing hand-weaving shops had no use in their trade for the fine fibers. The animals had subsequently been transferred to the San Luis Potosí haciendas of the junta's vice-chairman at that time, Sánchez y Mora, who offered to maintain the livestock free of charge. In the succeeding years, the existence of these animals had been all but ignored. A few had been sold to the state government of Zacatecas, some others had accompanied a colonization expedition to Upper California; but no demand for their wool had ever developed.[41]

Early in 1838, the junta bestirred itself to inquire of Sánchez y Mora about the remaining animals, and found itself unexpectedly presented with a bill for their maintenance. To save further expenditure, the junta resolved to sell the animals. Advertisements were placed in the press, but though a few inquiries were received, no one was willing to purchase the stock for cash. Two years later, in 1840, the animals were still grazing on Sánchez y Mora's property, while the junta was conducting a semiweekly auction to dispose of the two-hundred-odd head. How many were sold in this manner is not known, but apparently some were still held by the government even after the Banco de Avío was dissolved late in 1842.[42]

The machinery stored by the Banco de Avío in its Mexico City warehouse consisted principally of the partially ruined woolen textile plant originally intended for Querétaro, and a paper mill, which at one time had been assigned to Lucas Alamán, but subsequently had been returned. In addition to these major pieces of equipment, the warehouse bulged with boxes containing scores of spinning wheels, hand looms, and even two distilleries. The total value of this equipment cannot be precisely stated, but to acquire and transport just the paper mill and the woolen machinery to their present useless resting place had cost the Banco de Avío $60,000.[43]

The junta first turned its attention to the manual equipment early in 1838. Over the preceding seven years, the original inventory, acquired in the United States, of one hundred looms and almost four hundred spinning wheels had been substantially reduced by sales and, apparently also, though to a very minor extent, by theft. But the junta in 1838 still had on its hands three hundred spinning wheels and forty-one looms, which represented an investment to the bank of $5,400. This equipment, it was decided, should be offered for sale at cost, preferably to poor people, the proceeds to be used as a revolving fund to purchase additional spinning wheels for similar distribution.[44]

In thus deciding to make the spindles and looms available at cost to impoverished artisans, the junta was acting to implement its predecessor's original purpose in ordering the equipment seven years before. However, there is some reason to believe that the junta's decision was also influenced by the recent charge of the federalist newspaper, *El Cosmopolita*, that the bank served only the wealthy when it should be aiding the poor. Be this as it may, the latter seems to have been in no rush to purchase the equipment, perhaps because the junta's insistence on cash excluded many potential purchasers who could not put out seven pesos for a spinning wheel, much less the fifty pesos required for a loom.[45]

The problem of disposing of the larger and more expensive equipment in the bank's possession, the paper mill and the woolen textile machinery, was unexpectedly solved for the junta by a chain of circumstances over which the members of this body could exercise little control. José Fauré, the French freight handler, emboldened, perhaps, by his native country's recent success in compelling Mexico to recognize a number of private claims, presented a demand against the bank for an indemnity running into tens of thousands of pesos. Transmitted formally to the Mexican government in 1839 by the French chargé d'affaires, the claim pertained to a freight contract entered into by the bank in 1832 for the transportation of textile machinery from the port of Veracruz to the cities of Querétaro and Celaya. Because of the violent uprisings that broke out that year, the bank had ordered Fauré to deposit the machinery at Mexico City and had directed that he be paid a lesser rate for the shorter haul than he would have received for taking the shipments to their original destinations. Fauré had apparently made no objection at the time, in 1833, nor at any time in the next six years. In June 1839, however, he suddenly insisted that he was entitled to an indemnity for nonfulfillment of contract, and demanded to be paid the freight charges he would have earned, plus interest for the delays suffered in collecting payment.[46]

Fauré's claim was referred by the junta to the *promotor fiscal* for an opinion on the legal aspects. This official, influenced perhaps by diplomatic as well as legal considerations, counseled without qualification that the claim was entirely justified. The junta thereupon came to terms with Fauré over the procedure for computing the indemnity, with the result that a figure of $41,762 was agreed upon.[47]

In view of the junta's inability to liquidate this debt in cash, Fauré, who was already the proprietor of a textile factory and a sawmill in addition to his freighting business, proposed that the bank compensate him with machinery. He offered to take off its hands the incomplete woolen-textile plant—the very one whose nondelivery to Querétaro had occasioned most of the indemnity. However, he proposed that this equipment should be debited to him at its current value, to be determined by appraisers chosen at the discretion of the junta, not at the figure carried on the bank's books, which included original cost plus transportation charges. In addition to the woolen plant, Fauré asked for the paper mill and the distilling apparatus. But here he was willing to be charged their original cost plus all additional expenses paid to deliver them to Mexico City. To both of these proposals the junta willingly agreed, and thus the last major pieces of machinery owned by the bank passed out of its possession.[48]

The liquidation of stored machinery, the sale of livestock, the placing of loan assets on a paying basis, and much of the other activity of the bank's officers from 1838 through 1840 had as its ultimate objective the resumption of lending. Far from considering the bank a moribund agency, the members of the junta still hoped to continue its primary function, that of aiding new enterprises. The principal obstacle, however, was the obvious one—lack of liquid funds.

Ever since January 1836, the Banco de Avío had been dependent on the Finance Ministry to make available the monthly allotments of $15,000 stipulated by law. The ministry, however, confronted with other more pressing demands, had not complied consistently with its legal obligation to the bank. But even had the monthly sums been provided religiously, the law specified that this money could only be used to satisfy obligations of the bank, including approved loans, that had been incurred prior to the above-mentioned date. This appeared to rule out the granting of new loans on such funds, though one exception had been made in the case of the $60,000 loan issued to Lucas Alamán in December 1836. This was the only new grant of funds voted and effected after January 1836, but it was rationalized as being a revision of a loan approved before the cut-off date.[49]

In the spring of 1838, the prospect of obtaining funds from the Treasury to provide new loans, or even to pay off the uncashed drafts remaining from the old ones, far from improving, grew dimmer still. In April, the French began blocking the principal revenue-producing ports, and the government was faced with utter bankruptcy. In this crisis, ironically enough, it was the Banco de Avío that came to the aid of the Treasury. At the request of the finance minister, Eduardo Gorostiza, the junta turned over to him in November two drafts for $83,000 issued against Estevan de Antuñano, and payable when his debt to the bank fell due. Gorostiza was able to discount them at once, and thus place his hands on much-needed cash, though at a considerable loss from the drafts' face value.[50]

In cooperating with Minister Gorostiza, the members of the junta were placing patriotism above legality. The law creating the Banco de Avío had specifically prohibited the diversion of its capital to alien purposes, but the junta accepted Gorostiza's assurance that the money would be returned as soon as possible after the blockade ended.[51]

Meanwhile, the junta found itself besieged with applications for funds for a variety of undertakings. Many of these requests were for textile factories to be set up in various parts of the country. This was a natural aftermath of the successful pioneer work in the textile field, and of the recent enactment of a law excluding cotton yarn and yard goods.[52] But interestingly enough, the junta also began to receive an increasing number of requests to aid in the establishment of iron foundries and machine-tool works.

Apparently the first person to advocate the necessity of such works for any sort of industrialization was the country's pioneer textile manufacturer, Estevan de Antuñano. The Puebla entrepreneur, foreshadowing the economic thinking of some of his countrymen a century later, placed his finger on one of the most critical problems of the industrial development of his day.

The attempt to promote mechanical and rural industry by importing tools from abroad, as had been done since 1831, is not only uneconomical, but precarious and slow. . . . As long as we don't have tool factories in the country, foreign technicians will not be brought over as they should, nor will good machinists be trained who could handle the repair of parts which daily fall into disrepair in the new type establishments. The consequence is that these plants can't be kept running, national wealth cannot be created through them, nor civilization, nor power.[53]

As if in response to the need pointed out by Antuñano, several individuals, foreigners and Mexicans, appealed to the Banco de Avío to underwrite the costs of constructing metallurgical works. The junta received a variety of plans which called on the bank for sums ranging from $40,000 to $140,000. One of these was even presented by the French textile operator and transportation magnate, José Fauré, who outlined a plan for building a foundry to produce textile machinery, steam engines, and farm tools. Another plan was submitted by the Yankee machinist Benjamin Brundred, who had already built in his New Jersey plant the equipment installed in one of the Puebla cotton mills. A third proposal came from the owners of the Miraflores iron foundry, which had already produced a few pieces of farm machinery based on United States models. These requests, however, all involved sums far beyond the resources of the bank and the junta was reluctantly compelled to postpone action upon them.[54]

Nevertheless, the Banco de Avío was not wholly incapable of providing industrial capital during 1838. The very assets that had enabled it to make the emergency advance to the Treasury also made it possible to grant two industrial loans. The junta had received requests from two private firms, one the constructor of a textile factory in Jalapa, the other of an iron foundry in Tlascala, for loans that would be granted in the form of time drafts issued against Estevan de Antuñano. The latter, whose textile plant in Puebla was now in prosperous condition, expressed his willingness to accept drafts issued in favor of these firms to be paid when his notes fell due, provided that the junta would reduce his obligations to the bank by the face value of the drafts so issued.

The junta saw in these proposals not only an opportunity to give timely assistance to two substantial enterprises, but also the chance to place more of its loaned capital on an interest-paying basis. The money in Antuñano's possession earned no interest because of the exemption voted him by Congress in 1836; in the hands of other borrowers, the same funds could soon provide the bank with much-needed income. Accordingly, the junta, after examining the details of the individual proposals, and after having heard reports on the character of the entrepreneurs and the adequacy of their collateral, approved loans of $56,000 and $40,000 respectively to José Welsh and Company of Jalapa, a firm of

English merchants, and to Saracho Mier and Company, the proprietors of the iron foundry, La Vizcaína, in Tlascala.[55]

The Banco de Avío, by relending some of its original capital, thus found it possible to provide two sizable loans at a time when the government was totally incapable of supplying the agency with additional funds. Yet from the viewpoint of the borrowers, the arrangements were not so satisfactory as if the bank had been able to make the loans in cash. They had to assume the obligation of repaying the face value of the loans, and to pay interest on the full amounts, whereas the actual cash they received from negotiating the time drafts must have been considerably less. How the Jalapan firm fared in cashing its drafts is not known, but the proprietors of the Tlascalan foundry subsequently complained that they were forced to accept a 43-percent loss to obtain immediate cash from Antuñano.[56] Such was the latter's profit for redeeming his debt to the bank seven years in advance of its due date.

The two loans just described were the first to be granted by the Banco de Avío since the change in the junta's personnel took place in the autumn of 1837. It is worth noting that in processing the applications, the new officials displayed a caution that stood in refreshing contrast to the carelessness shown by some of their predecessors. Not only did the junta observe the correct procedure of referring the requests to a committee for study (a procedure set forth in the standing regulations, though not always followed), but the officials also sought legal advice on technical matters pertaining to the validity of the proffered collateral.[57] This collaboration of men with legal training in the loan-granting activities of the junta was an innovation long overdue. The art of drawing up escrituras that would fully protect the bank from unscrupulous borrowers had not been well practiced in the past, and much of the present junta's difficulty in dealing with delinquent clients had arisen from the vagueness and imprecision of the loan agreements entered into by its predecessors. The sad history of past loans was at least teaching a lesson for the future.

But the opportunity to practice this lesson was limited by a shortage of funds, without which the junta could do little to satisfy the many requests it received for assistance. The possibility of utilizing Antuñano for other loans was practically ruled out by the fact that his debt was almost completely repaid as a result of the two loans mentioned above, and the emergency advance made to the government during the French blockade. The end of that blockade, however, in the spring of 1839 raised the hopes of the junta that the Treasury would not only repay this advance, but also make available at least a part of the funds to which the bank was entitled under the $15,000 monthly allotment arrangement enacted by Congress in 1836. As of September 1839, the unpaid allotments alone amounted to over $457,000.[58]

The junta, accordingly, in the summer and fall of that year, gave its approval to four loans totaling $110,000, three of them for the expansion of cotton-textile plants already in operation in Mexico and Veracruz, the fourth for a glass factory under construction in Puebla. Two of the loans were advanced in the form of re-endorsed drafts that had been issued and accepted at a customhouse prior to January 1836, and hence were eligible for payment from the monthly allotment fund; the other two grants took the form of bills drawn by the junta on the finance minister specifically against the $83,000 temporary advance made by the bank to the Treasury the year before.[59]

But in not one of the four instances did the Treasury honor the paper issued against it. The borrowers who had received the re-endorsed drafts returned them to the bank after six months of vain attempts to get them accepted; the recipients of the bills did the same. The Finance Ministry thus not only persisted in denying the bank the funds stipulated in the 1836 law, but also reneged on an explicit promise made during the blockade to repay the extralegal loan that the junta gave at that time of crisis.

Against this indifferent treatment, the members of the junta raised their voice in frequent protest. They pleaded with the authorities to provide it with some source of revenue so that the bank could resume its functions, but to no avail. In each reassignment of public revenues that was made in 1839 and 1840, the Finance Ministry brushed aside the claims of the bank and of those luckless individuals who tried to present its paper for payment.[60]

The persistent refusal of the government to supply further funds to the Banco de Avío could not but dishearten its officials. As they themselves pointed out to the president late in 1840, their position was an embarrassing one:

We are at the head of a beneficial establishment whose basic laws are still in force, and we can't carry them out. What are the consequences? We reject requests which are directed to it in accordance with those very laws; we are unable to satisfy legitimate protests made to it for nonfulfillment of its contracts; we see regretfully the ruination of certain industrial undertakings because they need assistance. . . .[61]

The despair of the officials could only be deepened by time, for the succeeding months merely confirmed the hopeless position of the bank as a supplier of industrial capital. It is true that out of the income received by the bank from interest and other payments, the junta was able to eke out four modest loans ranging in size from $500 to $6,000;[62] but after 1840, apparently even such loans could no longer be made.[63] By the end of that year, the Banco de Avío to all intents and purposes had ceased to function as an industrial loan agency. It continued to keep tabs on its existing investments, to insist on the fulfillment of its contractual rights in the various loans, and, in some instances, to grant extensions for their repayment; but the day when the Banco de Avío could make a significant contribution either in money or in equipment toward the erection of a power-driven factory had definitely passed.

THE END OF THE BANK—AN APPRAISAL

It has often been observed that government agencies, once created, are difficult to abolish. The history of the Banco de Avío after 1840 seems to support this observation, for, although it was no longer able to fulfill its primary purpose of supplying industrial capital, it continued to exist in a kind of suspended animation for two more years. This does not mean that suggestions were lacking for the transfer of its assets and/or its powers to other bodies.

One such suggestion came from within the bank's own management early in 1841. Miguel Barreiro, vice-chairman of the junta and also a member of the Chamber of Deputies, proposed to the latter body that the Banco de Avío be merged with another state bank that had been set up to redeem the copper money then in circulation, to form a new institution to be known as the Banco del Crédito Público. This bank would have no responsibility for promoting industry, but, as the proposed name indicated, would devote itself exclusively to public-debt operations.[1] Barreiro's plan, which called for the termination of public financing of industry, and the diversion of Banco de Avío capital from its original purpose, aroused little enthusiasm in Congress. Support did materialize for another plan, however, one that called for the continued utilization of that capital for industrial development.

The originator of this proposal was an association of manufacturers, the *Sociedad para el fomento de la industria nacional*. Known generally as the *Junta de Industria*, this body had been organized in 1839 by the large textile manufacturers of Mexico City. It had subsequently expanded, with the formation of comparable groups in several provincial cities. Its membership was open to the proprietors of any size shop, but control was carefully retained in the hands of the largest operators by a provision of its charter that restricted voting rights for the selection of officers to those who employed more than thirty persons.[2] The Junta de Industria was thus the contemporary version of the modern big businessmen's association; and it was hardly a coincidence that many of its factory-owning charter members were simultaneously debtors of the Banco de Avío.[3]

The association's proposal for utilizing the bank's assets was part of a general scheme to convert the Junta de Industria from a voluntary body into an all-inclusive guild with official responsibility for protecting the interests of domestic industry. The head of the new organization would be an executive committee, presided over by the interior minister, but selected by the Junta de Industria of Mexico City. Under the plan, the loan assets of the Banco de Avío would be turned over to this executive committee, which would use the interest earnings for its own expenses and have authority to make additional loans when the state of the funds permitted.[4]

Initial congressional reaction to this proposal was favorable, despite the fact that it would convey control of the bank's assets to a body essentially controlled by private manufacturing interests. The Committees of Industry and Finance jointly studied the proposal, which had been embodied in a bill introduced by four deputies, and recommended its acceptance with minor modifications, none of which lessened the manufacturers' power to select the officials of the proposed body. Indeed, the committees sought to gloss over the implication of transferring Banco de Avío assets to such a group by criticizing the existing management.

Since the investment of funds will be made under the responsibility of the treasurer and the accountant, we shall avoid in the future the continued distribution of money with so much liberality and so little discretion as was the case in the past, when considerable sums were lost because they were given to persons who had not secured their responsibility.[5]

Such an attack on the bank directors was demonstrably unfair. Not since the reorganization of 1837 had they concluded a loan without first requiring adequate security and the completion of the legal formalities. It was, moreover, the height of disingenuousness to criticize the bank's management for lack of prudence, and simultaneously to recommend transfer of its assets to a privately controlled body, some of whose leading members had themselves defaulted on obligations to the bank.[6]

How honestly and efficiently the Junta de Industria would have administered those assets is a moot question, for, before the Congress could act on the proposed legislation, it was unexpectedly dissolved. The political storm that had been gathering in several quarters against the administration in power burst forth in the summer of 1841, sweeping before it the entire constitutional structure established five years before. In its place, enjoying full dictatorial power, settled General Santa Anna. To be sure, the Junta de Industria sought to persuade the dictator to approve their plan for absorbing the assets of the Banco de Avío,[7] but Santa Anna had his own ideas for the future of the agency.

With the entire government subject to his whims, Santa Anna displayed none of the restraint that had characterized his predecessors, or even his own previous administrations. In the past, however pressed the government had been for funds, it had always refrained from alienating the loan assets of the bank.[8] It had, moreover, refused to permit borrowers to repay their debts in Treasury certificates or other public paper, thus preserving those assets from depreciation. But now the dictator looked upon the bank's assets as disposable items on a par with any others possessed by the government. In his anxiety to obtain ready cash, he was prepared to alienate them at a fraction of their original worth. The results of this policy may be seen in table 4, which lists the income reported by the Tesorería General de la Nación from the liquidation of Banco de Avío assets during 1842. Credits that the bank valued, including interest due, at almost $240,000 were disposed of for $150,000. But what is more striking is the fact that only $81,000 was received in cash; the balance consisted of public debt certificates, many of which, it may safely be assumed, had cost their possessors far less than their face value.

The alienation of bank assets did not stop with those listed in table 4. During 1842 the government endorsed three additional credits, valued at over $48,000, to a private dealer in transactions that apparently produced no direct return, since the Treasury listed none in its accounts.[9] And in 1843, the government sold a note listed by the bank at $61,000 for $10,000 in cash and twice that amount in copper money certificates.[10]

With this piecemeal liquidation of the bank's loan portfolio, it was only a matter of time before the agency itself was abolished. On September 23, 1842, General Santa Anna issued the decree of dissolution. A lengthy preamble justified the step on two main grounds: first, that the bank could no longer fulfill its assigned purpose because most of its capital had been consumed; and second, "that the spirit of enterprise in this field had been spread in the Republic to the full extent its true happiness requires, and it no longer needs the protection and encourage-

TABLE 4

Treasury Income from the Disposal of Banco de Avío Assets in 1842

Description of Asset	Listed value	Amount received	Received in cash	Received in paper
Cocolapam textile factory, note and interest due[a]	$ 63,959	$ 63,959	$ 28,000	$ 35,959
Tlalpam Co., note	88,500	50,000[b]	50,000	—
F. Puig, note	10,000	—	—	—
Tlalnepantla Co., note	3,330	2,000	0	2,000
Welsh & Co., interest due	4,058	4,058	0	4,058
Welsh & Co., note	56,000	17,062[c]	25	17,037
Cayetano Rubio, note[d]	12,000	12,000	2,556	9,444
Lucas Alamán, note	1,500	1,500	500	1,000
	$239,347	$156,579	$ 81,081	$ 69,498

a. The debt was originally owed by Lucas Alamán.

b. The Tlalpam and Puig notes were sold in a single transaction that involved other payments, but only $50,000 was posted in the ledger as income from these notes.

c. The purchaser turned in $35,000 but only $17,062 was credited as income from the sale of the note.

d. This debt had its origin in the loan to the Celaya Co. in 1832.

Sources: Libro común de cargo de la Tesorería General de la Nación, 1842, 2, 696r–698v, MS in AGN; MSS in AN, Madariaga, 1842, 602v–603v.

ment which the Banco de Avío could provide."[11] Whatever one might say about the sincerity of the second reason, there is no denying the weight of the first. Without new sources of capital, and with many of its best loan assets sold to meet other needs of the government, there was no point in maintaining a separate agency. Thus was ended, twelve years after it began, the first attempt by a Mexican government to develop industry with public funds.

At various times during its checkered career, the Banco de Avío was the object of bitter attack. In the years since its dissolution, it has usually been treated with either scorn or indifference. A reappraisal of its significance for the development of industrial activity is certainly in order. First, however, it is necessary to eliminate the confusion that has arisen over the amount of capital available to the bank during its entire career. Several writers, accepting as accurate the statement in Santa Anna's decree of dissolution that the bank had never received its entire legal assignment of one million pesos, have confidently asserted that the maximum capital available to it was approximately $600,000.[12] They have derived this figure from the accounts published by the bank for the period prior to 1835, and from the unwarranted assumption that its funds were limited to those it had received from customhouses prior to the suspension of payments ordered in March 1833. The fact is that the Treasury continued to advance funds to the bank, either directly to its officers, or by making payments to third parties on its behalf. The records of the Treasury from July 1, 1833 to December 31, 1842, but excluding 1840 for which no data is available, show expenditures for the Banco de Avío totaling $733,898.[13] To be sure, this figure is inflated by the inclusion of the value of drafts which were subsequently voided,[14] but there can be little doubt that the net outlay was at least a half million pesos. And when this is added to the $560,000 which the bank received from customs duties before March 1833,[15] it is obvious that the agency had access to a sum that more than equaled its assigned capital.

This can also be demonstrated by examining the bank's investments in loans and machinery acquisitions. Table 5 summarizes the overall lending operations of the agency during its twelve-year history. It is clear that loans totaling $1,295,520 were authorized, but that the net amount advanced to borrowers was only $773,695. Chaotic fiscal conditions, which forced the cancellation of over $500,000 in drafts and Treasury orders, account for the difference. Nevertheless, the value of completed loans, when combined with the $245,271 invested in major machinery collections,[16] produce a total of $1,018,966. From the financial viewpoint, then, the Banco de Avío was not quite so small an operation as some have contended.

In view of the fact that the agency was primarily intended to develop the textile industry, it is well worth determining the extent to which the bank's investments in loans and machinery adhered to this purpose. The last column of table 5 makes it clear that only twenty-seven of the thirty-seven approved borrowers actually received funds. These twenty-seven had requested loans to develop twenty-nine distinct undertakings. Table 6, which classifies these undertakings by type of activity, reveals that while only twelve were in the cotton- and wool-textile field, these twelve received 71.1 percent of the total loaned to all enterprises, and that the cotton-textile field alone received over 65 percent. The agricultural undertakings, moreover, with three minor exceptions, were all devoted to the production of raw materials for the textile industry.

Similar emphasis on this industry is to be found in the bank's acquisition of heavy machinery. Of the $245,271 expended for this purpose, $180,018, or 73 percent, went toward equipment for cotton and woolen

TABLE 5   Summary of Banco de Avío Loans, 1830 – 1842

Date[a]	Borrower	Sum approved	Issued in specie	Issued in paper	Paper[b] dis-counted	Net total loaned
1830	Casarín	$ 4,500	$ 4,500	—	—	$ 4,500
	Lazo de la Vega	24,590	24,590	—	—	24,590
1831	Vallarta	600	600	—	—	600
	Sánchez[c]	5,000	5,000	—	—	5,000
	Tlalnepantla Co.	3,330	3,330	—	—	3,330
	Zacualpa de Amilpas Co.	68,000	40,000	28,000	28,000	68,000
	Antuñano & Co.	176,000	30,000	146,000	116,000	146,000
1832	Mexico Ind. Co.	131,000	51,000	80,000	40,000	91,000
	Puig	10,000	10,000	—	—	10,000
	Celaya Ind. Co.[d]	10,000	10,000	—	—	10,000
	Querétaro Ind. Co.	30,000	30,000	—	—	30,000
1835	Alamán	32,000	—	32,000	0	0
	Aldazoro	40,000	—	40,000	40,000	40,000
	Bracho	40,000	—	40,000	0	0
	Domínguez	8,000	—	8,000	0	0
	Escandón	20,000	—	20,000	0	0
	Icaza	50,000	—	50,000	0	0
	Pacheco	30,000	—	30,000	30,000	30,000
	Pardo	50,000	—	50,000	50,000	50,000
	Prieto	15,000	—	15,000	15,000	15,000
	Puebla Hospicio	40,000	—	40,000	0	0
	Roa	50,000	—	50,000	50,000	50,000
	Ruiz	30,000	—	30,000	20,808	20,808
	Sodi	32,000	—	32,000	1,200	1,200
	Victoria	100,000	—	100,000	0	0
1836	Arista	2,000	—	2,000	2,000	2,000
	Barrera	16,000	—	16,000	0	0
1837	Alamán	120,000	—	120,000	60,000	60,000
	Saracho Mier & Co.	40,000	—	40,000	40,000	40,000
	Welsh & Co.	56,000	—	56,000	56,000	56,000
1839	Ainslee	20,000	—	20,000	0	0
	Fauré	20,000	—	20,000	0	0
	Puebla Glass Co.	10,000	4,167	5,833[e]	0	4,167
1840	Díaz	4,000	—	4,000	4,000	4,000
	Font	1,000	500	500	500	1,000
	Guerrero	6,000	—	6,000	6,000	6,000
	Samudio	500	500	—	—	500
Total		$1,295,520	$214,187	$1,081,333	$559,508	$773,695

a. Refers to date of first loan if more than one was granted.   b. Face values are listed; the borrowers often realized less in cash.   c. A. González Cruz assumed responsibility for this debt after 1832.   d. L. Alamán assumed the debt in 1837; Cayetano Rubio took it over in 1842, at which time the principal was increased to $12,000.   e. The remainder of $10,000 in drafts issued originally; the rest were returned to the bank for a like amount of specie.   *Sources: Informe y cuentas*, 1841; MSS in AGN, B/A 1 – 3.

TABLE 6

Type of Enterprises Financed by the Banco de Avío, 1830 – 1842

Type	No.	Value of loans	Percent of total loaned
Agricultural[a]	8	$ 74,528	9.6
Cotton textiles	9	509,000	65.8
Glass	1	4,167	0.5
Ironworks and machinery	4	110,500	14.3
Paper mills	1	20,000	2.6
Sawmill and building ornaments	2	4,500	0.6
Wax bleaching	1	10,000	1.3
Wool textiles	3	41,000	5.3
	29	$773,695	100.0

[a] Includes cotton gins, silkworks, apiaries, and a flax plantation.
Source: Informe y cuentas, 1841.

factories, the balance going into the purchase of paper mills.[17] The heavy stress on cotton manufacturing noted above in the loan allocations was also reflected in the purchase of textile machinery, since all but $40,242 of the $180,018 went to that field. It is beyond dispute, then, that the directors of the Banco de Avío over the twelve years of its existence did in fact adhere to the objectives set down in the bank statute, and that the primary goal, in practice as in theory, was the modernization of the cotton industry.

Granted the distribution of bank investments as set forth above, the all-important question remains: What did this expenditure of public funds accomplish? The answers offered by writers over the years have tended to repeat with variations the theme first sounded by an anonymous pamphlet in 1848:

This Banco de Avío was a veritable "Mount Parnassus" from which, under the pretext of establishing factories, large sums were extracted; the factories which actually reached the working stage with the use of those funds were rare. Consequently, it can be said that the real industry which the bank fostered was, with few exceptions, that of finding pretexts to draw the greatest sums from it while spending a small part for appearances' sake in some looms, wheels, or cylinders. The Lord knows how they have settled their accounts with the government.[18]

A similar view of the bank, reiterating the lack of accomplishment and the loss of its resources, may be encountered in the works of Juan Suárez y Navarro and Carlos Díaz Dufoo, to name only two.[19] It is a view that has been too readily accepted, especially by those who, like Díaz Dufoo, object on principle to the idea of state intervention in economic life, or, like Suárez Navarro, bear political animosity toward the founder of the bank.

A careful examination of the facts suggests that these writers have considerably distorted the picture of its achievements, ignoring its accomplishments and exaggerating its failures. The Banco de Avío, as has already been shown, advanced funds for twenty-nine enterprises; in addition, it made power-driven machinery available on credit for seven of these, and for two others which received no funds.[20] It is therefore to the thirty-one projects that obtained money and/or machinery that one must look for evidence to determine the effectiveness of the bank.

The best gauge for evaluating the productiveness of its loans is the history of the individual projects. Although it does not of itself prove that funds were used efficiently, the fact that a project evolved from the planning stage into an operating enterprise is both an indication of genuine purpose on the borrower's part, and also a measure of bank achievement. Table 7 classifies the thirty-one projects into those that were never completed, those that reached the operating stage but subsequently shut down, and those that were successfully operating in 1845, three years after the extinction of the bank. It will be seen that only ten projects, involving a little over 18 percent of the agency's total investment, proved to be complete fiascos. The other twenty-one achieved an operating status but for various reasons seven of these closed down prior to 1845. This left in existence as of that year only fourteen of the original thirty-one, but in these fourteen, the bank had placed over 57 percent of its total invested capital.

The major reverses took place in the agricultural, paper, and iron fields. Six of the eight agricultural ventures financed by the bank were complete failures, an indication that its efforts to promote raw-material production were ill conceived. Two of the three paper-mill projects also failed to materialize, chiefly through lack of will on the part of the assignee to carry them through.[21] The difficulties in the iron industry were of another order, for here the two principal bank beneficiaries managed to put their respective enterprises into operation, but technical obstacles, particularly the lack of suitable refractory stone, caused the paralysis of their blast furnaces. Both enterprises, it might be noted,

TABLE 7
Progress of Enterprises Receiving Banco de Avío
Capital in Loans and Machinery

Type of enterprise	Name of borrower	Capital invested in enterprises		
		Never in operation	Closed before 1845	Operating 1845
Apiary	P. Sánchez	$ 5,000		
	A. Vallarta	600		
Cotton ginning	C. Sodi	1,200		
	L. Ruiz			$20,808
Flax plantation	A. Prieto	15,000		
Silkworks	Lazo de la Vega	24,590		
	Tlalnepantla Co.	3,330		
	J. J. Díaz			4,000[a]
Glass mfg.	Puebla Glass Co.			4,167
Iron foundry	Zacualpa de Amilpas Co.		68,000	
	Saracho Mier & Co.		40,000	
	J. F. Samudio			500
Farm machinery	M. Arista		2,000	
Paper mfg.	L. Alamán	22,340		
	J. R. Pacheco	40,915		
	Puebla Hospicio			21,998
Sawmill	V. Casarín		3,000	
Building ornaments	V. Casarín	1,500		
Wax bleaching	J. R. Pacheco		10,000	
Textiles, cotton	V. Roa		72,320	
	R. Pardo		50,000	
	L. Alamán			60,000
	S. Aldazoro			62,320
	Antuñano & Co.			183,916
	Celaya Ind. Co.			12,275[b]
	J. I. Guerrero			6,000[a]
	Mexico Ind. Co.			145,945
	Welsh & Co.			56,000
Textiles, wool	Querétaro Ind.	70,242		
	J. Font			1,000[a]
	F. Puig			10,000
		$184,717	$245,320	$588,929

[a] Reported as operating in 1841; no further data available.
[b] The original Celaya Ind. Co. failed in 1833; the physical facilities and the debt were taken over by L. Alamán, who established a woolen mill in 1840. In 1845 the mill was owned and operated by C. Rubio.

Sources: Informe y cuentas, 1841; MDG, 1845.

continued to produce iron by other methods, but their main objective was not achieved.[22]

Granted that the bank's investments in these various undertakings remained fruitless, one should still view the results in proper perspective. The primary goal of the Banco de Avío, as stated so often in these pages, was the development of the textile industry, and it was precisely in this field that the most notable successes were won. As table 7 indicates, nine of the twelve bank-supported cotton and wool undertakings, including seven projected spinning and weaving factories, became going concerns. Moreover, in every instance but one, the government was able to recover some part of the capital advanced, either through repayment of the debt, or through sale of the note held against the loan.[23]

The conclusion to be drawn from these figures is clear. More than half the capital distributed by the Banco de Avío was utilized productively, at least to the extent of bringing formerly unknown enterprises into existence. This achievement cannot, of course, obscure the fact that considerable sums were invested without result. Much money was granted ill-advisedly; much was wasted; and some, to be sure, was taken by persons who had little intention of complying with their own stated purposes. Even of the sums utilized in the enterprises that came to life, it cannot be denied that greater results might have been achieved with less expense.

But in judging the investments of the bank and the efforts of those it financed, it must be kept in mind that both the officers of the agency and the entrepreneurs were engaged in introducing into Mexico industrial methods and techniques that were completely new to the country. In such pioneering work, mistakes are as inevitable as they are costly. In this case, it was a public agency that underwrote them, and by so doing, paved the way for private enterprise. In the cotton-textile field, the bank contributed directly to the establishment of some half-dozen spinning and weaving factories, and to the expansion of mechanical ginning in the agricultural areas. Indirectly, it provided other businessmen with an opportunity to gain experience, and gave them encouragement to enter the field. The fruit of this encouragement was the rapid development of a modernized cotton textile industry in the decade 1835 – 1845, a development that will be traced in detail in chapter 12.

THE PROTECTIONIST ERA,

1837 — 1846

Government assistance to domestic industries was not restricted to the capital spasmodically provided through the Banco de Avío; nor did the passing of this agency mean the end of official bodies specifically established to encourage industrial development. In the decade prior to the war with the United States, other inducements, in the form of tax concessions and tariff protection, were increasingly utilized to supplement the work begun by the bank. Moreover, when this lending agency finally disappeared in September 1842, a new establishment known as the *Dirección de Industria* (Bureau of Industry) was called into being to assume some of the functions of the defunct body, as well as new ones created by the growth of various industries.

The use of tax concessions to assist industrial enterprises followed closely the pattern laid down in the first decade of independence. Through legislative enactment, the products of specific domestic industries—textiles, paper, iron, and earthenware— were allowed to circulate without paying the alcabala or other local duties.[1] One difference, however, distinguishes the tax exemptions granted after 1836 from those given before. In the past, the authority of the federal government to suspend the incidence of state-established taxes had been challenged, and as a result, Congress had voted exemptions only in the districts under federal control.[2] The transition from a federal to a central form of government enabled the national legislature to make the exemptions nationwide in scope. In the past, to be sure, individual states had also waived the collection of duties on domestic products, but it had been done on a discriminatory basis, to favor the artisans and raw-material producers located within their respective boundaries.

In fact, it was the continued tendency of the departmental govern-

ments (which replaced the states under the centralist system) to dis-
criminate against Mexican-made textiles produced beyond their respective borders that made the granting in 1837 of a nationwide tax
exemption so significant to the new industrialists. Only the year before,
Estevan de Antuñano, proprietor of what was still the country's largest
spinning factory, complained that his Puebla-made goods were subject
to higher duties in some departments than foreign goods were. As a
consequence, he said, he was forced to sell his textiles chiefly in Mexico
City, where they were exempt from all charges.[3]

It was to eliminate such internal barriers to the sale of domestic textiles, as well as to improve their competitive position vis-à-vis foreign
goods, that the law of May 23, 1837, was adopted. Under the terms of this
law, the exemption from all duties previously enjoyed by cotton, wool,
and silk textiles just in the federal district was extended to the entire republic, and was made applicable also to raw cotton and cotton yarn.[4]

To prevent foreign textiles from taking advantage of this privilege, a
system of checks on the domestic industry was established. Each manufacturer was required to report to the alcabala collector of his district
the exact number of looms and spindles he possessed, and the specific
types and amounts of goods he produced. In turn, he had to allow the
revenue officials to make periodic inspections of his establishment to
verify the information. All goods were to bear the stamp of their manufacturer, and had to be counterstamped by the alcabala collector in
order to circulate without payment of duties.[5]

These regulations impeded, but did not prevent, the fraudulent circulation of foreign textiles in the guise of native ones. Instances were
reported of domestic manufacturers located near the borders of the
country who "nationalized" imported goods with their own stamps; in
other instances, foreign textiles were found circulating with the stamp
of nonexistent factories.[6]

Equally disturbing to the textile industry were the attempts of individual departments to levy local taxes on the sale of domestic textiles, or
on the raw material that entered into their manufacture, despite the explicit wording of the law of May 23, 1837. The Puebla assembly invoked a
transit tax in 1844 on textiles produced outside the department, and on
all ginned cotton passing through it. In that same year, the legislature of
Veracruz imposed a fifty-centavo duty on every hundred pounds of
ginned cotton introduced into the manufacturing towns, whether of
departmental or nondepartmental origin. The Veracruz duty was revenue-producing in intent, not a measure to aid local manufacturers, as

in the case of the Puebla tax, but nevertheless it was just as much a violation of the 1837 law. Manufacturers' representatives protested against these departmental measures, and the Consejo de Gobierno, whose opinion was sought by the government, advised the executive to declare them void.[7]

The issue of locally imposed taxes was not, however, permanently resolved at this time. The overthrow of the centralist system, and the resumption by the departments of their statehood in 1846, introduced a new and more widespread phase of discriminatory taxation. A discussion of this phase is beyond the scope of the present study, but it might be said that one of the most vexing problems confronting the federal government after the conclusion of the war with the United States was how to restrain the state authorities from utilizing their tax powers to the disadvantage of national industries.[8] The shortsighted, narrowly localistic view that had characterized the economic policies of the state governments in the first ten years of independence had undergone little change, apparently, in the two decades that followed.

Much more important to domestic industry, and to the country as a whole, than the matter of tax exemptions was the question of tariff protection. Because the cotton-textile industry was the most important one involved, and because the ramifications of protecting this industry were widespread, attention will be directed primarily to the tariff measures affecting the production and sale of domestic cottons.

It will be recalled that from the birth of independence, artisans, farmers, and interested merchants had labored to obtain legislation prohibiting the import of competitive types of cotton goods; but these efforts had been without success until 1829, when, with the active support of General Guerrero, a law to that effect was adopted. This law, it will be remembered, was suspended at once, and the following year, after the overthrow of Guerrero, the suspension was continued indefinitely so as to provide funds for the Banco de Avío. For the next five years, the "cotton bloc" of artisans and farmers and their representatives in Congress fought persistently but unsuccessfully to have the 1829 law restored. Foreign textiles continued to enter the country, subject to the not inconsiderable duties established in the tariff act of 1827.[9]

In 1836, however, a series of shifts in government policy began to take place, which culminated in the establishment of a comprehensive system of prohibitions, and in the creation of a domestic monopoly for the producers of cotton and cotton artifacts. The first step was taken in August 1836, when the unicameral legislature banned, with but one dis-

senting vote, the further entry of raw cotton. The import status of foreign cotton had been in doubt since 1830, for the applicable tariff laws
were not consistent.[10] To remedy this situation, representatives from
the cotton-growing departments of Veracruz and Oaxaca successfully
introduced a bill in April 1836 to have the importation of foreign-grown
cotton in both the ginned and seeded state declared illegal.[11]

The adoption of this law was of far-reaching significance, for it established the principle that the more modern type textile industry, still in
its infancy, would have to depend exclusively on raw materials produced within the country. Far from opposing this principle, the proprietors of the new spinning factories gave it their support, for they apparently saw in the cotton growers a political ally who could help them
obtain legislation favorable to their own interests.[12] These manufacturers, it seems, gave little thought at the time to the possibility that in linking the growth of their industry to that of cotton farming, they might be
placing a hobble around their own legs.

The second step toward establishing a wholly protected market for
the domestic cotton industry was taken in March 1837 when the government, exercising the blanket authority delegated to it by the legislature on September 19, 1836, to revise existing tariff laws, promulgated a
decree that on its face met all the demands of the extreme prohibition-
ists. According to the terms of this act, one year after its publication, the
importation of every kind or class of foreign yarn and of *tejidos ordinarios de algodón* was to be absolutely forbidden.[13]

The willingness of the government to adopt such a measure requires
explanation. Traditionally, the executive power had been the one to oppose the prohibition of ordinary cotton goods. The Finance Ministry,
especially, had been sensitive to the fiscal implications of such a step,
and had been unwilling to accept an annual loss in revenue estimated
in the millions. Why, then, did the government reverse its attitude in
March 1837?

The original intention of the government officials responsible for the
tariff revision does not appear to have been to exclude the tejidos ordinarios, or all the varieties of yarn. In fact, the impression was widely
held in the final months of 1836 that they would even reduce the level of
duties established for such goods. So seriously did the cotton interests
anticipate this, that they brought pressure on Congress to limit the executive's authority to revise the tariff.[14] A resolution to forbid "any
change in the duties assigned by the present tariff to cotton yarn and
ordinary cotton textiles" was actually introduced into the legislature,

and won the support of the Committee on Industry.[15] Final action on this resolution, however, was made unnecessary by the government's decision, embodied in the tariff decree of March 11, 1837, to place the articles in question on the prohibited list.

The explanation of this fundamental shift in policy appears to lie in the increasing influence that the new manufacturers were able to exercise on the conduct of public affairs.[16] The personnel changes that accompanied the implementation of the new centralist constitution, formally adopted in December 1836, brought into important positions men sympathetic with the aspirations of the manufacturers. In the Consejo de Gobierno, newly constituted in the month of January 1837, the most prominent member was Lucas Alamán. Alamán's belief in the necessity of protecting the cotton industry, strongly expressed in the past, had lately been reinforced by his acquisition of a personal interest in a large cotton-spinning mill.[17] It seems reasonable to believe, therefore, though explicit proof is lacking, that Alamán, together with other manufacturers, was instrumental in persuading President Justo Corro and the Finance Ministry to accept the new policy. The task may have been facilitated by the fact that from December 19, 1836, until March 22, 1837, the position of minister was held, not by a figure of political importance, but by one of the permanent underofficials serving in a caretaking capacity.[18]

Examination of the details of the March 11, 1837, tariff act suggests that government officials had tried to effect a compromise between the needs of the Treasury and the interests of the consumer on the one hand, and the protectionist demands of the cotton industry on the other. In the past, the customary waiting period before restrictive tariff changes went into effect had been six months. But in the case of the cotton textiles and yarns now added to the excluded list, it was carefully specified that a full year should elapse. During that period, these goods were to enter on payment of duties considerably smaller, in most cases, than those collected in the past.[19]

Apparently it was hoped that the intended period of grace, plus the reduction of duties, would produce a substantial increase in government revenue. Merchants could be expected to lay in heavy stocks of goods, which they knew would no longer be available; the lowered duties would discourage smuggling; and the result would be a rise in the volume of legitimate imports, with consequent improvement in customs collections. If such were the expectation, it was realized only in part. The importation of cotton artifacts during the year did undergo an extraordinary increase. British export statistics show that more cotton yarn was shipped to Mexico in the single year 1837 than in the preceding five years put together.[20] But apparently much of the increase entered through extralegal channels. The duties collected on cotton goods, instead of rising, actually declined from the level obtained in previous years.[21]

The heavy influx of yarns and yard goods did not fail to arouse the apprehensions of the domestic-cotton interests. Working through their departmental assemblies, they bombarded the national government with petitions to reduce to six months the grace period before the prohibitions took effect. But the Finance Ministry was adamant in its refusal, explaining that the twelve-month period had been deliberately fixed so as to reconcile all the interests affected.[22]

When the year did elapse, however, Mexico was involved in a serious diplomatic crisis with France. Confronted with a heavy loss of revenue because of the blockade of Gulf ports, the government of President Bustamante was in no hurry to reduce its income further by ordering the prohibitions into effect. Months passed, and still no steps were taken. The manufacturers, in dismay, turned to Congress for action, and, finally, on October 20, 1838, a decree was enacted declaring the prohibitions in effect as of the previous March 18, but exempting from confiscation the goods that had entered Mexico since that date.[23] Thus, at long last, the ports of Mexico were legally closed to cotton yarn of any description, and to the varieties of cloth covered by the term *tejidos ordinarios de algodón*.

But law and reality in Mexico are often two distinct things. Such was certainly the situation after the enactment of the prohibitory decrees. The customs service, weakened by corruption and inefficiency, was unable to enforce the decrees effectively; smuggling of foreign cottons persisted to the detriment of both the home manufacturing interests and the national treasury. The Pacific ports seem to have been especially vulnerable to the entry of illicit goods, perhaps because their remoteness from centers of authority made effectual supervision difficult. But the Gulf ports, from Tampico to Matamoros, also served as a highway for prohibited goods, particularly when federalist insurrectionaries held control over them, as was the case in 1838 and 1839. Thus, despite the presence on the books of prohibitory legislation, the cotton manufacturers frequently complained of an inability to dispose of their goods profitably.[24]

Perhaps the most discouraging blow to the industry's desire for complete protection came, not from lowly customs employees or revolutionaries, but from generals holding high positions under the government. On two occasions, once in May 1839, and again in September 1840, the commanding officer in the Matamoros area issued orders to permit the entry of the illicit cotton goods. The second instance was the more serious, not only because of the volume of goods involved, but also because of its political consequences.[25]

On September 30, 1840, the minister of war, General Juan Almonte, authorized General Mariano Arista, in command at the port of Matamoros, to allow the entry of foreign yarn so as to obtain funds to meet the needs of his troops. Arista had previously written to the war minister describing the plight of his command, and explaining a proposal, submitted to him by local merchants, whereby they would be willing to provide $50,000 in specie, provided that cotton yarn would be allowed to enter in a volume sufficient to require the payment of this sum in customs duties.[26] With the permission of the war minister, General Arista proceeded to make contracts with various British merchants to permit the importation of over two million pounds of unbleached yarn, an amount considerably in excess of the current annual production of all Mexican spinning factories.[27]

Meanwhile, in Mexico City news of the war minister's action aroused an immediate storm of protest in the Senate. Almonte, appearing before that body on October 2, promised to rescind the authorization given to Arista, but he allowed nearly three weeks to elapse before sending the countermanding order, long enough, his critics subsequently charged, to permit the merchants to place their orders.[28]

In further reaction to these events, a group of cotton manufacturers petitioned to have the *Poder Conservador* issue a ruling on the legality of Almonte's September 30 order. At the same time, the Senate acted to bring impeachment charges against the war minister after hearing testimony from Finance Minister Javier Echeverría that he had been periodically supplying General Arista with funds to meet the needs of his command. Nevertheless, when the Chamber of Deputies met to act on the charges, a majority voted to absolve Almonte on the grounds that his intentions had been patriotic. The *Poder Conservador*, on the other hand, ruled Almonte's September 30 order a violation of the constitution, and hence null and void.[29]

This decision failed by far to put an end to the unfortunate episode. The British merchants, with the support of their diplomatic representative, took the position that the action of the Chamber in acquitting

Almonte gave full legality to the contracts entered into with General Arista. They therefore presented the government with two alternatives: either allow the entry of the yarn in accordance with the original agreements; or indemnify the merchants for the losses they sustained from abrogation of the contracts.[30] The precarious state of the national treasury made acceptance of the second alternative all but impossible. But to allow the yarn to enter meant to expose the government to other and equally embarrassing consequences.

The French government also had an interest in the tariff situation, deriving from the fact that French nationals had invested considerable capital in the textile industry. When it appeared that President Bustamante might allow the yarn to enter, the French envoy protested that his countrymen had invested in the domestic industry under the guarantees offered by the prohibitory laws. He pointed out that they, too, would demand an indemnity if their interests were ruined as a result of the negation of those laws.[31]

If this were not enough to give the Bustamante government reason to hesitate, it also found itself flooded by petitions opposing the entry of foreign yarn.[32] These petitions demonstrated the existence in Mexico of a widespread body of opinion favoring preservation of the prohibitory legislation, a body of opinion, moreover, that transcended the usual political lines. Individuals who had little in common on other matters found themselves in accord on this. The profederalist editors of *El Cosmopolita*, whose vitriolic blasts against Lucas Alamán and other conservative leaders have been noted earlier, now opened their columns approvingly to the statements signed by Lucas Alamán; and such diverse figures as conservative ex-President Justo Corro, federalist chieftain Juan Álvarez, and the opportunist General Santa Anna were all voicing similar criticism of the Arista tariff violation.[33]

Naturally each had his own reason for taking this position. The editors of *El Cosmopolita*, however sincere their belief in tariff protection, saw a good opportunity to discredit a conservative regime. In the case of Justo Corro and Juan Álvarez, both came from regions in which cotton growing or manufacturing was important, and their attitude was consonant with the interests of their home areas.[34] Santa Anna, on the other hand, was probably moved most by the opportunity to gain support from the growing number of textile manufacturers for an attempt to seize the presidency. But regardless of the diversity of motive, all agreed that the prohibitory laws should be maintained inviolate.

Faced by the dilemma of conflicting diplomatic pressures, and seeing its prestige weakened among its own supporters, the Bustamante administration carefully refrained from taking any definite action. The Congress, meanwhile, in February 1841, enacted an ambiguously worded resolution authorizing the government to resolve the differences with the British merchants, but on the basis of not allowing the disputed goods into Mexican ports.[35] This resolution did not suggest how the differences were to be resolved, and the government continued along its indecisive course.

Possibly the least-anticipated result of the Almonte-Arista assault on the prohibitory laws was its contribution to the downfall of the government. It is not intended here to trace the course of political events, but what should at least be mentioned is the effect of the yarn controversy on the overthrow of President Bustamante.

The cotton textile industry had recently been undergoing a period of difficulty. Costs of production had been rising as the result of a sharp increase in raw-material costs brought on in part by crop failures; at the same time, despite the tenor of the laws, large quantities of foreign *manta* were appearing in various towns of the interior, underselling the domestic product.[36] Several manufacturers, unable to reduce prices to meet this competition, had suspended operations;[37] others, presumably, had to accept a loss in profits. In these circumstances, the action of a cabinet member in blithely ignoring the prohibitory legislation must have come as a final irritant to the hard-pressed industrialists. They were willing, therefore, to support General Santa Anna in his bid for power, hoping thereby to obtain a government that would be a more consistent defender of their interests.

The exact role played by the manufacturers in the uprising of August-September 1841 remains to be determined. Suffice it to say that the industrialists subsequently acted as if they believed their contribution to Santa Anna's victory to have been a crucial one.[38] Through their organization, the Junta de Industria, they attempted to exercise a dominant influence on the economic policies of the new government. In this they were not altogether without success, as the record of the next three years, to be discussed presently, will show.

But the manufacturers erred if they thought Santa Anna would consent to being a mere puppet. A few months after his seizure of power, a crisis developed in the relations between the Junta de Industria and the new government. The manufacturers attempted to force the resignation of the finance minister, Ignacio Trigueros, whom they regarded as hostile to their interests. Santa Anna, however, supported his minister,

and made it very plain who was boss.[39] In the forthright words of the
editor of the official gazette: "The Junta de industria, which last year
took relish in the results of its opposition to a vacillating and timid government, falls into error if it supposes that the present circumstances
are similar, and that it will be permitted to create a new power in the
state which could threaten the government. . . ."[40]

Despite this seemingly bitter exchange, the record of the Santa Anna
regime reveals that industrial interests, as represented by the Junta de
Industria, did exert considerable influence on official policy. Within a
month of assuming power, General Santa Anna agreed to put into force
a radical measure for controlling smuggling, which industrialists had
long been urging. In the past, goods confiscated as contraband were
disposed of at court auctions. Equipped with appropriate documents,
these goods had subsequently circulated in legitimate trade. This practice, however, had enabled ingenious smugglers to ship illicit goods
through the country under the guise of articles that had already been
confiscated and legitimized. To close this loophole, manufacturers had
been recommending the outright destruction of all goods declared to
be contraband.[41] On October 21, 1841, President Santa Anna ordered
that thenceforth all raw cotton, yarns, or *mantas* whose entry was prohibited should be burned as soon as they were seized.[42]

Further evidence of the influence of the industrialists is to be seen in
the lowering of the taxes imposed on factories. On April 5, 1842, the Finance Ministry first announced a schedule of direct taxes to be collected on a variety of economic activities. Included was a levy of three-
fourths of one *real* per month on each spindle in the cotton mills.[43] The
imposition of this tax was one of the principal reasons why the Junta de
Industria had sought the firing of the Finance Minister.[44] Although this
request, as mentioned earlier, had been warmly rejected, the government did agree to reduce the tax to a mere one-eighth of a *real*.[45]

The willingness of General Santa Anna to heed the desires of the cotton interests, growers as well as manufacturers, was put to its severest
test in his efforts to solve the vexing problem of the Arista yarn contracts
inherited from the previous regime. In need of funds to consolidate his
own position, the dictator obviously could not accept a solution that involved the payment of an indemnity. But would he accept a settlement
profitable to the Treasury but objectionable to the cotton industry? An
opportunity to do so was offered in January 1842, when the merchants
holding the contracts demanded action. They pointed out that the government stood to receive over $700,000 in duties if the goods were per-

mitted to enter. Moreover, in a move to weaken industrial objections, they offered a modification of the original terms. Instead of the 2.7 million pounds of white and grey yarns which were directly competitive with domestic products, they proposed to introduce only 1.8 million pounds of these types, and in place of the balance to bring in 100,000 pounds of colored yarn and 188,000 pounds of sewing thread. The latter items, they claimed, were noncompetitive.[46]

President Santa Anna refrained from acting on these proposals until he had consulted the Junta de Industria. But at the same time that he submitted the proposals to that body for comment, he suggested that the industrialists, as principal beneficiaries of the prohibitory laws, would want to help out the Treasury.[47] The reply he received was hardly encouraging. The junta explained that the present distressed state of the industry prevented the manufacturers from providing any monetary assistance, but, at the same time, it urged the president to reject the proposals as extremely harmful to the textile industry.[48] Santa Anna accepted this recommendation, and dropped the proposals.[49]

The final settlement of the yarn contracts issue came in June 1842. The record of the negotiations has not come to light, but it appears that the government's determination not to antagonize the cotton growers and manufacturers was responsible for the favorable result. The merchants agreed to introduce a total of only 700,000 pounds of yarn, none of which was to be in the category of the white or grey *hilaza* generally produced in Mexican mills. The total was to be made up exclusively of sewing threads and colored yarns. It is understandable why the finance minister proudly characterized the settlement as one that, while providing some relief to the Treasury, did not conflict with the interests of the domestic industry.[50]

The special status enjoyed under the new regime by domestic manufacturers and by producers of industrial raw materials was further demonstrated late in 1842 with the incorporation of these groups into an industrial guild. The idea of such an organization had been repeatedly urged by the Junta de Industria, which first presented a plan for one early in 1841.[51] That plan, it will be recalled, involved the absorption by the new body of the functions and assets of the Banco de Avío. General Santa Anna, as described in the previous chapter, had shown no enthusiasm for this feature of the plan, and had proceeded to liquidate the lending agency in his own way. The final dissolution of the Banco de Avío in September 1842, did, however, increase the need for a mechanism to maintain liaison between the government and the industries it was seeking to help. It was to meet this need that the government finally adopted an organizational plan drawn up by the Junta de Industria. On December 2, 1842, acting-President Nicolás Bravo decreed the formation of an industrial guild, and the establishment of its executive organ, the *Dirección General de la Industria Nacional.*[52]

The structure of the new organization was patterned largely after the mining guild of colonial days. Membership was obligatory for the owners, managers, and principal employees of factories employing over twenty workers in the manufacture of textiles (cotton, silk, wool, hemp, or flax), earthenware, glass, paper, and iron. In addition, farmers who raised cotton, silk, flax, or hemp, and the owners of more than four thousand head of sheep were required to join. Voluntary membership was open to the proprietors of any industrial shop, and to all other farmers.[53]

All members were to be organized in regional *juntas de industria*— either those already in existence or new ones to be formed. The existing juntas were to adapt their by-laws to conform with the new conditions. These regional juntas were to elect executive committees of five to seven members, who were to carry out the various duties enumerated in the decree. One of these was to select representatives to attend the general court of the guild *(junta general de la industria mexicana)* which was to meet biannually in Mexico City.[54]

This general court was to elect the members of the Dirección General, the central executive of the entire guild. A director, vice-director, three deputies, and four alternates made up this body. All but the alternates were to serve four-year terms. The appointment of the director and vice-director was actually to be made by the president of the Republic from a slate of three names *(terna)* presented by the general court; the other members of the Dirección General were appointed directly by the electing body.[55]

The functions of the director and his associates were set forth in detail in the organic decree. These duties were: to serve as a channel of communications between the government and the regional juntas; to promote the establishment of these juntas; to acquire and disseminate the latest technical information from abroad; to hold exhibitions of domestic products; to promote primary education, religious instruction, and habits of saving; to assist in the repression of smuggling by naming special observers to report violations; to collect statistical data; and to prepare annual reports on the state of industry with recommendations for its improvement. The Dirección was to be responsible to the

Ministry of Finance for funds, and for matters pertaining to the control of smuggling.[56]

To meet the expenses of the Dirección, the government assigned to it one-third of a new fund to be created from the receipts of the spindle tax, and from a special levy of two to five centavos per vara collected on the various types of foreign cloth whose importation was permitted.[57] In addition, the Dirección was to receive the fines imposed on manufacturers who might try to pass off prohibited foreign goods as their own product.[58]

In order to get the Dirección into operation at once, the decree provided that the Junta de Industria of Mexico City should substitute for the general court in the first exercise of its electoral functions.[59] Accordingly, the industrial association in the national capital drew up slates for the directorship and vice-directorship, and submitted them to the government. Acting-President Bravo in each case appointed the first one named. In this manner, Lucas Alamán, who had founded the Banco de Avío and served as its first chairman, became the first director-general of national industry. Antonio Garay, the current head of the Mexico City Junta de Industria, was named vice-director.[60]

Under the leadership of Lucas Alamán, and with the assistance of an able secretary, a Guatemalan, Dr. Mariano Gálvez, the Dirección devoted itself energetically for the next four years to its assigned duties. Mention might be made in passing of two of its many activities. An attempt was made to establish vocational schools in the fields of agriculture and industrial crafts, and the useful practice of collecting and publishing industrial statistics was begun.[61]

The Dirección survived the downfall of General Santa Anna's regime in December 1844, but it underwent a basic reorganization two years later when the federal constitution of 1824 was revived. The ties that linked the regional juntas to the central body were broken, as control over the former was vested in the state governments together with the right to collect the spindle tax.[62] The Dirección itself lost its independent status, and was transferred to a newly established *Dirección de Colonización e Industria*.[63] Eventually, in 1853, this body became one of the principal components of the newly created *Ministerio de Fomento*, the bureaucratic progenitor of the modern secretariats of *Economía Nacional* and *Agricultura y Ganadería*.[64] Thus a direct link exists between the agency established in 1842 to promote the interests of manufacturing and agriculture and its twentieth-century counterparts.

A study of the tariff legislation of the Santa Anna period reveals that the use of prohibitions to protect cotton farmers and manufacturers was continued more or less without change. The first tariff decreed by the dictator on April 20, 1842, was intended to be a liberal measure which, by lowering the ad valorem from 30 percent to 25, would discourage smuggling, enlarge the volume of legal trade, and, it was hoped, increase the collection of revenues. Nevertheless, still preserved were the prohibitions on raw cotton, cotton yarn, and unfigured cloth, white or grey, that had less than thirty threads to the quarter inch. Dropped from the excluded list were figured weaves and mixtures; and the base line for determining the permitted qualities of fast-color printed and striped goods was reduced from thirty threads to twenty-six.[65]

These innovations brought considerable criticism both from individual manufacturers and from the Dirección de Industria.[66] The latter body pointed out, after the tariff act had been in operation a year, that the changes had enabled foreign commission merchants to evade the prohibitory sections of the law. Unfigured cloth of less than thirty threads with a single red thread woven into it was being introduced as striped goods (lienzos rayados); and fabrics that were pure cotton save for a few linen threads were brought in as mixtures. The Dirección proposed that all cotton cloth having less than thirty threads, white or grey, plain, striped, or figured, whether mixed with other materials or not, should be excluded.[67] This recommendation found favor with the government and was incorporated into the next general tariff act issued by Santa Anna, that of September 26, 1843.[68]

This second venture by the dictator into tariff-making constituted a sharp reversal from the trend of the first one. The failure of the 1842 act to bring about the hoped-for increase in customs revenues, or even to prevent them from dropping, led Santa Anna to restore the ad valorem rate of 30 percent.[69] Moreover, the list of prohibited goods in fields other than cottons was radically extended.

The origin of this extension lay in pressures placed upon the government by various industrial groups who wanted the same kind of protection as that granted to the cotton industry. General Santa Anna, in all probability seeking to enhance his popularity, capitulated unconditionally to such pressures. In a special decree issued on August 14, 1843, and incorporated substantially without change into the general tariff act of September 26, he ordered the addition of some 180 articles—chiefly metal products—to the existing list of prohibited goods.[70] Presented as a measure to protect industry and provide employment, this action rather unwisely denied entry to a wide variety of tools and instruments essential to the very activities it was supposed to assist. So short-sighted, indeed, was this measure that the Dirección felt called upon to condemn the sections that excluded iron implements not made in the Republic.[71] These prohibitions, however, remained on the books until after the overthrow of Santa Anna, and the adoption of a new general tariff act in October 1845.

During the Santa Anna regime, the list of tariff prohibitions inherited from the past was not only lengthened as shown above, it was also protected against possible attack by the use of constitutional guarantees. Heretofore, the prohibitory clauses of the tariff acts had been the result of legislative enactments, or of executive decrees issued under a grant of legislative authority.[72] Accordingly, the legislature could alter them through the simple adoption of a new law. However, when the new constitution, the so-called *Bases Orgánicas*, was drawn up under Santa Anna's direction in June 1843, the power of the legislature to change existing prohibitions was severely circumscribed. Title IV, article 67, of this document read: "The Congress shall not repeal or suspend the laws prohibitive of the introduction of articles prejudicial to national industry without the previous consent of two-thirds of the departmental assemblies."[73] In effect, this clause meant that as long as the constitution was in force, the few departments basically concerned in the raising of cotton or its manufacture could obstruct any change in the existing prohibitory regulations.

It might readily be supposed that this constitutional provision was the exclusive brain child of a minority of conservative politicians, or perhaps just another gesture of Santa Anna to win popular favor. That Santa Anna approved it for this reason need not be doubted, nor can it be denied that the authors of the *Bases Orgánicas* were in large part members of the propertied, clerical, and military classes. Yet the adoption of the provision cannot be so simply explained. There is evidence that political forces with little sympathy for Santa Anna's pretensions or for the *fueros* of church and army also wanted the constitutionalization of the prohibitive laws.

This evidence is to be found in the attitude displayed by the members of the Constituent Assembly that was elected in 1842, a body in which liberal and federalist sentiment predominated, despite the hostile attitude of Santa Anna. This assembly produced two drafts for a constitution. One, the work of the extreme federalist, or *exaltado*, minority, would have openly restored the federal system; the other, the proposal of the *moderado* majority, called for a system that was federalist in practically everything save for the use of the term. As is well known, General Santa Anna and the conservatives who supported him found neither draft to their liking, and to extricate themselves from an embarrassing situation, they had the assembly abruptly dissolved.[74] The important thing to note, however, is that the proposed constitutions of both the moderate majority and the federalist minority contained provisions for protecting the existing prohibition laws. Article 81, paragraph one, of the majority draft is practically a word-for-word anticipation of the article later adopted in the *Bases Orgánicas* and it undoubtedly served as its model.[75] The corresponding article of the minority draft differed somewhat, by requiring the approval of state legislatures for the imposition of new, as well as for the repeal of existing, prohibitions, and by reducing from two-thirds to a simple majority the number of state bodies whose consent was necessary.[76]

From these facts, it can be concluded that the preservation of the existing prohibition laws had truly become a national policy that transcended traditional political differences. This is not to say that opposition to these laws was nonexistent. Merchants and Treasury officials, among others, were bitterly critical of the prohibitory system.[77] But as we have seen, the major political factions, conservatives, moderates, federalists, were all in accord that the laws should be preserved.

With the adoption of a constitutional provision for safeguarding existing prohibitory measures, the philosophy of protectionism may be said to have reached its highest point since independence. Yet already the cost of the prohibitions was weighing heavily not only on the Treasury and on the consumer, but paradoxically on the very interests it was intended to help. More and more, the manufacturers of cotton textiles were coming to realize that the exclusion of raw cotton, which they had so readily championed in 1836, conflicted fundamentally with their own interests. The earlier assumption that farm and factory could expand in parallel fashion had been disproved by the force of events.

Despite the existence of an assured market, cotton production failed to keep pace with the growing demands put upon it. The explanation for this lies in a combination of natural and human factors. A scarcity of labor on the humid, disease-ridden coasts where cotton was traditionally grown prevented any large increase in output; and periodic calamities such as windstorms and unseasonal rains took their toll of existing production. A further complicating factor was the activity of speculators, who bought up the reduced crops for resale at considerable profit.[78] The result was that after 1839, by which time factory construction had undergone a notable expansion, shortages and exorbitant prices began to characterize the raw-material market.[79] New elements of uncertainty and increased costs were thus introduced into the manufacturing industry.

This situation brought about the first break in the previously united front of manufacturers and farmers. In 1840, a number of leading Mexico City fabricators, with the vociferous support of the Pueblan entrepreneur Antuñano, pressed the government to permit the entry of foreign cotton.[80] This request, however, was opposed by many other manufacturers as well as by all cotton growers, and failed to influence the authorities.[81]

The persistence of scarcity cotton prices in 1842, and the consequent closing of several factories, induced many manufacturers to renew their request for the admission of foreign cotton. Some manufacturers were still opposed to the idea, especially those in control of the Puebla Junta de Industria. That body assailed the requested alteration in the prohibitory laws as a threat to the interests of the farmers and a dangerous precedent for manufacturing interests.[82] The newly created Dirección de Industria, however, took up the cudgels in behalf of the admission of cotton, and presented a plan to reconcile the interests involved. It recommended the retention of the law prohibiting foreign cotton, but with the proviso that whenever the price of domestic cotton rose above eighteen pesos the quintal in the Veracruz market, foreign cotton should be permitted to enter with a single duty of four pesos. This procedure, it was claimed, would assure the farmer of a remunerative price, and guarantee the manufacturer adequate supplies at reasonable cost.[83]

The patent shortage of raw cotton led General Santa Anna to agree to the entry of foreign supplies, but not according to the plan suggested by the Dirección, nor in a manner pleasing to most manufacturers. Instead of granting a general right to introduce the needed raw material, he gave an exclusive privilege to one mercantile firm to import 60,000 quintals during 1843. The company agreed to pay the government six pesos per quintal, or $360,000 in cash within two months, and, in turn, was assured that no other permit would be granted that year. At the close of the year, a second permit was issued under similar terms, this time for 20,000 quintals.[84]

With these two concessions, the urgent need for cotton was met temporarily, but the problem of high prices persisted. The creation of a monopoly to dispose of a limited supply of foreign cotton was hardly the way to achieve a permanent reduction in cotton prices. Yet without such a reduction, the Dirección de Industria gloomily predicted, manufacturers would be unable to increase their sales, and the cotton industry would inevitably decay. Domestic harvests, it argued, could not meet the demand; the only way was through importation.[85] But any move to establish a general right to import cotton now had to contend with the constitutional provision that required the prior assent of two-thirds of the departmental assemblies.

The cotton manufacturers nevertheless were not without hope that such consent might be obtained. Throughout 1844 and into the following year, they labored to win over hostile opinion. One result was a greater consolidation of outlook within the ranks of the manufacturers themselves. Several industrialists in Puebla and Jalisco, who had formerly been opposed to any easing of the prohibitory laws, changed their minds, persuaded probably by the continuance of cotton shortages and high prices, but possibly also by the stream of propagandistic writings issuing from the pen of Estevan de Antuñano.[86]

This greater unity of opinion among the industrialists facilitated the taking of a definite position by the first general court of the industrial guild. Meeting in Mexico City in December 1844, just after General Santa Anna's grip on the government had been broken, this body proposed the unlimited entry of foreign cotton under a duty of eight pesos per quintal, a sum sufficient, it was claimed, to allow domestic cotton to sell on the farm at twenty-four pesos. The prohibition was to be fully restored, however, when domestic production, as revealed in a three-year average, should be sufficient to meet the demand. In the meantime, to encourage production, it was proposed that four pesos of the duty collected on each imported quintal should be set aside to create the capital for a new Banco de Avío, and half of this body's resources be applied to the financing of cotton growers.[87]

The newly established government of General José Joaquín de Herrera, naturally anxious to obtain additional revenues, was quite receptive to the idea of relaxing the prohibition on cotton. But article 67 of the constitution still had to be hurdled. In an effort to break down the opposition of cotton-growing departments, the minister of justice called a meeting of cotton growers and members of the Dirección. The latter proposed to guarantee the purchase of 20,000 quintals of domestic cotton at a price of twenty-five pesos, provided the growers would consent to the entry of foreign cotton under an eight-peso duty. But the growers could not be persuaded to agree; and the necessary two-thirds of the departmental assemblies refused to approve the lifting of the prohibition.[88]

In view of these circumstances, it is not surprising that the general tariff reform undertaken in 1845 did nothing to alleviate the cotton situation. The legislature, in authorizing the executive to draw up a new act, laid down the principle that all prohibitions that were in effect when the *Bases Orgánicas* were adopted in June 1843 were to be maintained. This did allow the elimination of the scores of items that Santa Anna proscribed in his decree of August 14, 1843, but the long-standing bans on yarns, textiles, and, of course, raw cotton were still preserved.[89]

Prevented, thus, from opening the ports to foreign cotton, the Herrera government still had one other plan for accomplishing the goal. It turned to the idea of constitutional reform. A recommendation to change article 67 was drawn up and submitted to the legislature. There it actually gained a favorable vote in the Chamber of Deputies, but a majority of the Senate, fearing that all prohibitory decrees would thus be jeopardized, voted against the measure.[90] The upshot was that another year passed, the Herrera government itself was overthrown, but the law prohibiting the import of raw cotton remained undisturbed.

The year 1846, however, finally saw a change in the status of the prohibitions. The new occupant of the presidential seat, General Mariano Paredes, shared none of the legal inhibitions of his predecessor. Within three weeks of seizing power, he issued a decree that temporarily permitted the entry of foreign cotton through the ports of Mexico and San Blas, under the considerable duty of ten pesos per quintal.[91] Thus, at last, the long-awaited prospect of unlimited supplies of raw cotton was apparently at hand. But the lifting of the prohibition had been deferred too long to be of much advantage to the cotton factories, because less than four months after the ban was raised, the United States, from whose farms the manufacturers hoped to obtain their cotton, was at war with Mexico.

This survey of the lengthy efforts to suspend the ban on raw cotton demonstrates how inflexible the prohibitory measures, adopted in the decade prior to the war, had become. The original purpose of these laws, as we have seen, was to encourage the development of an integrated cotton industry from the raw-material to finished-goods stage. But even when this goal was found to be impractical, and the manufacturing industries themselves were being endangered by its continued pursuit, it proved a political impossibility to obtain a relaxation of the laws.

Had the manufacturers been willing to accept a system of protective duties in place of the prohibitions on yarn and cloth, elimination of the raw-material ban might well have been obtained. But the industrialists for the most part were unalterably opposed to the slightest easing of those laws favoring their own products. In fact, even as they pressed for relief from the shortages and high prices caused by the prohibition on raw cotton, some manufacturers were seeking to extend the scope of the prohibitory measures to include better grades of cloth than those already under exclusion.[92]

Still, the stream of pamphlets, articles, and expositions that had accompanied the five-year controversy over the import of cotton could not fail to have weakened the case for maintaining the system of prohibitions. The arguments of the manufacturers in behalf of lifting the ban on cotton could be turned, as some of them had realized, against the very laws that favored their interests. After all, why should the manufacturers be entitled to enjoy a closed market at the expense of both consumer and the public treasury? Could not a system of protective duties be devised that would safeguard the industry, provide some revenue to the government, and at the same time, not confront the consumer with the necessity of purchasing smuggled goods if unsatisfied with the domestic product?

The conviction that the prohibitory system had outlived its usefulness did not become really widespread until after the end of the war with the United States. But already in 1846, among responsible government officers, and, surprisingly, even within the ranks of industry, this idea was winning support.[93] As Antonio Garay, for four years vice-director of the Dirección General de Industria and now head of the newly organized Dirección de Colonización e Industria, phrased it: "All that the government need do in behalf of the manufacturing industry is to [provide] well-calculated duties on imported foreign merchandise and to [assure] the abundance of raw materials so that [our] products can be reasonable, compete with foreign goods, and supply the public with its needs at low prices."[94] With these words, Garay was calling for the end of an era in the history of government promotion of industry.

12

THE NEW TEXTILE INDUSTRY

The purpose of the Mexican government in undertaking the various measures described in previous chapters—the direct loans, the exemptions from taxes, and the protective tariffs—was, of course, to establish mechanical industries on the style of those developed abroad. By these various means, officials hoped to induce private capital to invest in the manufacturing fields, and through the establishment of such industries, to provide new sources of employment and income to the population.

The industrial field of primary interest, it has already been shown, was the manufacture of textiles, especially the production of cotton goods. It was to develop a mechanized cotton industry that the largest expenditures were undertaken, and that the greatest sacrifices in terms of public-revenue reduction and consumer deprivation were made. It is, therefore, of considerable importance to inquire into the progress made by this industry, to examine the extent to which the hoped-for goals of investment and employment were achieved.

In 1837, at the time of the adoption of the ban on cotton-goods imports, and the enactment of the nationwide tax exemption on domestic textiles, Mexico had four cotton-spinning mills in operation, and four others in various stages of construction. All of the former had come into existence with the aid of capital supplied by the Banco de Avío, and were utilizing the machinery provided by that agency.[1] Of the latter, one had obtained a substantial government loan,[2] and two were receiving technical assistance from Estevan de Antuñano, whose own factory, the first to begin regular operations, had been the principal beneficiary of the government's assistance program.[3] The fourth was the small unsubsidized venture of Pedro Sáinz de Baranda, the pioneer textile entrepreneur of Yucatan.[4]

The expansion of mechanized spinning proceeded much more rapidly in the eight years after 1837 than in the seven before; the reason was the pioneer work of the earlier period and the new incentives provided by the government in the form of tax relief and tariff protection. By the end of 1840, the number of spinning mills in active operation was at least seventeen, and it more than doubled in the next two years. The rate of increase declined thereafter, but the absolute number continued to rise, reaching forty-seven in 1843 and fifty-one in 1844. Five more factories opened their doors the following year, but the suspension of four older ones left a net total of fifty-two. These fifty-two mills had 113,813 spindles in operation, or fourteen times as many as the approximately 8,000 in use eight years before.[5]

Accompanying this mechanization of cotton spinning, but not so complete nor so far reaching, was the transformation of cotton weaving. Just as had been the case in European countries, the power loom did not everywhere, or at once, supersede manually operated apparatus, and the number of handlooms in the country continued to far outnumber those moved by power. Nevertheless, the latter did spread fairly rapidly in the principal textile centers. In Puebla, where there had been but sixty such looms in 1838,[6] the number increased almost ninefold to 530 by 1843.[7] In that same year, Mexico City had 385 power looms, and in the entire country, the total number stood at 1,889.[8]

Because of the widespread dispersion of handlooms in homes, shops, and factories, it is not possible to do more than estimate the number in use in the country. Figures submitted to the Dirección de Industria by the governors of eight departments late in 1843 add up to 5,538, though some of these looms were idle at the time.[9] Not included, however, were the looms in twelve other departments, including the two most important, Mexico and Puebla. In the former, there were 802 handlooms known to have been active just in the capital city in 1843, and in the principal city of the latter department, 1,275 handlooms were reported in use in 1841.[10] It seems safe to conclude, then, that the number of handlooms actively employed in the entire country was well in excess of 7,500, and that the over-all total, hand-operated as well as power-driven, was at least 9,500.

The geographical distribution of the new spinning factories constructed in the decade 1835 – 1845 followed a pattern that was quite similar to that of the old handicraft industry. As table 8 reveals, Puebla retained its traditional position of leadership, with almost 38 percent of the total operating spindles in 1845. Second place was held by Mexico

TABLE 8

Location of Cotton-Spinning Mills in Operation, 1845

Department	Number of factories	Spindles in use	Percent of all spindles
Puebla	20	42,812	37.6
México	8	21,868	19.2
Veracruz	7	19,807	17.4
Jalisco	4	11,588	10.2
Durango	5	5,520	4.9
Querétaro	2	4,800	4.2
Sonora	1	2,198	1.9
Coahuila	2	1,960	1.7
Michoacán	1	1,668	1.5
Guanajuato	2	1,592	1.4
	52	113,813	100.0

Source: MDG, 1845, table 4.

with just under 20 percent. In each case, the factories were located in or near the capital city of the department. The most important deviation from the colonial pattern was the emergence of Veracruz as the third leading department, with slightly more than 17 percent of the operating spindles. Here it was the highland towns of Jalapa and Orizaba where six of the seven factories listed for the department were located. Next in importance to Veracruz was Jalisco, which, in late colonial times, had almost equaled Puebla in the value of its cotton manufactures. These four departments accounted for almost 85 percent of the total number of spindles operating in 1845.

For an industry that grew up under the sponsorship of the government, the location of the individual factories was determined principally by economic considerations, to be discussed presently, and only in a secondary way by political factors. In one respect, however, a political directive did exercise an influence on the free choice of locations. In order to combat the possible use of domestic factories as a shield for smuggling foreign textiles, a practice in which certain Pacific coast manufacturers were said to have engaged, General Santa Anna, in 1842, forbade the establishment of new cotton factories within twenty-five leagues of the coast; in addition, he ordered that all factories already established in the proscribed area be transferred to the interior within a five-year period.[11] Protests from the assemblies of the coastal departments subsequently led to the rescission of the second part of the order, but the ban on future construction was enforced.[12]

The location of the new spinning mills was the result of a combination of economic considerations. The availability of capital in the community and the willingness of its possessors to risk it in an industrial venture were certainly fundamental elements. But there were other factors of an objective nature that existed apart from the human one of entrepreneurs: the presence of water power, proximity to raw-material sources, availability of labor, closeness to potential markets. No one of these in itself explains the geographical distribution of the mills, for it is apparent that individual entrepreneurs differed in the importance they placed on each of them.

Certainly the availability of water power was the primary consideration in the erection of the Orizaba and Jalapa mills. The proximity of these towns to cotton-farming areas was not, in itself, a sufficient enough factor to create a manufacturing center, as evidenced by the relative unimportance of these communities as textile producers in the handicraft era. Nor does it appear that their market possibilities or labor situation underwent any marked change as to warrant by themselves the construction of factories in their midst. It was their advantageous location near rivers with a continuous flow in all seasons that enabled these towns to become prominent centers of the newly created mechanized industry, and that, parenthetically, allowed Orizaba to become Mexico's premier textile city in the twentieth century.[13]

Water sites played a significant role in the location of many other mills. Of the forty-seven in existence in 1843, thirty-three had been placed on streams, and depended on water as their principal source of power.[14] The selection of water sites, however, was complicated by seasonal variations of rainfall, which is characteristic of Mexico, and instances were not lacking in which animal power was used as a supplementary force. In one extreme case, which suggests a considerable lack of foresight on the part of the entrepreneur, a mill was erected on a stream that was dry or useless fully eight months of the year.[15]

If the availability of flowing water exercised a considerable influence on factory locations, so did proximity to markets. The cities of Puebla and Mexico, located in what was the most populous part of the country, had 54 percent of the nation's cotton factories, and 56.8 percent of the spindles. With the mills located close to the potential market, the bulk of their output could be disposed of without incurring heavy freight charges for long shipments on mule-back or wagon. Of course, the factories in these cities had to obtain their raw materials from a considerable distance, and pay the necessary charges, but because the freight on raw cotton was consistently less than that on finished goods, it was more economical to transport the raw material great distances than it would have been the completed fabrics.[16]

Mexico and Puebla had the added attraction of having in their midst hundreds of trained weavers. Whether the entrepreneur set up a weaving department in his own factory, or sold his yarn to independent shops, or distributed it in a putting-out system to artisans laboring in their own homes, the advantages of locating close to the workers were plain.

The combined factors of proximity to the consumer and to trained labor appear to have played the decisive role in the location of the ten mills reported in 1843 as relying exclusively on animal power. Eight of these were established in Puebla, the other two in Mexico.[17] Although animal power was more expensive than harnessing streams, it provided flexibility of location, with a smaller immediate outlay, than the use of a steam engine would have required, and with a fuel problem far easier to solve. It was the lack of coal and the difficulty of obtaining a substitute that probably limited the number of mills reported as utilizing steam power in 1843 to three out of the forty-seven.[18]

The availability of capital as a fundamental factor in the location of factories was mentioned above. Needless to say, had it not been for the investment of funds on a massive scale, the transformation of the textile industry that took place between 1830 and 1845 would not have occurred. It is desirable, therefore, to examine this investment, to inquire into its extent, its origin, and its effectiveness.

Reliable statistics are not available on the amount of capital that was poured into the several score cotton-spinning and weaving plants constructed prior to 1846. However, we do have the estimates of two contemporary foreign observers. The U.S. Minister to Mexico, Waddy Thompson, referring apparently to the status of the industry in 1842, placed the value of the capital invested in it at $8 million.[19] Another American official, Brantz Mayer, who was secretary to the legation in that same year, guessed the figure to be closer to $10 million.[20] A modern scholar, whose effort to recalculate the value of the investment resulted in a somewhat lower figure, concluded nevertheless that the $8 — 10 million figure for 1842 was "sufficiently on the mark."[21] Given the fact that the industry continued to expand over the next several years, a range of $10 — 12 million for 1846 does not seem unreasonable.[22]

The origin of the capital invested in the cotton industry can be traced to three principal sources. One, of course, was the Banco de Avío acting for the government; another was the Mexican investor; the third was foreign. The government's contribution to the total is easily determined. Approximately $650,000 was invested by the Banco de Avío in the cotton industry.[23] But the respective amounts invested by the native Mexican and the foreigner cannot be readily differentiated. In any case, it is obvious that private sources were responsible for the bulk of the capital invested in the cotton industry. In the over-all picture, the contribution of the Banco de Avío may appear small, but it was the first to be invested in the industry, and it served the essential purpose of stimulating the still-greater private investment.

In this connection, it is worth pointing out how wrong Carlos Díaz Dufoo was when he described the industrialization program as "an effort which basically was inspired by a sentiment of ill will toward foreign capital, since—as Dr. Mora says—the purpose was to nationalize the industries founded and supported by that capital."[24] One purpose, it is true, was to establish industries in Mexico that could supply goods that might otherwise be imported from foreign factories; but only in the sense that the profits of these factories might be affected could the program be called antiforeign. Actually, the government was quite eager to have foreign capital invested in the textile industry. The records of the Banco de Avío show that of the six spinning factories it financed, one was wholly owned by a firm of Englishmen, and another was largely a French-owned enterprise.[25] The numbers of foreigners who invested in the industry under the protection of the tariff laws are further evidence that a "sentiment of ill will toward foreign capital" had little to do with the government's efforts to promote manufacturing.

Foreigners who invested capital in the textile industry were frequently resident merchants desirous of extending the scope of their activities beyond strictly commercial ventures. Experienced artisans and machinists, however, were also among those who established cotton factories.[26] The nationalities represented were many: French, English, Spanish, North American, and German.

The French were the first foreigners to establish spinning mills, that branch of the cotton industry that required the greatest capital outlay. French capital contributed to the construction of the two largest mills to operate in Mexico in the period up to 1846.[27] But Englishmen were quick to follow, and, in terms of individual factories, constructed a larger number than the French did.[28]

Among the English factory owners, interestingly enough, were two men who had been serving their homeland as vice-consuls: Joseph Welsh of Jalapa and Eustace Barron of Tepic. In their consular capacity, Welsh and Barron had an official interest in protecting the Mexican market for British textiles. How they succeeded in reconciling their personal interests with their official duties is not completely clear, but charges that Barron's factory in Tepic was being used to "nationalize" illegal imports does suggest one answer.[29] Most of the English textile operators, however, seem to have entered the industry in good faith, as evidenced by their conduct during the yarn-contracts controversy of 1840 – 41. At that time they protested against the attitude of their own diplomatic representative, Richard Packenham, for siding with the British merchants who had received the questionable contracts in their efforts to introduce several million pounds of yarn. The textile operators of English extraction accused Packenham of arbitrarily and illegally denying them their right to His Majesty's protection because they were in competition with manufacturers in England.[30]

Mexican capital invested in the cotton industry appears to have come, like the foreign, largely from commercial establishments. In the case of the first factories, merchants abandoned their previous enterprises and devoted themselves and their capital exclusively to their new ventures.[31] But eventually, when the proprietors of large mercantile firms became interested in manufacturing, they were able to transfer a part of their capital and still continue to engage in commercial or financial transactions. Such was the case when leading agiotistas invested in cotton factories.

Despite the common belief that these moneylenders were engaged in too lucrative a business to be interested in industrial enterprises,[32] the fact is that the most famous, or perhaps most infamous, agiotistas did invest considerable sums in textile factories. Cayetano Rubio, Antonio Garay, and Felipe Neri del Barrio all had heavy industrial interests, and their factories were among the best equipped in the country. Rubio's Hercules plant in Querétaro was valued in 1844 at $800,000;[33] Garay's Magdalena mill in Mexico, in which French capital was also invested, had a reported value of $1 million in 1846.[34] Undoubtedly, the goal of these men was profit, but perhaps they wanted to obtain it in enterprises at once more productive to the country and less unpopular with their contemporaries than through speculation in the public debt. At any rate, the agiotistas did make a sizable investment in textile manufacturing, an investment that some of their critics have been loath to admit.

The over-all investment in the cotton industry from sources public and private, native and foreign, as stated earlier, was in the vicinity of $10 − 12$ million. For such a sum, it would seem that more might have been accomplished than the construction of fifty-odd spinning factories with less than 125,000 spindles, and the establishment of a few thousand power looms.[35] Yet various reasons explain the high cost of establishing a mechanized industry in Mexico.

One fundamental factor was the necessity of purchasing all machinery abroad, and of depending on foreign sources when parts were needed for repairs.[36] This would not have been so expensive had it not been for the primitive transportation system existing in the country. The era of railroads was still thirty years in the future, even though the first concession for a line to connect Veracruz and Mexico had been granted in 1837.[37] With the existing system of wagon transport, imported machinery landed at Veracruz often doubled in cost by the time it reached the capital city. For factories located closer to the ports, transport costs were naturally less, but, as we have already seen, the bulk of the industry was erected around the cities of Mexico and Puebla.

Another factor contributing to the excessive cost of establishing factories was the necessity of relying on foreign technicians to assemble the machines and to direct their operation during the first few years. In order to attract such personnel to Mexico, it was necessary to offer higher salaries than they earned at home, and to provide other inducements, such as travel expenses and long-term contracts. If it happened that their services could not be utilized at the time of their arrival in Mexico, these technicians nevertheless constituted a fixed charge that increased the over-all cost of the enterprise.

The instability of political conditions must also bear considerable responsibility for the high cost of industrial construction. International difficulties as well as internal disturbances inflicted serious and costly delays on entrepreneurial plans. Funds promised could not be obtained; machinery ordered could not be delivered. Unanticipated delays were a burden common to many industrial enterprises.[38]

Such delays and their inevitable expense were not always the result of political circumstances. Plain misfortune dogged the steps of some manufacturers. The classic experience of this sort was suffered by Estevan de Antuñano, who, anxious to expand his factory, ordered machinery from the United States, only to have three successive shipments lost at sea.[39] Small wonder that his factory, La Constancia Mexicana, has been regarded as the aptly named symbol of the perseverance needed to overcome the obstacles to Mexican industrial development.

A final explanation of the high cost of some industrial construction is one peculiar to the times and to the people concerned. The men who built the very first textile factories were doing more than introducing a new technology into Mexico; they were trying to overcome the weight of traditional attitudes. Well aware of the long-standing preference for investment in real property, they wanted to give their factories a solidness and even a beauty that would symbolize for their countrymen the permanence and the desirability of the industrial era they hoped to introduce. Their buildings, consequently, were designed with an eye to appearance as well as to function.[40] Madame Calderón de la Barca gives us this description of Antuñano's Constancia:

> It is beautifully situated, and at a distance has more the air of a summer palace than of a cotton factory. Its order and airiness are delightful, and in the middle of the court in front of the building is a large fountain of the purest water. A Scotchman, who has been there for some time, says he has never seen anything to compare with it, and he worked for six years in the United States.[41]

This factory could hardly be called typical, but still Madame Calderón's words suggests that in Mexico the concept of essential expense was not quite the same as that held in Manchester or Lowell.

Granting that the cotton industry underwent the expansion and received the investment described in previous pages, it is appropriate to consider the impact that the industry had on both employment and working conditions within Mexico. One of the most frequent justifications for providing public assistance to the industry was that it would thereby be able to provide useful jobs to unemployed or underemployed citizens. To what extent, then, did the industry fulfill this expectation?

The construction of spinning mills, the installation of power looms, and the general expansion experienced by cotton manufacturing prior to 1846 might be expected to have influenced opportunities for employment in various ways. The erection of factories would have called for large numbers of skilled construction workers; the operation of the mills would have opened up jobs in the various tasks connected with manufacturing yarn and cloth. But in addition, as the consumption of raw materials increased, and the volume of finished goods grew, the agricultural and transport industries also would have expanded. Finally, as worker incomes in these various fields rose, an increased demand for consumer goods and services should have followed, with a resulting expansion of employment in other fields.

It is not possible with the available data to depict exactly on a countrywide basis the employment changes that resulted from the growth of the cotton industry. Fortunately, however, we do have some information on the employment situation in Orizaba, the site of the Cocolapam textile factory; and a study of what took place in this city may be suggestive of general trends.

Prior to the establishment of what became the largest spinning mill in the country, Orizaba had no handicraft cotton industry to speak of. A census of 1831 speaks of twenty-nine individuals who made a living weaving cotton.[42] The coming of the factory revolutionized the economy of the town. A survey taken in 1839, while the factory was still only partially operative, showed that the number of weavers had risen to 160, with eighty others in the apprentice stage.[43] As the factory reached full production, employment opportunities expanded. At the close of 1841, it was said that over 1,200 persons were engaged in the various tasks related to the production of yarn and its conversion into cloth, and that they were receiving a total of $5 – 6,000 a week in wages.[44] In the same year, it was reported that, largely because of this factory, the population of Orizaba had risen to 24,000 from the 17,000 living there before its construction.[45]

The effects of the factory were not limited to the absorption of workers in specifically manufacturing tasks. The 1839 survey, which was made while the factory was still under construction, showed that certain classes of skilled workers had enjoyed significant increases since the previous census of 1831. Table 9 presents a comparison of the trades that underwent expansion. The sharp rise in construction workers, masons, and carpenters was surely a reflection of the increased building activity connected with the factory; and the rise in the number devoted to shoeing or loading animals, or carrying merchandise on their backs attests to the growing need for transportation services caused by operations of the factory. But the expanded number of artisans in crafts providing goods and services directly used by the consumer can also be explained as secondary or tertiary effects of the factory. The increased purchasing power pumped into the community by the wages paid to

TABLE 9
Growth of Skilled Crafts in Orizaba, 1831 – 1839

Kind of craft	No. in 1831*	No. in 1839 (less apprentices)	No. in 1839 (including apprentices)
Weaver	29	160	240
Carpenter	64	112	122
Mason	81	144	428
Brickmaker	35	37	43
Tinsmith	0	11	15
Blacksmith	73	69	81
Painter	16	14	18
Harnessmaker	17	15	19
Farrier	0	13	15
Liveryman	0	8	10
Porter	0	25	25
Embroiderer	0	2	2
Hatter	20	17	25
Tailor	75	65	111
Shoemaker	90	148	192
Barber	0	20	24
Soapmaker	0	10	12
Combmaker	0	4	4
Wax chandler	15	12	17
Tallow chandler	24	18	27
Baker	48	47	55
Miller	0	15	15
Gunsmith	0	4	6
Silversmith	0	12	16
Watchmaker	0	3	3
Musician	30	22	42
Singer	0	0	6
Fireworks maker	0	11	15
Totals	617	1,018	1,588

* It is not known whether these figures include apprentices or not.

Sources: Estadísticas del estado libre y soberano de Veracruz. Cuaderno primero que comprende los departamentos de Orizaba y Veracruz, y la memoria del Gobierno (Jalapa, 1831), p. 5; Manuel de Segura, "Apuntes estadísticos del distrito de Orizaba formados el año de 1839," Boletín del Instituto Nacional de Geografía y Estadística 4 (1854): 32.

employees of the factory in all likelihood stimulated much of the increase in the number of shoemakers and barbers, millers and soap-makers, and provided the wherewithal for supporting a larger number of entertainers. More money in the hands of factory employees meant more business for the town as a whole, and even the makers of fireworks could profit.

There is no reason to believe that the Cocolapam mill's impact on the Orizaba economy was not duplicated by other factories in other areas. Reports coming from Durango, where five mills were established, certainly attest to the positive influence that manufacturing industry exerted on employment there.[46] Similar effects should have been felt in Puebla, Mexico, Jalapa, Querétaro, and many other places. The consequences of the factory development, moreover, must have been transmitted to agriculture through the constantly increasing demand for cotton, to transportation through the growing volume of goods requiring shipment, and to service industries in and around the various factory towns.

In directing attention to the job-creating aspects of the new industry, one should not overlook the fact that at the same time it destroyed some existing jobs. The female hand-spinners (hilanderas), who had managed to support themselves in past years despite entries of foreign yarn, were now unable to compete with the machine-spun products of domestic factories. Deprived of this employment, some of them, nevertheless, may have earned a living in the new jobs opened up by the factories.

Exactly how many individuals were employed in the cotton industry in all Mexico is a subject on which contemporary observers were far from agreement. Madame Calderón de la Barca, on a visit to Puebla, heard reports that the factories of that city were "already giving employment to thirty-thousand individuals."[47] Yet, at about the same time, Brantz Mayer was estimating the number employed in the entire country at the same figure.[48] This discrepancy probably arises in part from the enthusiasm of Madame Calderón's informants and in part from a different concept as to what constituted an employee of the cotton industry. The figures cited by the author of Life in Mexico must have included not only those directly working in the factories, but everyone whose livelihood depended in any way on the industry, including, perhaps, laborers on distant cotton plantations. Brantz Mayer, on the other hand, appears to have been considering only those directly engaged in the manufacturing process. Even so, on the basis of what is known about the number of looms operating in the country and about the working staff of individual factories, his estimate of approximately thirty thousand workers for the entire country still seems extremely high.

Although accurate employment figures for the cotton industry as of 1845 are not available, it is possible to arrive at an approximation of the numbers employed by extrapolating from data available for other years. Reports submitted by eleven spinning mills that were operating in three different cities in 1841 reveal a labor force of 1,618 to handle 37,800 spindles.[49] Dividing the number of spindles by the number of workers gives an average labor efficiency ratio for the eleven factories of 23.3 to 1, although, as table 10 reveals, the individual factories varied in efficiency from a low of 18.5 to a high of 25. On the assumption that the industry average of 23.3 still prevailed in 1845, when 113,813 spindles were in operation, the labor force required at that time by the fifty-two spinning factories would be 4,885. To this number must be added those workers employed in weaving operations. As of 1843, the cotton industry had an installed capacity of 1,889 power looms.[50] By 1845, the total can be conservatively estimated at 2,100. Data on power shops in Puebla and Orizaba in 1841 indicate that an average of five workers were needed for every three looms in use.[51] If this average still prevailed in 1845, the 2,100 power looms would have required a force of 3,500. The number of work-

TABLE 10
Labor Efficiency in Eleven Cotton-Spinning Factories, 1841

Location	Factory name	No. of spindles	No. of workers	Ratio spindles per worker
Puebla	Constancia	7,500	300	25.0
	Patriotismo	6,000	250	24.0
	La Teja	2,500	100	25.0
	Benevolencia	1,500	80	18.8
	Amistad	1,000	50	20.0
	Mayorazgo	2,500	100	25.0
	Dos Hermanos	500	20	25.0
Jalapa	La Libertad	1,200	65	18.5
	Victoria	600	30	20.0
	Industrial	3,000	158	19.0
Orizaba	Cocolapam	11,500	465	24.7
Totals		37,800	1,618	Av. 23.3

Source: Semanario de la industria mexicana 1, no. 21 (1841): 2, nos. 4, 8 (1842).

ers employed in spinning and weaving by the modernized sector of the cotton industry would thus have amounted to 8,385 as of 1845.

This number, however, may in fact exaggerate the size of that labor force. Jan Bazant, in a study of the Puebla cotton industry in 1843, contends that labor efficiency in its spinning mills averaged thirty-two to one, and that weaving operations employed an average of one worker for 1.05 looms, figures that compared very favorably with contemporary English and United States factories.[52] If these efficiency ratios held for the entire cotton industry in 1845, the total labor force then would have consisted of 3,556 in spinning, 2,000 in weaving, or a total of no more than 5,556.

While the efficiency of weaving operations may have improved between 1841 and 1845 to the point where the Puebla average was applicable to the industry as a whole, it is difficult to believe that the thirty-two to one spindle : worker ratio was now typical of the nation's spinning plants. Indeed, nine years later in 1854, when the cotton-textile industry employed 10,316 persons to operate 161,860 spindles and 4,393 power looms, the spindle : worker ratio was only twenty-six to one, not much above the most efficient factories of 1841.[53]

It seems safe to conclude, then, that the labor force employed in the fifty-two factories in 1845 lay somewhere between the 5,556 extrapolated from the Bazant calculations and the 8,385 extrapolated from the 1841 data. However, any analysis of the impact of the industry on employment must take into consideration that there were still some 7,500 handlooms in the country, which provided employment for another 15,000 individuals, and that countless others were employed in the raising, cleaning, and transportation of raw cotton.

The makeup of the factory labor force, the conditions under which it worked, the wages it received, are all matters that deserve a comprehensive treatment that is not possible here. A few generalizations will be offered, however, with the understanding that they are tentative, and subject to revision by future research.

Employment of women and children was characteristic of a number of the new spinning mills, especially in nontraditional areas. In Puebla, however, considerable prejudice existed against having women work alongside men in the factories, and even Antuñano, who had publicly urged the hiring of women and children in a pamphlet published in 1837, employed a work force that was only 10 percent female in his Constancia factory in 1843.[54] In contrast, women outnumbered men in cotton factories in Durango, Sonora, and Querétaro, and were a noticeable

part of the labor force in the nation's largest spinning mill, the Cocolapam plant in Orizaba.[55]

Employment in the textile factories does not seem to have been
accompanied by the restrictions on personal freedom that were characteristic of some colonial obrajes. True, during working hours, a rigid
discipline was maintained, with conversation and smoking forbidden;
but after hours, the workers enjoyed full freedom. There were instances,
however, in which orphans were apprenticed for training to factory
owners, and it must be presumed that the owners took steps to insure
the constant presence of their charges. That such apprenticeship
was not without its compensations, though, is seen in the fact that
the young men serving in the factories were exempted from military
service.[56]

At least some employers were aware of a broader obligation to their
workers than might be expected. Schools were established for workers'
children in at least two factories. In one of these, moreover, the em-
ployer contributed jointly with his workers to a medical fund that paid
for the services of a doctor and an apothecary.[57] It is not at all unlikely
that similar practices were followed elsewhere.

The hours of work required of the factory hand varied from mill to
mill; some operated a ten-hour shift, others as much as sixteen. In 1843,
the most typical day was one of twelve hours.[58] The work week, however, was broken up by the many religious festivals celebrated in Mexico. It was estimated in 1836 by one factory owner that fully one-fifth of
the potential working time was lost in this way.[59]

The frequency of holidays had aroused relatively little concern in the
past, when the direct cost of such idleness was borne chiefly by the individual worker in the form of wages lost. But with the heavy investment
in capital equipment, the owners of the factories found that they, too,
were paying for the frequent stoppages. It was considerations such as
this that may explain the efforts of the Mexican government in 1836 to
obtain papal consent to a reduction of holidays. Pope Gregory XVI was
amenable to the idea, and issued a brief allowing Mexicans to work on
all days except Sundays and sixteen other specified days. But because
of the strenuous objections of certain members of the Mexican clergy,
the circulation of this brief was prevented until 1839.[60] The granting
of the *pase* in that year, however, made possible a work year of two
hundred and ninety-seven days, but whether it was observed is open
to question.

A discussion of the complex topic of wages is beyond the scope of the present study. It is hoped, however, that some student of Mexican labor history will undertake to answer questions such as these: How did the development of mechanized factories in the cotton industry affect the existing pattern of wages? How did the earnings of the factory workers compare with those in other occupations? What did the introduction of power looms do to the earnings of artisan weavers? Did the wages paid to weavers directly employed by the factories differ from the earnings of independent weavers who purchased their own yarn?[61]

If the rise of the mechanized cotton industry was of considerable significance in stimulating employment, it was also important for its effect on the consumer of cotton products. The hope had been extended by government officials in 1830, when the program of direct assistance was first begun, that Mexican factories would eventually be able to supply the home market with all its needs at prices comparable to those of goods produced abroad. As time went on, less and less was said of this latter expectation, and attention was directed rather to the increasing volume of manufactured goods, and to the reduction in their price as compared with the price of similar goods produced under handicraft methods.

Of the growing volume of production after 1837, there can be no doubt. Table 11 presents the statistics compiled by internal revenue collectors on the volume of yarn and manta that passed through their offices for the official stamp allowing them to circulate free of duties. These statistics should not be confused with actual production figures,

TABLE 11
Cotton Manufactures Presented for Revenue-Office Stamp, 1838–1845

Year	Yarn (pounds)	Manta (32 vara pieces)
1838	63,123	109,305
1839	32,565	124,948
1840	557,591	88,096
1841	1,014,004	195,758
1842	777,116	217,851
1843	No report	279,739*
1844	1,632,111	507,565
1845	2,783,774	641,183

* For ten months only.
Sources: MDG, 1843–1845

for the volume of yarn converted into cloth, or otherwise disposed of, within each revenue district is not recorded; neither is the amount of cloth sold locally within the producing district. Nevertheless, for what they are, these figures do give an idea of the sharp upward trend of production in the eight-year period indicated.

A more exact idea of the total output of yarn may be inferred from the manta production figures. Since eight pounds of yarn were normally consumed in the weaving of one thirty-two-vara piece of manta, the 641,183 pieces presented for stamping in 1845 represented 5,129,464 pounds of yarn.[62] But the Dirección de Industria, on the basis of the large number of looms whose output was not reflected in official figures, estimated manta production for 1845 to have been no less than 1 million pieces. [63] This would have meant that the yarn production of Mexican mills was at least 8 million pounds, a figure quite within the capacity of the existing spindles.

If the precise output of the cotton industry is subject to uncertainty, the same may be said for its value. At the beginning of 1845, the Dirección de Industria estimated that the cotton manufactures produced in the year just concluded were worth at least $8 million. This figure was reached, however, on the basis of an assumed, rather than a known, output.[64] Less than two years later, in December 1846, the head of the newly created Dirección de Colonización e Industria asserted that the combined value of cotton and woolen output—there were at this time five mechanized woolen mills—stood at over $15 million, and this figure, he intimated, was an understatement.[65] If this assertion can be accepted, the value of cotton goods alone must have been in the vicinity of $12 million. This would have meant that the output of the cotton industry had equaled in value the current annual mintage of precious metals, an achievement of no little significance in a country whose mines were universally regarded as the principal source of national wealth.[66]

Price considerations were as important as factory capacity in determining the output of the industry. The Mexican consumer, although legally barred from purchasing imported goods equivalent to the domestic varieties, still could supply himself to some extent with smuggled merchandise, and, moreover, retained the alternative of using imported linens and better quality cottons if the price of domestic cottons was too high. The home industry was thus not free from all competitive pressures, and had some incentive to lower prices. The incentive grew stronger as the number of producing units expanded, and competition for the existing market increased.

TABLE 12

Manta Prices in Mexico City, 1835 – 1843

Year	Reales per vara	Pesos per pieza
1835	2 1/2	9.50[a]
1836	2 3/4	10.50[b]
1839	—	8.62[c]
1842	2	—
1843	2	7.50
1845	—	5.63

a. On lots of 16 to 100 pieces.
b. On lots of 50 pieces or over.
c. On lots of 20 – 50 pieces.
Sources: La Lima, Oct. 15, 1835, Apr. 12, 1836, May 11, 1839; Brantz Mayer, *Mexico As It Was and As It Is*, p. 315; *MDG*, 1843, p. 25; *El Siglo XIX*, June 12, 1845, p. 4.

The benefits received by the consumer, in terms of lowered prices, are indicated in table 12. The wholesale price of domestic manta in Mexico City dropped from $9.50 the piece in 1835, to $7.50 in 1843, to $5.63 two years later. In the same period, the retail price dropped from 2 1/2 reales the vara to two reales as of 1843, a reduction of 20 percent. Given the wholesale price in 1845, the price per vara was probably just over 1 1/2 reales; this meant a 40-percent decline in retail price since 1835.

Compared to the price of manta produced earlier under handicraft methods, the reduction was even greater. The traditional price for the twenty-two-inch-wide manta *(manta de dos tercios)* sold in Mexico City in colonial days had been two reales. But the cloth produced after 1835 ran to thirty-four and thirty-five inches in width. Similar cloth produced completely by hand methods would have sold for three reales. Thus the Mexican consumer of 1845, in paying 1 1/2 reales, was enjoying a saving of 50 percent over the cost of domestic cloth sold prior to the establishment of the machine industry.[67]

The reduction obtained in the price of manta provides a criterion for judging the fundamental policy decision made by the Mexican government in 1830 to foster industrial mechanization. The Mexican consumer in 1845 still paid at least 50 percent more than what imported cloth would have cost him, were it introduced on a duty-free or near-free basis. But it is unrealistic to compare the price of domestic and foreign goods on this basis. In 1830, when the Bustamante government was faced with forming an economic policy, the choices open to it were either simply to continue the protection of the handicraft industry, a policy undertaken by its predecessor in the passage of the 1829 prohibitory law; or to try to effect the modernization of that industry. A third alternative of allowing the free entry of foreign textiles just did not exist. Such a policy would have meant abandoning completely the thousands of individuals who in the past had derived their income from the growing and processing of cotton. Given these circumstances, the government chose to use public funds to stimulate the transformation of the handicraft processes. The result was the creation of an industry that, although still requiring protection, was able to present the consumer with products considerably cheaper than those wrought by handicraft methods. Seen in this light, and taking into consideration the positive effects of the industry on employment, the decision made in 1830 was the correct one.

This is not to absolve the officials of the government then or in succeeding years from the mistakes they made in implementing this policy decision. The use of prohibitory measures, instead of protective duties, to follow up the start made with grants of money was especially unwise. The chief rationalization for the former was that they were easier to enforce than a duty system; but experience did little to justify this claim. The system of prohibitory measures, moreover, introduced an element of inflexibility, which, as we have seen, was unfortunate, not only for the government or the consumer but for the cotton manufacturer as well. A duty system that permitted the entry of raw cotton while guaranteeing the consumption of the domestic crop would have enabled factory owners to sell more at lower prices.

The prohibitory measures had a further defect. They helped fix in the minds of the factory owners the belief that they were utterly dependent on them. Consequently, the frequent rumors that poverty-stricken governments might abandon the system sent periodic shudders through the entire industry. The industrialists appear to have devoted more time to protesting against possible raising of the prohibitions than to finding ways and means of reducing their costs so as to be in a better position to compete with foreign goods. This psychology of absolute dependence was one of the negative aspects of government intervention in industry.

But after all is said against it, the fact remains that as of 1846, a mechanized textile industry had been created; the level of employment in manufacturing, agriculture, transportation, and other fields had been raised, and concomitantly the income of a goodly number of working people. The creation of this industry, moreover, was not a transitory achievement. It was to survive the shock of foreign invasions and civil wars; it was to witness the growth of plant capacity and of the volume and variety of output; and it was to constitute, in the hands of its predominantly Mexican entrepreneurs, a viable and profitable sector of the economy well before the economic transformations of the Porfirian era.[68]

POSTSCRIPT:

RECENT WRITINGS ON THE ECONOMIC

HISTORY OF THE EARLY REPUBLIC

In the more than twenty years since the Spanish edition of this book appeared, the period that it treated—the first several decades of Mexico's independent existence—has received relatively limited attention from economic historians. In contrast to the volume and variety of studies by Mexican and foreign scholars that focus on the latter part of the nineteenth century, the Early Republic, in the words of a noted Mexican economic historian, "continues to play the role of the poor relation."[1] Nevertheless, to enable the reader to appreciate the kinds of studies that have, in fact, been produced, the contributions that have been made to our understanding of the economic realities of that early period, and the range of topics that still call for research, this postscript is appended.

It should be noted at the outset that no new research has been undertaken on the Banco de Avío itself; no additional manuscripts or other sources related to it have been uncovered. On the other hand, a collection of most of its known annual reports, together with other documents, did appear in a volume issued in 1966.[2] As will be noted below, the growth of the textile industry and the careers of certain entrepreneurs have received serious, if selective, attention, but the bulk of what has appeared in book and article form in the past two decades focuses on other dimensions of the Early Republic: economic ideas and political forces; the role of the Church; the economic role of elites and foreigners; studies of haciendas; public finance and fiscal problems.

Surveys of Mexican ideas on economic development, including those of the Early Republic, have appeared in anthologies and texts, like those of Jesús Silva Herzog and Diego López Rosado, but by far the most systematic analysis of those ideas is incorporated in Jesús Reyes Heroles's study of Mexican liberalism.[3] Reyes Heroles, in this massive work, examines a wide gamut of contemporary writings, including pamphlet literature and parliamentary speeches, in an effort to establish the essential qualities of Mexican liberalism. He places special emphasis on the issue of protectionism versus free trade, an issue that was hotly debated during the Early Republic, and on the related issue of the role of government in general in directing or regulating economic activities. In this connection, he pays considerable attention to the Banco de Avío and to the economic ideas not only of its founder, Lucas Alamán, and its principal beneficiary, the pioneer industrialist Estevan de Antuñano, but also to the ideas of its critics, especially Lorenzo de Zavala, José María Luis Mora, and Mariano Otero.

Some of this same ground is covered, although from a different perspective and with different conclusions, by the United States scholar, Charles Hale. In a masterful work, devoted in large part to dissecting Mora's ideas, Hale takes issue with Reyes Heroles about the nature of the differences between liberalism and conservatism where economic issues were involved. Alamán, in Hale's perception, had a far less integrated economic outlook than Reyes Heroles contends.[4] What is clear is that neither of these works, nor the various dissertations that have been devoted to Alamán, exhausts Mexican conservatism as a topic for research.[5]

Our understanding of the role of the Catholic Church in the economy and society of the Early Republic has been enhanced by a series of recent studies dealing with such topics as tithe collections, administration of nunneries, and church-state financial relationships. We are now aware, for example, that the compulsory collection of tithes after independence contributed more to governmental coffers than to the Church.[6] This would explain the lack of enthusiasm, even on the part of presumably pro-Church conservatives, to have compulsory tithe collection restored once the short-lived anti-clerical Gómez Farías regime abolished it.

New light on the Church's role as a lending agency and accumulator of wealth is provided in Michael Costeloe's slender volume, *Church Wealth in Mexico* (Cambridge: Cambridge University Press, 1967). Costeloe directs attention to a little-known agency that functioned within each archdiocese in Mexico as the steward and administrator of properties received through legacies and endowments entrusted to its care. Known as the "Juzgado de Testamentos, Capellanías y Obras Pías" and managed for the most part by laymen, this agency functioned as a banking institution, making small loans secured by real estate to merchants and landowners. Costeloe sees the juzgado as exercising "a monopoly in the availability of investment capital" and, once the Banco de Avío disappeared, as "the only institution in the country able to provide capital for investment purposes."[7] In offering this judgment, Costeloe seems to overlook the role that merchant firms played as lenders of capital. Nevertheless, his detailed study of juzgado operations within the archbishopric of Mexico, the wealthiest in the country, provides a convincing picture of small-loan operations in a capital-poor era. Moreover, Costeloe presents a thoughtful reassessment of the effects of Church lending on such issues as property concentration and agricultural development.

Another major contribution to our understanding of the economic role of the Church is Jan Bazant's *Los bienes de la Iglesia en México (1856 – 1875)* (Mexico: El Colegio de México, 1971). While concerned primarily with analyzing the secularization process that was initiated in 1856, Bazant reviews earlier efforts to sell off nationalized real estate. His work makes it clear that conservative as well as liberal governments did not hesitate to extract loans from the Church to meet their expenses, a practice that Asunción Lavrín also documents in her study of nunneries.[8] Bazant, moreover, provides a new estimate of the overall value of Church wealth in Mexico, an estimate far below the frequently cited calculation of the nineteenth-century liberal writer, José María Luis Mora. Far from possessing one-half of all the national wealth, as some have claimed, the Church's holding constituted no more than a fifth, or perhaps a quarter, of the total.[9]

Given this reduced share, it becomes all the more important to understand the distribution of private wealth and the role of private, as against ecclesiastical, capital in promoting or retarding economic development. While no definitive analysis based on convincing statistical evidence has emerged, a number of recent studies have begun to fill out the picture. Doris Ladd's *The Mexican Nobility at Independence 1780 – 1826* (Austin: University of Texas Press, 1976) stresses the survival of the exnoble families under the Republic, and their continuing economic importance in the spheres of landownership, mining, and credit. Richard B. Lindley, in his "Kinship and Credit in the Structure of Guadalajara's Oligarchy 1800 – 1830" (Ph.D. diss., University of Texas, 1976), points to the importance of British connections in the rise of a regional elite.

The nature and extent of foreign influence on the Mexican economy has also received a certain amount of attention in recent studies. Spanish merchants and property owners, those who elected to remain in Mexico after 1821, were not foreign in the same sense as other Europeans, but their legal status was altered by the adoption of legislation after 1827 ordering their expulsion. Did this expulsion result in a substantial loss of capital? Romeo Flores Caballero, in a study of the Spaniards in Mexican political, social, and economic life to 1838, argues that the numbers that actually left the country were fewer than one would suppose, and that many Spanish capitalists and merchants managed to escape the effects of the expulsion laws. Moreover, he notes that other foreign merchants had begun to replace Spanish merchants well before the enactment of the expulsion laws, thus reducing their economic effects.[10] Harold Sims, on the other hand, in his *La expulsión de los españoles de México (1821 — 1828)* (Mexico: Fondo de Cultura Económica, 1975), links the expulsions to sharp declines in government revenues, customs receipts, and the level of foreign trade.

The role of non-Spanish foreign merchants and capitalists in the economy of the Early Republic has yet to receive the systematic analysis it deserves. Nevertheless, advances have been made in the study of individual firms or business ventures. Robert Randall's *Real del Monte. A British Mining Venture in Mexico* (Austin: University of Texas Press, 1972) provides a detailed study of a mining undertaking that was launched in London amidst the speculative boom of the mid-1820s, only to collapse a quarter century later in a financial loss for the British investors, but a gain for their Mexican successors. Barbara A. Tenenbaum, in an article based on the correspondence files of a British merchant firm, argues that certain resident British merchants, intimating that the force of their government was behind them, did in fact influence Mexican commercial policy decisions, and that as a result "Mexico during this period was never able to develop a consistent and enforceable policy of protection. . . ."[11] This issue is by no means settled, and it would be very useful to have detailed studies of the activities of the other foreign merchants, United States, French, German, as well as British, who took up residence in Mexico in this period.

The study of Mexico's foreign trade during the Early Republic has received little attention from scholars in the past twenty years. One reason, perhaps, has been the limited nature of trade statistics, and the difficulty of constructing continuous time series for imports and exports. As a result, most discussions of foreign trade have tended to rely on Mi-

guel Lerdo de Tejada's statistical compilation that was published originally in 1853 and reissued in 1967.[12] For this reason, the appearance of
Inés Herrera Canales's *El comercio exterior de México 1821–1875*
(México: El Colegio de México, 1977), which was based on painstaking
work in archival and printed sources, constitutes a welcome advance.

Nothing comparable, however, exists with respect to domestic trade.
Except as incidental to the study of individual mining and agricultural
enterprises, little scholarly energy has been expended to produce a
comprehensive study of internal trade and transportation in the pre-
railway era. The general assumption is that in the absence of cheap
transportation, bulky goods of low unit value could not be shipped any
significant distances. But do we know enough about the actual rates
charged by muleteers and carters to move goods between specific
points in the Republic? What were the goods that did move beyond
local markets, and why? Who were the merchants who were active
in domestic trade? Harold Sims has established that in Durango, prior
to their expulsion, Spaniards comprised about 15 percent of the merchant class.[13] Did the same percentage prevail in other regions? Did
these merchants dominate local and regional trade, as against their
more numerous creole competitors? What were the economic effects
on domestic trade of the expulsion laws at federal and state levels?
Did foreign merchants of other nationalities introduce new credit practices, goods, or capital into domestic trade? The list of questions that
can be raised is almost limitless; it can only be hoped that future scholars will find in domestic trade and transportation an attractive field to
investigate.[14]

In contrast to the limited research on trade-related topics, substantial attention has been directed to the study of haciendas, the system of
large estates that was a major legacy of colonial society to independent
Mexico. Scholars in Mexico, the United States, and Europe have all contributed to advancing the frontiers of knowledge about this important
subject. As a result of detailed, primary-source-based histories of individual estates or land-holding families, the older stereotype of the
hacienda as an essentially self-sufficient entity, held more for prestige
than for profit and worked by a resident labor force that was controlled
through bondage, has given way to a more complex, or, one might say,
a pluralistic view. It is now clear that significant regional variations
characterized the operation of haciendas; it is also becoming evident
that the early nineteenth century was a time of troubles for many hacienda owners.

Contributing to the new understanding has been a series of longitudinal studies that examines specific properties from their acquisition in the colonial period to well into the nineteenth century. Notable among these are the works of Jan Bazant on San Luis Potosí, David Brading on the Bajío area, Ward Barrett on the Cuernavaca sugar hacienda established by Cortés, and Charles Harris III on the Sánchez Navarros of Coahuila.[15] From these studies, as well as from the work of other scholars, it would appear that the hacienda system was shaken by the independence struggle. In the Bajío and eastern Jalisco areas, as Brading has demonstrated, a partial breakup of large estates took place in the following decades. In Chalco, south of Mexico City, hacienda owners found it more and more difficult to obtain workers from increasingly independent villages.[16] Evidence also exists of individual owners selling off, or even giving away, hacienda lands, and of Indian villages invading hacienda properties.[17] As a result of the above-mentioned studies, and others under way, the haciendas of the Early Republic may eventually be viewed in a different light from those of either the colonial or the Porfirian eras.

Linked to the problems of the agricultural and other economic sectors, to the heated controversies over tariff rates and import prohibitions, and to the fate of the Banco de Avío itself, was the inability of Mexican governments of the Early Republic to raise sufficient tax revenues to meet their expenses. The connection between fiscal difficulties and the political instability that characterized this period has long been assumed, but detailed historical studies of its fiscal philosophy, taxation administration, and deficit financing methods have been rare. Recently, scholars have begun to pay attention to these issues, encouraged, perhaps, by the studies that have appeared on the financial and monetary aspects of the last years of colonial rule.[18]

Among the recent works that might be mentioned is a series of publications by Carlos J. Sierra on the legislative and organizational history of the relevant governmental agencies: the Finance Ministry, Treasury, and Customs. Sierra has also published documents that deal with the history of specific taxes.[19] In the area of foreign financial relations, a recent major contribution is Jan Bazant's *Historia de la deuda exterior de México (1823 – 1946)* (Mexico: El Colegio de México, 1968). Bazant analyzes the tangled web of financial arrangements with foreign creditors that originated in the 1823 Goldschmidt and Barclay loans; he also offers balanced judgments on the impact of these arrangements on Mexican policy objectives.

The reasons for the failure of Mexican governments to raise sufficient tax revenues, and the methods of deficit financing they resorted to after further foreign borrowing was ruled out in 1827, are explored in an as-yet-unpublished volume by Barbara Tenenbaum. Entitled "Mexico in the Age of the Moneylenders, 1821 – 1857," this study focuses on the relationship between a succession of impecunious administrations and the small group of merchant financiers who advanced them funds at exorbitant rates. A study of the role and influence of these moneylenders, known pejoratively in their own day as agiotistas, has long been needed. Tenenbaum examines the extraordinary influence they acquired over Mexican governments of every political coloration; at the same time, she notes the positive role they played in promoting a national economy through investing their profits in geographically dispersed mining, industrial, and manufacturing enterprises.[20]

Tenenbaum's data comes in part from a recent collective study of Mexican entrepreneurs that was undertaken by a research seminar at the Department of Historical Investigations of the National Institute of Anthropology and History. Published under the rather ambitious title, *Formación y desarrollo de la burguesía en México. Siglo XIX* (Mexico: Siglo Veintiuno Editores, 1978), this study is one of the first to exploit the wealth of data in notarial and judicial archives to reconstruct the careers of businessmen. Essentially a collection of case studies, this volume provides a detailed and often fascinating picture of the growth of certain business houses from relatively modest beginnings in the Early Republic into powerful, diversified establishments that played important roles in the economic life of the second half of the century.

One of these establishments, that of Martínez del Río, was heavily involved in the cotton-textile industry;[21] and, indeed, it is this industry more than any other that has attracted scholarly attention over the past twenty years. Again, it is Jan Bazant who has made the most significant contributions with his quantitative studies of productivity, profits, and wages.[22] Bazant's calculations of the high profits earned by the Puebla factories of Estevan de Antuñano makes explicable the decision of agiotistas to channel funds into the textile industry. It is clear now that as a result of investments by Martínez del Río and others, textile production survived the wartime trauma of 1846 – 1848 and continued to expand well into the next decade.[23] The later history of this industry, its growth and transformation after 1870, can now be followed in Dawn Keremitsis's monograph *La industria textil mexicana en el siglo XIX* (Mexico: Secretaría de Educación Pública, 1973).

While primary attention has been paid to the financial and technical aspects of textile production, increased interest has also been shown in the study of the working classes. A significant contribution to understanding the distinctions that existed within these classes has been made by the Argentine sociologist, Torcuato Di Tella.[24] In turn, Frederick Shaw, using data culled from police and court records, has produced a convincing portrait of the life of the Mexico City artisan during the Early Republic.[25] Still needed are studies that examine in detail the labor force that was used in the new factories, studies that would tell us who the workers were, where they came from, what and how they were paid, and how and to what extent their lives and working conditions were changed by the growth of the factory system.

This review of writings on the economic history of the Early Republic should not be allowed to close without reference to certain innovations that go beyond the publication of the individual monograph. One is the recent application to that history of the methods associated with the "new" or "cliometric" school of economic historians, with their use of statistical inference based on economic theory. The leading innovator of this approach, insofar as Mexico is concerned, has been Professor John Coatsworth of the University of Chicago. His work in article and book form has already challenged deeply held views about Mexico's economic performance in the nineteenth century, and the reasons for its failure to grow at rates comparable to those of the United States during the first half of that century.[26] Another development has been the effort to explain the Mexican economic experience within a conceptual framework that stresses Mexico's dependency on the developed world. While some attempts at explanation suffered from naivete about the realities of Mexican history,[27] a recent collaborative study makes sophisticated use of the research findings of both Mexican and foreign scholars.[28]

Finally, mention should be made of some of the improvements in research facilities and tools available now, in contrast to a generation ago. At the Archivo General de la Nación, which has recently moved into spacious and specially renovated quarters, holdings that were once deposited in practically inaccessible locations like the Casa Amarilla have been integrated into the main collection and inventoried.[29] Access to notarial records, with their wealth of data for economic and social history, is also improving. At the Archivo General de Notarías in Mexico City, a new listing of notaries and their respective files was recently completed. Moreover, a project is now underway to provide a comprehensive index to all persons and institutions mentioned in the notarial records for selected years of the nineteenth century.[30]

Paralleling the progress with manuscript sources have been measures to facilitate the identification and location of printed sources, including often elusive government and periodical publications. Comprehensive bibliographic guides now exist to enable the economic historian of today and tomorrow to locate statistical data and other materials relevant to his or her tasks.[31] It remains to be seen how these various advances will be utilized to promote understanding of the Early Republic.

APPENDIX

A

Text of the Law of October 16, 1830

1. A Banco de Avío for the promotion of national industry will be established with a capital of one million pesos.
2. For the time necessary to provide this capital and no longer, the permission for entry into the ports of the Republic is extended for the cotton goods prohibited by the law of May 22, 1829.
3. One-fifth of the total duties accrued, or which shall in the future be yielded by the importation of the goods mentioned in the previous article, shall be applied to the funds of the bank.
4. In order to make needed sums available promptly, the government is authorized to borrow against the portion of the customs duties assigned to the bank. A loan of up to 200,000 pesos is authorized at the lowest possible interest, but not to exceed 3 percent per month and for a period not to exceed three months.
5. For directing the bank and managing its funds, a junta will be established under the chairmanship of the minister of relaciones composed of a vice-chairman and two members, with a secretary and two clerks if needed. The members of this junta will not enjoy any salary for the present, and will be replaced one each year starting with the junior member. The government may reappoint the outgoing member if it seems convenient. For the secretary and clerks, able-bodied pensioners will be employed, who will serve at the salary established for their former positions. The government will formulate the regulations by which this junta will be ruled in discharging its functions; and, henceforth, when the fund earns profits, Congress will establish the salaries which the members of the junta and other employees of the bank are to receive.
6. The funds of the bank will be deposited for the present in the casa de moneda in Mexico City at the disposal of the minister of relaciones, who, in conformity with decisions of the junta, will issue the sums that are necessary. When, through the increase of the funds, an office will be required to manage them, one will be established with the necessary employees, after congressional approval of their number and salary.
7. The junta shall arrange for the purchase and distribution of the machinery needed to develop the distinct branches of industry, and shall grant under legal requirements and guarantees, the capital needed by the various companies that are formed, or by the individuals who are engaged in industry in the states, district, and territories. The machinery shall be provided at cost, and the capital at an annual interest of 5 percent,

with a fair period fixed for the return of the principal. The capital, by remaining in circulation, shall serve as a continuous and permanent stimulant to industry.

8. The income from the interest yielded by the sums mentioned in the previous article shall be assigned to pay the salaries of the junta members and other employees of the bank and for its expenses. Any surplus shall be added to its capital.

9. The junta shall present and publish its accounts annually together with a report that describes the state of national industry and its subsequent advances.

10. Although preference shall be shown to the cotton- and wool-textile fields, and to the raising and processing of silk, the junta may likewise devote funds for promoting other branches of industry or agricultural products of importance for the nation.

11. The government may assign up to 6,000 pesos annually from the bank's funds as prizes for the various branches of industry. These prizes will be awarded at the recommendation and on the basis of a report by the junta.

12. The funds of the bank shall not be diverted to other purposes for any reason or pretext; nor shall the junta engage in gifts, functions, or make any outlay alien to its purpose.

B

Text of the Questionnaire circulated by the

Banco de Avío December 15, 1830

Office of the Banco de Avío
for the Promotion of
National Industry

Inasmuch as the promotion of the various branches of national industry is the objective of this office according to the law of October 16 of the current year, our plan is to begin with the fields of cotton and woolen textiles, the raising of silkworms, and, consequently, the planting of mulberry trees, and the propagation of bees. Since all climates are not equally suitable for these products, and, moreover, since the combination of particular circumstances makes certain regions more suitable for a given crop or kind of husbandry, this office requests that all true lovers of the greatness of the Republic cooperate by responding with the information in their possession to the following questions.

COTTON

1. Is the climate suitable for its cultivation?
2. Is cotton already being grown?
3. If the answer is yes, what kind of seed is used? Send a sample of the cotton.
4. How many arrobas are produced annually?
5. What is done with the cotton? Is it exported? If so, where? Is it processed locally?
6. In this case, what kinds of textiles are produced and what is the annual output?

WOOL

7. Is the area suitable for raising sheep?
8. Is sheep raising carried on now? What kinds of wool are produced? Send a sample of each.
9. What use is made of the wool?
10. If there are any woolen-textile factories, identify them and indicate what their products are.

MULBERRY TREES

11. Are the climate and terrain of your village adapted to the growing of mulberries?
12. If the answer is yes, are any growing?
13. How many? How long have they existed? Does anyone remember who planted them?
14. Discuss the condition of the various trees, distinguishing the white from the black, known commonly as the female and male mulberry.
15. Do the inhabitants show any inclination to develop them?

SILKWORMS

16. Are there any silkworm seeds?
17. Do the natives of your area devote themselves to nurturing them?
18. What use is made of them?
19. How do they wind the filament?
20. If the terrain and climate are suitable for planting mulberries, but there are no silkworm seeds, what is the closest place where silk is cultivated, and from which the seed can be obtained?
21. Have any attempts been made to bleach and wind the silk? What method has been followed?
22. Is any [financial] support needed for this kind of industry? Specify.

BEES

23. Is the climate favorable, or not, for increasing the number of bees? What animals hostile to bees have been observed?
24. Is there an abundance of vegetation whose flowers are suitable for supporting them?
25. Are there any apiaries?
26. If yes, how many boxes?
27. How many swarms does each beehive produce annually? How many pounds of wax are obtained from them? How many pounds of honey?
28. Is any encouragement needed for this activity? Specify.
29. If none of the above activities exists, or, if, in addition to them, there are other natural or manufactured items produced, what are they? Indicate the state of backwardness or progress of each one, and identify the individuals who are most given to experimentation and observation. What assistance do they need, and what security can they give for the capital that might be advanced and for the interest that would be required at the rate of 5 percent annually.
30. Is there ceramic clay in the vicinity of the village?
31. What use is made of it? Is this for fine or ordinary ware? Report on everything you have observed about this type of industry and on the means for improving it.

Replies should be numbered and follow the sequence of the questions, because one of the purposes of the office in circulating the questionnaire is to systematize its work. With the information obtained, it will achieve accuracy in its operations and a prudent economy in impending expenses. It will also be able to apply its efforts with greater success to the most important branches of industry, or to those that, because of the abundance of elements they offer for their improvement, require assistance. Hence, not only the individuals to whom these questions are sent directly, but all those who hear about them, should regard themselves as invited to get in touch with this office, to advise it about the products mentioned in the questionnaire, and, especially, about whatever they know concerning any other industrial activity. Any residents within or without our republic who are interested in its prosperity should give this office their ideas on how to achieve it.

Mexico, December 15, 1830

Ramón Rayón
Lic. Basilio José Arrillaga.

C

List of Manuscript and Printed Responses to

Banco de Avío Questionnaire of December 15, 1830

State and community described	Submitted by	Present location of document
Chiapas		
Acala	Fr. Torivio Corro	SMGE[a]
Bachajón	Fr. Tomás de Aguilar	SMGE
Coaquitepeque	Fr. Francisco de Lara	SMGE
Moyos	Fr. José María Solano	SMGE
Ocosingo	Fr. Manuel Paniagual	SMGE
Ocosocuantla	Fr. Eustaquio Zabadúa	SMGE
San Carlos	Fr. Valentín Solís	SMGE
San Juan Cancú	Fr. Francisco de la Fuente	SMGE
San Nicolás Tenango	Fr. Francisco de la Fuenta	SMGE
Tila	Fr. Manuel Solano	SMGE
Zocoltenengo	Fr. Eugenio Córdoba	SMGE
Chihuahua		
Chihuahua	José Agustín Escudero	AGN, B/A[b]
Colima		
Colima	R. Maldonado et al.	RO[c], July 5, 1831
Durango		
Cuencamé	Miguel Miranda (prefect)	SMGE
Guanajuato		
Acámbaro	Francisco Zambrano	RO, Feb. 24, 1831
Jerécuaro	Ayuntamiento	AGN, B/A
León	Br. Gabriel Zámano	AGN, B/A
Pénjamo	Cayetano Bravo and Miguel Navarrete	RO, May 8, 1831
Salvatierra	Basilio Peralta	RO, Feb. 11, 1831
Silao	Ignacio Gutiérrez	RO, Feb. 8, 1831
Tarandacuao	Ángel López and J. J. Zimavilla	RO, Mar. 28, 1831

Appendices

State and community described	Submitted by	Present location of document
Valle de Santiago	Juez Ecclesiástico	*RO*, Feb. 9, 1831
Yuriapúndaro	Manuel Juncal	*RO*, May 2, 1831
Guerrero		
Tixtla Guerrero	Ayuntamiento	SMGE
Zumpango del Río	Ayuntamiento	SMGE
Hidalgo		
Tecozantla	Francisco Medalla	*RO*, Dec. 19, 1831
Yahualica	Br. Luis María Hurtado	SMGE
Jalisco		
Autlán	Ayuntamiento	SMGE
Purificación	Martínez	SMGE
Tomatlán	Blas Betancourt	SMGE
Zapopam	Colegio de María Santísima	SMGE
México		
Altajayucan	Br. José J. Gavito	SMGE
Chimalhuacán	Fr. José María Moreno	SMGE
Morelos	Fr. Manuel Zavalza	SMGE, also *RO*, May 15, 1831
San Bernadino Tasquillo	Br. José Lucas Colín	SMGE
Tlálpam	José Miranda (prefect)	SMGE, also *RO*, Jan. 23, 1831
Xochimilco	Agustín Vallarta	*RO*, Mar. 7, 1831
Ystacalco	Fr. Manuel Espinosa de los Monteros	SMGE
Zumpango	Junta de Industria	SMGE
Michoacán		
Angamacutiro	Joaquín de Madrigal and Vicente Pérez	SMGE
Angamacutiro	José Antonio Gutiérrez	*RO*, May 28, 1831
Cuneo	Juan José Pastor Morales	SMGE
Huango	Juan José Pastor Morales	SMGE
La Piedad	Ayuntamiento	SMGE
Tanhuato	Ayuntamiento	SMGE
Nuevo León		
Linares	Ayuntamiento	AGN, B/A
Monterrey	José Francisco Arroyo	*RO*, May 28, 1831
Monterrey	Br. Francisco Arze Rosales	AGN, B/A
Oaxaca		
Ejutla	Rafael José de la Lanza	*RO*, Jul. 16, 1831
Jamiltepec	Francisco Esteves	*RO*, May 12, 1831
Miahuatlán	José V. Rodríguez	*RO*, Jul. 16, 1831
Nochistlán	José A. Domínguez	*RO*, Jun. 6, 1831

State and community described	Submitted by	Present location of document
Oaxaca	José A. Domínguez	*RO*, Jun. 6, 1831
Tehuantepec	Mariano Conde	*RO*, May 22, 1831
Puebla		
Tehuacán	Alejandro Bozán	*RO*, Mar. 17, 1831
Tepeaca	Mariano Calderón	SMGE
Querétaro		
Querétaro	J. Antonio del Razo et al.	*RO*, May 24, 1831
Querétaro	Miguel García et al.	*RO*, Jun. 28, 1831
Sonora		
Álamos	Ayuntamiento	SMGE
Altar	Ayuntamiento	SMGE
Altar	Luis Redondo	SMGE
Arizpe	Ayuntamiento	SMGE
Buenavista	Ayuntamiento	SMGE
Buenavista	Br. J. J. Herreros	SMGE
Hermosillo	Ayuntamiento	SMGE
Hermosillo	Francisco Escobosa	SMGE
Oposura	Ayuntamiento	SMGE
Oposura	Fr. Francisco Robles	SMGE
Ranchito	Víctores de Aguilar	SMGE
San Miguel Horcasitas	Fr. Pedro A. Martínez	SMGE^d
Sta. Magdalena, Alta Pimería	Fr. José María Pérez Llera	Beltrán
Tabasco		
Cunduacán	Juan M. de Torres	*RO*, May 1, 1831
Huimanguillo (cantón)	José María Iglesias (prefect)	SMGE
Huimanguillo	Francisco Picachi	SMGE
Veracruz		
Córdova	Antonio González	SMGE
Jalapa	Tomás Illanes	SMGE
Huatusco	Miguel María Muñoz	*RO*, Jun. 24–25, 1831
Orizava	Manuel Monte Argüelles and Juan de Orbegosa	SMGE
San Andrés Tuxtla	Juan Francisco Cadena	SMGE
San Antonio Huatusco	Ayuntamiento	SMGE
Sitio del Rosario	Manuel Urgell	SMGE
Songolica	Agustín Amador	SMGE
Totula	Miguel María Muñoz	*RO*, Jun. 24–25, 1831
Veracruz	Francisco Arrillaga	SMGE, also *RO*, Jul. 1, 1831

State and community described	Submitted by	Present location of document
State Undetermined		
Cantón Militar de las Villas	Unsigned	SMGE
Hacienda de Tilapa	Antonio Magito	SMGE
Jiménez (ciudad)	Ayuntamiento	SMGE
Misión de San Luis	Fr. Antonio Peyri	Beltrán
San Lucas	José Manuel Ortíz	SMGE
Santa Cruz	José A. Valenzuela	SMGE
Areas now within the United States		
Misión de Santa Cruz,		
Alta California	Fr. J. J. Aumano	SMGE
Sante Fe, New Mexico	Melchiades A. Ortega	*RO*, May 9, 1831
Tucson, Arizona	Teodoro Ramírez	*RO*, May 9, 1831

a. The Sociedad Mexicana de Geografía y Estadística (SMGE) possesses most of the manuscript responses. These originally composed expediente 29 of the Banco de Avío files. This expediente was turned over to Marcos Esparza in June and September 1831 with the idea that he would draw up a "manufacturing statistic" from the material. Lack of clerical assistance and the uneven nature of the coverage discouraged Esparza. The espediente was later in the hands of Pablo de la Llave. It is not known how or when it came into the possession of the Sociedad.

b. The files of the Banco de Avío in the Archivo General contain some of the manuscript replies. See expedientes 56, 65, 72, and 118.

c. The *Registro oficial (RO)* published a good many of the replies and also correspondence that, strictly speaking, was not in reply to the questionnaire, but which was stimulated by it. See especially the issues of May 16 – 17 for José A. Escudero's comments on Chihuahua, and the issues of Oct. 15 – 17 for Melchiades A. Ortega's supplementary statement on New Mexico.

d. Señor Ramón Beltrán, Director of the Biblioteca Histórica de Hacienda, Mexico City, possesses a copy of the original questionnaire and a handful of responses in manuscript.

D

Chairmen of the Junta

of the Banco de Avío

Name	Title	Term
Lucas Alamán	Relaciones minister	Oct. 16, 1830 – May 20, 1832
J. M. Ortíz Monasterio	Acting minister	May 21, 1832 – Aug. 19, 1832
Francisco Fagoaga	Relaciones minister	Aug. 20, 1832 – Dec. 24, 1832
Bernardo González Angulo	Relaciones minister	Dec. 26, 1832 – Apr. 26, 1833
Carlos García	Relaciones minister	Apr. 27, 1833 – Dec. 15, 1833
Francisco Lombardo	Acting minister	Dec. 16, 1833 – Jan. 10, 1834
Francisco Lombardo	Relaciones minister	Jan. 10, 1834 – Jan. 22, 1835
J. M. Gutiérrez Estrada	Relaciones minister	Jan. 23, 1835 – Jun. 1, 1835
J. M. Ortíz Monasterio	Acting minister	Jun. 2, 1835 – Jul. 8, 1835
Manuel Díaz de Bonilla	Relaciones minister	Jul. 9, 1835 – Oct. 28, 1835
J. M. Ortíz Monasterio	Acting minister	Oct. 29, 1835 – Jan. ?, 1837
Joaquín Iturbide	Acting interior minister	Jan. ?, 1837 – Apr. 22, 1837
Manuel Peña y Peña	Interior minister	Apr. 23, 1837 – Oct. 17, 1837
José A. Romero	Interior minister	Oct. ?, 1837 – Mar. 9, 1838
Luis Cuevas	Acting minister	Mar. 9, 1838 – Mar. 22, 1838
J. J. Pesado	Interior minister	Mar. 23, 1838 – Dec. 13, 1838
Juan Rodríguez Puebla	Interior minister	Dec. 13, 1838 – Dec. 16, 1838
Joaquín Iturbide	Acting minister	Dec. 16, 1838 – Dec. 20, 1838
Manuel Eduardo Gorostiza	Interior minister	Dec. 21, 1838 – Dec. 26, 1838
Agustín Pérez de Lebrija	Interior minister	Dec. 26, 1838 – Apr. 26, 1839
Juan de Dios Cañedo	Interior minister	Apr. 27, 1839 – May 18, 1839
José A. Romero	Interior minister	May 18, 1839 – Jul. 27, 1839
Luis Cuevas	Interior minister	Jul. 27, 1839 – Aug. 18, 1840
Juan de Dios Cañedo	Acting minister	Aug. 18, 1840 – Sep. ?, 1840
José Mariano Marín	Interior minister	Sep. ?, 1840 – Dec. 8, 1840
José María Jiménez	Interior minister	Dec. 8, 1840 – Sep. 28, 1841
Crispiano del Castillo	Justice minister	Oct. 10, 1841 – Feb. 22, 1842
Pedro Vélez	Justice minister	Feb. 22, 1842 – Sep. 22, 1842

Abbreviations and Spanish Terms

Used in Notes

AGN   Archivo General de la Nación, México

AMP   Archivo de la Secretaría Municipal, Puebla

AN   Archivo General de Notarías, México

B/A   Papers of the Banco de Avío, AGN

Com.   Ramo de Industria y Comercio, AGN

DG   *Diario del Gobierno de los Estados Unidos Mexicanos*

Exp.   Expediente, file of papers related to a single transaction

Ind.   Papers of the Sección de Industria, AGN

Leg.   Legajo, bundle of loose papers or group of expedientes tied together

MDG   *Memoria sobre el estado de la agricultura e industria . . . que la Dirección general de estos ramos presenta . . . 1843 – 1845*

Ramo   A specific collection within the AGN

RO   *Registro Oficial del Gobierno de los Estados Unidos Mexicanos*

Note: Citations to Archivo General de Notarías documents will use only the last name of the officiating notary, the year of the document, and the folio number.

NOTES

CHAPTER 1

1. A contemporary writer estimated that of a total population of 6 million in 1810, about 1,320,000 natives lived in economic isolation, offering nothing for sale and purchasing nothing in return. Juan López Cancelada, *Ruina de la Nueva España si se declara el comercio libre con los extranjeros* (Cadiz, 1811), pp. 11 – 13.
2. Miguel O. de Mendizábel, "Las artes textiles en México," *Obras Completas* (Mexico, 1947), 6:452 – 53, 481, 492.
3. Miguel Lerdo de Tejada concluded that such goods were increased in price by 75 percent by the time they reached the consumer. *Comercio exterior de México desde la conquista hasta hoy* (Mexico: Rafael Rafael, 1853), p. 23.
4. "Reglamento y aranceles reales para el comercio libre de España a Indias de 12 octubre de 1778," AGN, Ramo de Bandos, 10:431.
5. Spanish-made textiles of wool, cotton, flax, and hemp paid no export duties on leaving the mother country, and were also exempt from the *almojarifazgo* on entering the colonies. Ibid.
6. Conde de Revillagigedo, *Instrucción reservada que el conde de . . . dió a su sucesor en el mando, marqués de Branciforte. . . .* (Mexico, 1831), pp. 109 – 10.
7. Ibid., p. 109. Domestic textiles were not universally exempt from the alcabala, though of course they were free of the duties collected at the ports. However, cotton textiles woven by Indians were entirely free of the alcabala as were cotton, wool, and silk fabrics woven and sold within the limits of Mexico City. Fabián de Fonseca and Carlos de Urrutia, *Historia general de real hacienda* (Mexico, 1845 – 1853), 2:62.
8. Revillagigedo to Diego de Gardoqui, México, Aug. 31, 1793, *Boletín del Archivo General de la Nación* 2 (1931): 49.
9. For a discussion of unemployment, see "Cuadro de la situación económica Novo—Hispana en 1788," Secretaría de la Economía Nacional, *Documentos para la historia económica de México* (Mexico, 1934), 2:13.
10. *Instrucción reservada*, p. 93.
11. For this reason the trade ordinance of 1778 dropped the duties on raw wool that entered Spain from the colonies. Joseph M. Gálvez to Viceroy Aranjuez, May 21, 1785, MS in AGN, Com., 18, exp. 1, fol. 1.
12. *Instrucción reservada*, p. 92; López Cancelada, *Ruina de la Nueva España*, pp. 15 – 17.

13. Oaxaca, once a thriving silk-weaving center, had 7 looms devoted to silk manufacture and 500 to cotton in 1793. *Instrucción reservada*, p. 91.

14. "Los Mayorales del Arte maior de la Seda sobre ordenanzas para la mezcla de seda y algodón," 1796, MS in AGN, Com. 18, exp. 8, ff. 50 – 58. The prohibition on mixing cotton with silk was lifted in 1796.

15. "Bando del Sr Marqués de Croix en 11 de Jun^o de 1767 que . . . prescribe reglas p^a el trato de los sirvientes," AGN, Ramo de Bandos, 6:68.

16. Alexander von Humboldt, *Political Essay on the Kingdom of New Spain*, trans. John Black (London: Longman, Hurst, Rees, Orme and Brown, 1811), 3:463 – 64.

17. "Bando de 4 de Octr de 81 por el citado Sr Mayoraga, insertando el del Sr Croix de 11 de Junio de 67 para que se fixe en los Obrages de Querétaro donde se ha notado que no se observa," AGN, Ramo de Bandos, 11:387.

18. MSS in AGN, Com., 8, exp. 12, ff. 265 – 68, 273 – 75; MSS in AMP, 224, ff. 226 – 29.

19. Weavers in ordinary *(maestros de llano)* could qualify as specialty weavers *(maestros de labor)* and thus be permitted four additional looms. For a copy of the ordinances adopted by the cotton weavers of Mexico City in 1776, see "Reformación de la antigua ordenanza del gremio que antes era de tejedores de algodón y hoy lo es también de seda y metales," 1809, MS in AGN, Com., 18, exp. 10, ff. 137 – 41. These regulations differ from those issued in 1757 and printed by Francisco del Barrio Lorenzot, *El trabajo en México durante la época colonial* (Mexico: Secretaría de Gobernación, 1920), pp. 176 – 78.

20. "El gremio de algodoneros sobre el exterminio de los Intrusos y cumplimiento de sus ordenanzas en lo que expresen," Feb. 18, 1796, MS in AGN, Com., 21, exp. 4, ff. 126 – 29.

21. MSS in AGN, Com., 18, exps. 4, 6, 9, 10.

22. MSS in AGN, Com., 18, exp. 10, ff. 180 – 236.

23. Ibid., fol. 236v.

24. Lucas Alamán, *Historia de México*, 2d ed. (Mexico: V. Aguero y Comp., 1883 – 1885), 1:131, 158.

25. "Noticias de Fábricas, Molinos, Yngenios, Lagunas, Ríos y Puentes," MS in AGN, Ramo de Historia, 74, ff. 407 – 55; Humboldt, *Political Essay*, 3:462; *Instrucción reservada*, p. 91.

26. "Provincia de Guadalajara. Estado que demuestra los frutos y efectos de agricultura, industria y comercio . . . en al año de 1803 . . . ," *Relaciones estadísticas de Nueva España de principios del siglo XIX*, Archivo Histórico de Hacienda, Colección de documentos publicados baja la dirección de Jesús Silva Herzog, no. 3 (Mexico, 1944), p. 110.

27. "Noticias . . . de Real Hacienda, Comercio, Agricultura, Minería y Artes de la provincia de Guadalajara reino de la Nueva Galicia," Sept. 6, 1804, ibid., pp. 119 – 21.

28. MS in AGN, Com., 8, exp. 12, fol. 271.

29. Humboldt, *Political Essay*, 3:463; Letter signed J. Antonio del Raso, *RO*, May 11, 1831.

30. "Noticias estadísticas de la intendencia de Puebla," *Relaciones estadísticas*, p. 54.

31. This is a conservative estimate, since the three provinces mentioned above accounted for close to 50,000 and there were other important textile centers in the intendancies of Mexico, Valladolid, and Guanajuato. The large number engaged reflects, of course, the low technological state of the industry. The cleaning, carding, and spinning of the fibers were all done by hand.

32. Humboldt, *Political Essay*, 3:462.

33. José M. Quirós, *Memoria de estatuto. Idea de la riqueza que daban a la masa circulante*

de Nueva España sus naturales producciones en los años de tranquilidad y su abatimiento en las presentes conmociones (Veracruz, 1817), table opp. p. 30.

34. For an adverse appraisal of Quirós's statistical methods, see Robert S. Smith, "José María Quirós, 'Balanza del Comercio Marítimo de Veracruz' e ideas económicas," *El Trimestre Económico* 13 (1946−47): 701.

35. Mendizábel, "Las artes textiles en México," p. 490, n. 2.

36. The role of mercantile credit in the production of cotton before 1810 is discussed in "Informe y cuentas que el Banco de Avío presenta," Jan. 1, 1832, *Memoria de la secretaría . . . de relaciones interiores y exteriores* (Mexico, 1832), appendix, pp. 17−18, 23.

37. "Apuntes estadísticos de la intendencia de Veracruz," *Relaciones estadísticas*, p. 21.

38. Freight rates fluctuated according to circumstances, but the cost of a mule load *(carga)* of about 400 pounds from Veracruz to Puebla was rarely under twelve pesos and usually fifteen pesos or more. See quotations in *El Águila Mejicana* (Mexico), July 28, Aug. 7, 1828; *El Censor* (Veracruz), May 30, 1830; Feb. 16, Aug. 28, 1831; July 5, 17, 1835.

39. These prices are for the period prior to the outbreak of violence in 1810. *El Correo Semanario Político y Mercantil* (Mexico), Mar. 14, Apr. 18, June 13, 1810.

40. Letter signed Francisco Arrillaga, *RO*, July 1, 1831.

41. Humboldt, *Political Essay*, 3:18−19. The cotton gin was established at Alvarado by some Catalonian merchants. López Cancelada, *Ruina de la Nueva España*, p. 16.

42. "Noticias estadísticas de la intendencia de Puebla," pp. 54−57.

43. Figures for the years 1799−1800 are not included. The statistics were compiled by the *Real Aduana* of Mexico City and are to be found in the *Gazetas de México* 4−13 (1789−1805). The *tercio* was half a mule load and contained at this time 7 arrobas or approximately 175 pounds.

44. "Expediente formado sobre . . . observansia de las ordenanzas del Gremio," 1803, MS in AMP, 224, fol. 274.

45. A prior permit, issued on Nov. 18, 1797, and rescinded seventeen months later, excluded articles prohibited under existing regulations, and hence maintained the ban on foreign cotton goods. *La libertad del comercio en la Nueva España en la segunda década del siglo XIX*, Archivo Histórico de Hacienda, no. 1 (Mexico, 1943), intro., pp. 6−7.

46. Lerdo de Tejada, *Comercio exterior*, tables 19−21.

47. Ibid.; *Comercio extrangero por el puerto de San Blás en los años 1812 a 1817*, Archivo Histórico de Hacienda, no. 2 (México, 1944).

48. Quirós, *Memoria de estatuto*, p. 25.

49. R. A. Humphreys, ed., *British Consular Reports on the Trade and Politics of Latin America, 1824−1826*, Camden Third Series, vol. 63 (London: Royal Historical Society, 1940), p. 303.

50. For comment on artisan unemployment in Mexico City see "Informe que dieron los señores . . . prior y cónsules del real tribunal del consulado de México," Sept. 16, 1818, *La libertad del comercio*, p. 147.

CHAPTER 2

1. Decree of Feb. 13, 1822, Manuel Dublán and José María Lozano, *Legislación mexicana*, 34 vols. (Mexico: Edición Oficial, 1876−1904) 1:594.

2. Ibid., pp. 563−64, Decree of Nov. 22, 1821.

3. See Fausto de Elhuyar, *Memoria sobre el influjo de la minería en la agricultura, industria, población y civilización de la Nueva España* (Madrid, 1825), pp. 1–8, 72.

4. *Gaceta Imperial de México* 2, no. 13 (Mar. 28, 1822).

5. "Arancel general interino para gobierno de las aduanas marítimas en el comercio libre del imperio," Dublán and Lozano, *Legislación mexicana*, 1:567–86.

6. Written or printed music, pictures and designs, unboundbooks (save for those contrary to religion and morals), and surgical instruments.

7. The other items freed of duties were mercury, flax, plants or seeds unknown in Mexico, and live animals. These animals were subsequently defined as those exotic to Mexico. Decree of Aug. 1, 1822, Dublán and Lozano, *Legislación mexicana*, 1:618.

8. For these debates see *Diario de las sesiones de la soberana junta provisional gubernativa del imperio mexicano* (Mexico, 1821), pp. 112–20. A comparison of the final prohibitory list with one originally presented in the *Soberana Junta* reveals the omission of a lengthy list of foodstuffs. See *Arancel general interino e instrucción para gobierno de las aduanas marítimas en el comercio libre del imperio mexicano* (Mexico, 1821), chap. 3.

9. The others were leaf tobacco, wrought wax, vermicelli noodles, metallic braid, silk braid, and wheat flour. The last was added in an amendment dated Jan. 14, 1822. Dublán and Lozano, *Legislación mexicana*, 1:588.

10. The value of foreign cotton goods classified as manta was not given in the tariff act, and consequently had to be fixed by port appraisers. The Veracruz and Alvarado customs established the figure of 37 1/2 centavos (3 reales) per vara if 33 inches or more in breadth, and 25 centavos (2 reales) if under 33 inches. Miguel Lerdo de Tejada, *Comercio esterior*, tables 31, 32. The cost of American manta varied from 12 to 15 cents a yard. *Niles Register* 31, p. 257 (Dec. 23, 1826).

11. *Gaceta Diaria de México* 1, no. 68 (Mar. 9, 1826).

12. Prior to 1810, 22-inch material (manta de dos tercios) sold in Mexico City for 2 reales; in 1827, according to a Puebla deputy, the current cost was 2 3/4 reales. Remarks of deputy Carlos García, reprinted in *El Poblana* (Puebla), Supplement to no. 3, Mar. 11, 1827.

13. Charles Mackenzie to George Canning, Xalapa, July 24, 1824, in Humphreys, *British Consular Reports*, p. 323; *A Sketch of the Customs and Society of Mexico* . . . (London: Longman & Co., 1828), p. 71.

14. [Diego Solís], *Específico y único remedio de la pobreza del imperio mexicano* (Guadalajara, 1822).

15. *Diario de las sesiones de la soberana junta*, pp. 185 ff.; *Actas del congreso constituyente mexicano* (Mexico, 1822–1823), 1, session of Mar. 4, 1822.

16. The debates preceding the adoption of this measure saw a motion introduced to raise the alcabala on foreign textiles to 40 percent. *Actas del congreso constituyente*, 2, session of Aug. 8, 1822; Decree of Aug. 9, 1822. Dublán and Lozano, *Legislación mexicana*, 1:626.

17. *Gaceta Imperial de México* 1, no. 17 (Feb. 6, 1823).

18. Justo Sierra, *Evolución política del pueblo mexicano*, 2d ed. (Mexico: La Casa de España, 1940), pp. 194–95.

19. *Diario de la junta nacional instituyente del imperio mexicano* (México, 1822–1823), pp. 256–59; Manuel Ortiz de la Torre, "Discurso de un diputado sobre la introducción de efectos estranjeros," *El Trimestre Económico* 12 (1945): 283–315.

20. Vicente Riva Palacio, ed., *México a través de los siglos* (México: Ballescá y Comp^a, 1888 — 1889), 4:100 — 101.

21. Decree of Oct. 7, 1823, Dublán and Lozano, *Legislación mexicana*, 1:681.

22. Law of Feb. 13, 1824, *Guía de la hacienda de la república mexicana* (Mexico, 1826), p. 36. Spanish troops in the harbor fortress of San Juan de Ulúa kept the port of Veracruz under intermittent fire until Sept. 1825.

23. Agustin Cué Cánovas, *Historia social y económica de México* (Mexico: Editorial América, 1947), p. 115.

24. *Memoria presentada . . . por el secretario . . . de relaciones esteriores e interiores* (Mexico, 1825), p. 37.

25. *Memoria que el secretario . . . de relaciones esteriores e interiores presenta* (Mexico, 1823), p. 49.

26. Letter of Francisco Arrillaga, *RO*, July 1, 1831; Decree of Oct. 8, 1823, Mariano Galván, comp., *Colección de órdenes y decretos de la soberana junta provisional gubernativa y soberanos congresos generales* (Mexico, 1829 — 1840), 2:192; Decree of Oct. 8, 1823, Dublán and Lozano, *Legislación mexicana*, 1:681.

27. Lionel Hervey to George Canning, Mexico, Jan. 18, 1824, in *Britain and the Independence of Latin America 1812 — 1830: Select Documents from the Foreign Office Archives*, ed. Charles K. Webster (London: Oxford University Press, 1938), 1:443 — 44.

28. J. R. Poinsett, *Notes on Mexico Made in the Autumn of 1822* (Philadelphia: H. C. Carey and I. Lea, 1824), p. 102. Poinsett, accepting Humboldt's estimate of $8 million, gives $4 million as their current value.

29. *Representación que la diputación provincial de Puebla hizo al Soberano Congreso en 12 de agosto de 1823* (Mexico, 1823); *Actas del congreso constituyente*, 4, session of May 1, 1823, remarks of Deputy Covarrubias; *Dictamen de las comisiones unidas de hacienda y comercio sobre prohibiciones de efectos* (Mexico, 1824), p. 1.

30. *Memoria sobre reformas del arancel mercantil que presenta el secretario de hacienda al soberano congreso constituyente leída en sesión de 13 de enero de 1824* (Mexico, 1824), pp. 6 — 7; and appendix, pp. 1 — 23.

31. Ibid., pp. 7 — 8.

32. Charles Mackenzie to George Canning, in Humphreys, *British Consular Reports*, pp. 315 — 17.

33. Dublán and Lozano, *Legislación mexicana*, 2:706 — 7. Nine articles were listed twice, making a total of 107.

34. *Dictamen de las comisiones unidas de hacienda y comercio sobre prohibiciones de efectos* (Mexico, 1824), p. 11.

35. The duty was based on 125 percent of valuation. Decree of Aug. 4, 1824, Dublán and Lozano, *Legislación mexicana*, 1:710.

36. Decree of Dec. 22, 1824, ibid., p. 748.

37. The various federal duties amounted to 48 3/8 percent. See Charles O'Gorman, Memorandum, Jan. 10, 1825, annex no. 2 and note, MS in Texas University Library, García Collection, Manning and Marshall Papers; see also Guillermo Prieto, *Indicaciones sobre el origen, vicisitudes y estado de las rentas generales de la federación mexicana* (Mexico, 1850), p. 212. Prieto arrives at a total duty of 45 1/4 percent by omitting the 3 1/8 percent *avería* (officially 2 1/2 percent, but computed on 125 percent of the tariff valuations).

38. Theoretically, such goods paid the alcabala once in the state where they were finally consumed. Decree of Aug. 4, 1824, Dublán and Lozano, *Legislación mexicana*, 1:711.

39. See Ortiz de la Torre, "Discurso de un diputado," pp. 283–315; *Dictamen de las co-misiones unidas de hacienda y comercio sobre prohibiciones de efectos*, p. 2; also the prize-winning essays of de la Torre and Juan W. Barquera on the topic of promoting national wealth and population in *Certamen científico que el nacional y más antiguo colegio de S. Ildefonso de México dedica a su antiguo alumno el Ciudadano Guadalupe Victoria* (Mexico, 1825). Barquera significantly had already published an edition of J. B. Say's *Treatise on Political Economy*.

40. *Informes y manifiestos de los poderes ejecutivo y legislativo de 1821 a 1904* (Mexico, 1905), 1:41.

41. Ibid., pp. 55, 69, 71.

42. *Memoria . . . de relaciones*, 1825, p. 44.

43. See Tadeo Ortiz de Ayala, *Resumen de la estadística del imperio mexicano* (Mexico: Herculana del Villar, 1822).

44. *Memoria de la secretaría . . . de relaciones interiores y esteriores* (Mexico, 1829), p. 15.

45. Luis Ugalde, who had bred his ewes with government-owned merino rams in 1826 and thus built up a flock of over 300 head by 1831, found himself unable to dispose of their wool. Luis Ugalde to Lucas Alamán, Tehuacán, July 31, 1831, MS in AGN, B/A, 1, exp. 122.

46. *Memoria . . . de relaciones*, 1823, p. 49; *Diario de las sesiones del congreso constituyente de la federación mexicana* (Mexico, 1824), 1, session of Apr. 9, 1824.

47. *Memoria de los ramos del ministerio de relaciones interiores y esteriores* (Mexico, 1826), p. 17.

48. Chamber of Deputies session, Apr. 25, 1826, reported in *El Sol*, May 11, 1826.

49. Law of May 18, 1826, Mariano Galván, *Colección de órdenes*, 4:52. The Chamber of Dep-uties, in which Zozaya was a prominent member, actually enacted a private bill em-bodying all his requests, but the Senate rewrote it into the general measure waiving only the alcabala duty. The warmest debates, incidentally, revolved around the issue of whether the federal government could grant exemptions from the alcabala in the states as well as in federal territories. The measure as enacted did apply to state-levied duties. *El Sol*, May 11–June 1, 1826.

50. Decree of Apr. 28, 1826, *Colección de los decretos, circulares y órdenes de los poderes legislativo y ejecutivo del estado de Jalisco* (Guadalajara, 1874–1877), 2:341; Decree of May 3, 1826, *Colección de los decretos y órdenes más importantes que espidió el con-greso constituyente del estado de Puebla* (Puebla, 1827–1832).

51. Chamber of Deputies, session of Mar. 7, 1825, in *El Sol*, Mar. 9, 1825; for import figures see Lerdo de Tejada, *Comercio exterior*, tables 33–34 and notes.

52. See the Nov. 25, 1824, session of the Congreso Constituyente reported in *El Sol*, Nov. 27, 1824. A tariff bill was passed in 1826 by the Chamber of Deputies, but the Senate failed to approve it before the session came to an end.

53. *Dictamen de la comisión primera de hacienda de la cámara de representantes del con-greso general de la federación sobre arreglo de aranceles para las aduanas marítimas* (Mexico, 1827), pp. 1–8.

54. Ibid., pp. 21–22.

55. See law of Nov. 16, 1827, Dublán and Lozano, *Legislación mexicana*, 2:26–46.

56. Chamber of Deputies sessions May 3–14, 1827, in *El Sol*, May 19–June 3, 1827.

57. Chamber of Deputies sessions May 10, 16, 17, 1827, in *El Sol*, June 4–17, 1827. Various state legislatures led by Puebla had recommended the exclusion of such fabrics.

58. The valuation of foreign manta had been left to the discretion of port appraisers with considerable confusion resulting. The 37.5 figure had been applied locally at Veracruz and Alvarado as early as 1823, and two years later had been made standard for all ports by a Finance Ministry directive. In October 1826, the ministry ordered an increase in valuation to 62.5 centavos, but the lower figure was restored by legislative enactment the following March, chiefly as the result of foreign protests. *Guía de la hacienda de la república. Año de 1828* (Mexico, 1828), pp. 230−32; Dublán and Lozano, *Legislación mexicana*, 2:6.

59. Chamber of Deputies session of April 27, 1827, in *El Sol*, May 11, 1827; Law of Feb. 1, 1828, Dublán and Lozano, *Legislación mexicana*, 2:58. This exemption was subsequently extended to cotton and wool yarn (ibid., p. 72).

60. *Decretos del congreso constituyente y del primero constitucional del estado de Guanajuato* (Mexico, 1834), p. 33; *Colección de los decretos . . . que espidió el congreso constituyente del estado de Puebla* (Puebla, 1827−1832), 2:128; *Colección de leyes y disposiciones relativas al ramo de hacienda del estado de México* (Toluca, 1876), p. 92; Amador Coromina, ed., *Recopilación de leyes . . . expedidas en el estado de Michoacán* (Morelia, 1886−1913), 4:36−37.

61. The state of Puebla was a notable exception in not limiting the tax exemptions to locally produced textiles. Such liberality probably had its roots in the belief that their fabrics had little to fear from the competition of those woven in other states.

62. Pablo Macedo, *La evolutión mercantil. Comunicaciones y obras públicas. La hacienda pública; tres monografías. . . .* (Mexico: J. Ballescá y Cᵃ, 1905), p. 70.

63. Ambiguous references to imported textile machinery in 1822 refer in all probability to manually operated equipment, *Diario de las sesiones de la soberana junta provisional*, p. 307; *Memoria . . . de relaciones*, 1823, p. 49.

64. For a detailed study of one such investment see Robert Randall, *Real del Monte. A British Mining Venture in Mexico* (Austin: University of Texas Press, 1972).

65. Ernesto Lobato López, *El crédito en México* (Mexico: Fondo de Cultura Económica, 1945), pp. 101−5.

66. J. M. Murguía y Galardo, "Extracto general que abraza la Estadística toda en su 1ᵃ y 2ᵃ parte del Estado de Guaxaca. Año de 1827" 2, 30 (unpublished manuscript in the possession of the University of Texas).

67. *Memoria en que el gobierno del estado libre de México dá cuenta . . . presentada el día 13 de marzo de 1828* (Tlálpam, 1828), p. 10.

68. See *Clamor de los artesanos o sea de los ciudadanos* (Guadalajara, 1827); also *Representación de la sociedad de artesanos y comerciantes dirigida al soberano congreso de la unión* (Guadalajara, 1828).

69. For a defense of this policy, with its reliance on prohibitions, see Romeo Flores Caballero, "Del libre cambio al proteccionismo," *Historia Mexicana* 19, no. 4 (Apr.−June 1970), 492−512.

CHAPTER 3

1. *Estatutos generales de la sociedad mexicana de industria agrícola y fabril* (Mexico, 1829); *El Amigo del Pueblo* (Mexico), July 23, 1828; *Correo de la Federación Mexicana* (Mexico), Apr. 27, 1829.

2. *Manifiesto del C. Vicente Guerrero, segundo presidente de los estados-unidos mexicanos a sus compatriotas* (Mexico, 1829), pp. 16 – 17.

3. Juan A. Mateos, *Historia parlamentaria de los congresos mexicanos de 1821 a 1857* (Mexico, 1877 – 1886), 5:327.

4. *Dictamen de la comisión primera de hacienda de la cámara de diputados sobre prohibición de géneros toscos de algodón y lana* (Mexico, 1829).

5. Mateos, *Historia parlamentaria*, 5:364.

6. Ibid., 443 – 48; *Correo de la Federación*, Mar. 11, May 18, 1829.

7. Mateos, *Historia parlamentaria*, 5:542; Lorenzo de Zavala, *Ensayo histórico de las revoluciones de Mégico desde 1808 hasta 1830* (Paris: P. Dupont, 1831 – 1832), 2:304.

8. For instances of this reasoning, see references in n. 4 above and in chap. 2, n. 67; see also *Economía interesante para la nación mexicana* (Guadalajara, 1826).

9. An estimated $12 million in capital was withdrawn from Mexico by the Spaniards driven out under the law of Mar. 20, 1829. Lucas Alamán, *Historia de México*, 5:640. For a recent study that questions the economic significance of the expulsion law of Mar. 20, 1829, see Romeo Flores Caballero, *La contrarevolución en la independencia* (Mexico: El Colegio de México, 1969), pp. 139 – 55.

10. See chap. 2, nn. 29, 57; see also *A los habitantes del estado de Puebla. Su congreso constituyente* (Puebla, 1825); *Memoria presentada al congreso de Puebla de los Ángeles . . . año de 1827* (Puebla, 1827), pp. 23 – 24.

11. Mateos, *Historia parlamentaria*, 5:312, 327, 542.

12. *Discusión habida en la sala de sesiones del honorable congreso de la Puebla sobre el proyecto del Ciudadano José María Godoy . . .* (Puebla, 1829), remarks of Deputy González. It is questionable that so many were actually in use. The deputy cited no authority for his statement.

13. The state government in 1825 had provided vocational fellowships for two craftsmen, Vicente Enríquez and José María Manso, to study textile and other industries in the United States and Europe respectively, and to bring back useful tools. Subsequently, funds were appropriated to finance public tests of the knowledge so acquired. It was reported by 1829 that 16 looms, as well as spinning apparatus, had been constructed in Puebla on the basis of foreign models. *Colección de los decretos . . . que espidió el congreso constituyente del estado de Puebla en los años de 1824 . . . 1831* (Puebla, 1827 – 1832), 1:80; 2:91, 103; *Memoria presentada al congreso constitucional de Puebla . . . por el secretario del despacho de gobierno. . . .* (Mexico, 1826), pp. 24 – 26.

14. Luis Chávez Orozco, *Historia de México* (México: Editorial Patria, 1947), pp. 220 – 23; *Dictamen de la comisión de industria de la cámara de diputados sobre el nuevo arbitrio para dar . . . medios de subsistir a la clase de gentes pobres de la república mexicana* (Mexico, 1829), pp. 3 – 4.

15. *Dictamen de la comisión de industria*, pp. 16 – 17.

16. Ibid., passim.

17. Ibid., p. 12.

18. *Discusión habida en la sala de sesiones*.

19. Luis Chávez Orozco, *Historia de México*, pp. 364 – 71.

20. *Dictamen de las comisiones unidas de hacienda, comercio, agricultura y artes de la honorable legislatura de Puebla sobre el nuevo arbitrio que propone el C. José María Godoy, Guillermo Dollar y Jorge Winterton* (Puebla, 1829).

21. *Discusión habida en la sala de sesiones*, remarks of Deputy Callejo.

22. Session of Feb. 25, 1829, reported in *Correo de la Federación*, Apr. 10, 1829; see also the speech that day of the Puebla deputy, Sr. Guadalajara, ibid., Mar. 21, 1829.

23. *Segundo dictamen de la comisión de industria sobre el proyecto de Godoy y Compañía* (Mexico, 1829).

24. Juan Ignacio Godoy, *Exposición que se dirige no a la Cámara sino en particular a cada uno de los señores diputados, presentando sólo hechos de los más notables* (Mexico, 1829), p. 5.

25. Ibid.

26. Ibid., pp. 6 – 7; J. I. Godoy, *Explicación de los estados que la ciudad de Puebla remitió a México para impugnar el proyecto del ciudadano Godoy* (México, 1829).

27. Pueblan artisans showed their appreciation of their representatives' successful fight against the Godoy project by weaving them fancy waistcoats. *El Patriota* (Puebla), Mar. 20, 1829, reprinted in *Correo de la Federación*, Mar. 26, 1829.

28. "Providencia de la secretaría de hacienda de 15 de junio de 1829," Basilio José Arrillaga, comp. *Recopilación de leyes, decretos, bandos, reglamentos, circulares y providencias de los supremos poderes y otras autoridades de la República mexicana*, 17 vols. in 16 (Mexico, 1834 – 1850), 1:136.

29. *Memoria . . . del estado libre de México* (Tlalpam, 1829), p. 14. Zavala was governor of the state of Mexico until he became finance minister a month after presenting the above report.

30. *Correo de la Federación*, May 13 and 14, 1829, editorials; see also Zavala, *Ensayo historico*, 2:304.

31. *Correo de la Federación*, Oct. 7 and 9, 1829.

32. Chamber session, Aug. 18 and 25, 1829, Mateos, *Historia parlamentaria*, 5:576 ff.

33. Manifesto signed by the deputies from Puebla. *Correo de la Federación*, Aug. 29, 1829.

34. Ibid.

35. "Circular de la secretaría de hacienda de 7 de diciembre de 1829," Arrillaga, *Recopilación, p. 362*.

CHAPTER 4

1. See Ortiz de la Torre, "Discurso de un diputado," p. 301; see also *El Águila*, Jan. 30, 1828.

2. *Correo de la Federación*, May 13, 1829.

3. *Balanza general del comercio marítimo por los puertos de la república mexicana en los años de 1825 – 1828*, 4 vols. (Mexico, 1827 – 1831).

4. *Balanza general*, 1827, n. 14.

5. "Informe del Departmento de cuenta y razón," Feb. 3, 1830, *RO*, Mar. 3, 1830.

6. Ibid.

7. *RO*, Mar. 3, 1830.

8. Chávez Orozco, *Historia de México*, p. 267.

9. José C. Valadés, *Alamán estadista e historiador* (Mexico: José Porrua e Hijos, 1938), p. 280.

10. Jared Sparks, "Gold and Silver in Mexico," *North American Review* 21 (1825): 434 – 35.

11. *Memoria de la secretaría de estado y del despacho de relaciones interiores y exteriores*, 1830 (Mexico, 1830), p. 30.

12. Ibid., p. 29.

13. Cf. "Indicaciones económico-políticas," *El Observador*, Mar. 10, 1830, pp. 29 – 46; see

also Mora's later statement of the economic liberal's position in *El Indicador de la Federación Mexicana*, Feb. 5, 1834.

14. *Memoria de . . . relaciones*, 1830, p. 29.

15. Law of Apr. 6, 1830, *RO*, Apr. 7, 1830.

16. The text of Alamán's recommendations is given in V. Filisola, *Memoria para la historia de la guerra de Tejas* (Mexico: I. Cumplido, 1848 – 1849), 2:590 – 612.

17. "Dictamen de la comisión especial de la integridad del territorio de la república," Feb. 25, 1830, *RO*, Mar. 3, 1830.

18. Law of Apr. 6, 1830, art. 16. The provisions of this article were extended to include promotion of the woolen industry. Law of Apr. 16, 1830, Dublán and Lozano, *Legislación mexicana*, 2:242.

19. Article 1 specified that the suspension would lapse on Jan. 1, 1831, except at Pacific ports, where it would continue until June 30, 1831.

20. In contrast, it specified that $500,000 would be set aside for the security and colonization measures in Texas, and another $300,000 as a special fund in case of a new Spanish invasion. Law of Apr. 6, 1830, arts. 14, 17, 18.

21. Circular of Apr. 3, 1830, *RO*, Apr. 7, 1830.

22. See below, chap. 5.

23. "Iniciativa de ley," July 5, 1830, *RO*, July 7, 1830.

24. Ibid.

25. M. Payno, "Un viaje a Veracruz en el invierno de 1843, carta 4ª," *El Museo Mexicano* 3 (1843): 163 – 64. The context of the accusation is as follows: "Around the year 1830, there was a very industrious and dedicated employee who worked next to an excellent old man, Don Ildefonso Maniau. In his free time, he began to consult books and to write up many drafts which soon formed a hefty notebook. That notebook contained nothing less than the proposal for a vocational school and the establishment of a national industrial bank. Various governmental magnates, of the type that have traveled in Europe and pass for men of great talents and political skills, in a word, one of those regrettably historical men, saw the project, took possession of it, modified it, varied it, and proclaimed himself its owner and author. Industry came into its own, and here we have a man, who at the same time that he established a factory with funds from the bank, strutted about with the glory of a national, humane, philanthropic idea. Meanwhile, the employee, who had been its author, remained in obscurity and misery, without even being able to provide his children with the elements of an education. This employee is a person very close to me, and for whom I have a tender and considerable affection."

26. José Manuel Payno y Bustamante was listed as the *oficial* of the *Primera Sección, Mesa Primera* of this department. *Guía de Hacienda de la república mexicana* (Mexico, 1825), p. 15.

27. Chamber of Deputies session of July 14, 1830, in *RO*, July 24, 1830. On Feb. 10, 1829, the original motion to prohibit the same textiles had been overwhelmingly adopted, 47 to 10. An analysis of the votes cast on the two occasions reveals that 21 of the 47 were not recorded as present on July 14; 7 were consistent in voting against allowing the textiles to enter; while 19 reversed themselves and voted in favor of it. Ten who had not been recorded on Feb. 10, 1829, and 4 who had voted "No" at that time also supported the bank motion. Mateos, *Historia parlamentaria*, 5:364.

28. See "Iniciativa de ley," July 5, 1830, arts. 1, 2.

29. Ibid., art. 3; *Estracto de las sesiones de la cámara de senadores del congreso de la unión* (Mexico, 1830), sessions of Sept. 24, Oct. 14, 1830.

30. The full measure of this opportunity may be gathered from the fact that the government was authorized to pay 3 percent *per month* for a loan to get the bank operating at once. The authority was never used. See Appendix A, art. 4.

31. Zavala, *Ensayo histórico*, 2:305; see also *El Faro*, no. 110, cited in *RO*, Nov. 15, 1830; *El Fenix*, Feb. 17, 1834.

32. *Dos años en Méjico ó Memorias críticas sobre los principales sucesos de la República ... desde la invasión de Barradas hasta la declaración del puerto de Tampico contra el gobierno del General Bustamante* (Valencia: Cabrerizo, 1832), p. 74.

33. Zavala, *Ensayo histórico*, 2:327, 325; *Dos años en Méjico*, p. 74; José María Bocanegra, *Memorias para la historia de México independiente* (Mexico: Impr. del Gobierno Federal, 1897), 2:163. Bocanegra, like Zavala, had been a cabinet member under Guerrero.

34. *RO*, Oct. 23, 24, 1830, Mar. 12, 1831.

35. See n. 19.

36. Customs duties collected on cotton goods in the fiscal year 1830 − 31 were $1,588,266. *Memoria que sobre el estado de la hacienda nacional presentó ... el ministro del ramo en julio de 1845* (Mexico, 1846), table opp. p. 122.

37. Foreign merchandise was required to pay a new 5-percent consumption duty (it already paid one such duty to the states) by a decree enacted while the bank act was under consideration. Decree of Aug. 24, 1830, Dublán and Lozano, *Legislación mexicana*, 2:283.

38. *Regeneración política de la república mexicana* (Mexico), Aug. 14, 1830; see also references cited in nn. 39, 40.

39. *Los males de la república y el modo de esterminarlos o sea Plan de espulsión contra coyotes y estrangeros* (Guadalajara, 1831).

40. Chamber of Deputies session of Aug. 27, 1831, in *RO*, Sept. 1, 1831. Pedro Azcué y Zalvide, *Contestación a los editores del Sol y del Registro o sea observaciones sobre el banco de avío* (Mexico, 1831).

41. Chamber sessions Aug. 27 to Sept. 24, 1831, in *RO*, Sept. 1 − Oct. 31, 1831; see also editorials in *RO*, Sept. 3, 15, 23, 1831. The legislatures of San Luis Potosí, Michoacán, Tamaulipas, Guanajuato, and Querétaro all passed resolutions opposing Azcué's efforts to destroy the bank.

42. *RO*, Sept. 23, 1831.

CHAPTER 5

1. MSS in AGN, Ramo de Gobernación, leg. 118, exp. 36; Libro de actas de la Junta establecida para la Dirección del Banco de Avío por ley de 16 de Octubre de 1830, MS in AGN, 1 v. (hereafter referred to as Libro de Actas), Nov. 5, 1830.

2. Sánchez Papers, MSS in University of Texas Library.

3. Less famous than his brother Ignacio, Ramón Rayón distinguished himself in the defense of Zitácuaro in 1811. For other details about his career, see Antonio García Cubas, *Diccionario geográfico, histórico y biográfico de los Estados Unidos Mexicanos* (Mexico: Murguía, 1888 − 1891), 4:425 − 26

4. Santiago Aldazoro, *Exposición presentada a la Cámara de diputados....* (Mexico, 1841), p. 11, n. 2.

5. Arrillaga is perhaps best known for his work in compiling legislative and executive decrees, which he began to publish subsequent to his appointment to the bank. See John T. Vance and Helen L. Clagett, *A Guide to the Law and Legal Literature of Mexico* (Washington: Library of Congress, 1945), pp. 26–27.

6. Libro de Actas, May 9, 1831.

7. Ibid., Dec. 30, 1830.

8. The salaries paid to the staff amounted to only $1,790 for the first year, certainly not a large amount for five men; in 1832 the junta raised the salaries to a total of $2,700 on the grounds that the increases were needed to preserve the honesty of the employees. Libro de Actas, Jan. 10, 1832.

9. Finance Ministry circular, Nov. 4, 1830, in Dublán and Lozano, *Legislación mexicana,* 2:297.

10. Libro de Actas, Nov. 19, 1830; May 9, 30, and Oct. 14, 1831.

11. Ibid., May 30 and June 10, 1831; Contaduría del Banco de Avío, Copia del Manual de Data en numerario, 1831, 1832, MSS in AGN, B/A, 1; "Informe y cuentas que el Banco de Avío presenta . . . ," Jan. 1, 1832, *Memoria de la secretaría . . . de relaciones interiores y exteriores* (Mexico, 1832), Doc. no. 2, p. 27.

12. The complete text is given in Appendix B.

13. Banco de Avío MSS in the Sociedad Mexicana de Geografía e Estadística, Mexico City.

14. Appendix C contains a list of the replies; those treating areas presently within the limits of the United States were published by the writer in the *New Mexico Historical Review* 24 (1949): 332–40.

15. Revillagigedo used the 1793 data in his famous confidential report to his successor, as did Baron von Humboldt in his *Political Essay;* the Consulado material has been published under the title *Relaciones estadísticas de Nueva España de principios del siglo XIX,* Archivo Histórico de Hacienda, no. 3 (Mexico, 1944).

16. Quoted from the editor's introduction to the first volume in the series, *Instrucción sobre el cultivo de moreras y cría de gusanos de seda. . .* , 2d ed. (Mexico, 1830).

17. In addition to the work cited in the previous note, these were *Memoria sobre las abejas, traducida del francés por el corresponsal de la junta directiva del Banco de Avío* (México, 1831); C. P. Lasteirie, *Tratado sobre el ganado lanar de España traducido del francés de orden del supremo gobierno. . . .* (Mexico, 1831).

18. Typical were the *Cartilla para colmenares* (Mexico, 1831) and the *Cartilla sobre cría de gusanos de seda* (Mexico, 1831), written by Tomás Illanes of Jalapa. The junta referred numerous manuscripts to the editors of the *Registro Oficial* for publication in its regular columns and in its supplement, the *Registro Trimestre.*

19. MSS in AGN, B/A, 1, exps. 48, 78, 118; Libro de Actas, Dec. 7, 1830 and Jul. 11, 1831; *RO,* Jan. 5, 1831; *Esposición que el tercer gobernador del estado hizo . . . el 2 de julio de 1832* (Oaxaca, 1832), pp. 26–27.

20. Libro de Actas, Nov. 9, 19, 1830; *RO,* Nov. 24, 1830; "Informe y cuentas," Jan. 1, 1832, pp. 23–25.

21. *RO,* Oct. 20, 1830.

22. The average U.S. spinning mill in 1831 had 1,500 spindles. See Victor S. Clark, *History of Manufactures in the United States,* 2 vols. (Washington, D.C.: Carnegie Institution, 1916–1928), 1:452.

23. *RO,* Apr. 16, 1831.

24. For a discussion of the ginning problem, see chap. 1.

25. Martínez Pizarro to Dirección del Banco de Avío, New Orleans, Jan. 15, 1831, printed in *RO*, Feb. 17, 1831, "Informe y cuentas," Jan. 1, 1832, p. 21.
26. Tomás Murphy to Dirección, París, Jul. 17, 1831, printed in *RO*, Oct. 1, 1831; Libro de Actas, Nov. 19, 1830; *RO*, Feb. 19, 1832.
27. Libro de Actas, Feb. 4, 1831; MSS in AGN, B/A, 1, exp. 88.
28. Curiously, the Libro de Actas makes no reference to this proposed legislation; conceivably Alamán did not consult his colleagues, but it is also likely that the matter was discussed informally, and not made part of the record.
29. *Memoria de la secretaría de ... relaciones* (Mexico, 1831), app. Inititiative no. 5, arts. 1, 2.
30. *Estracto de las sesiones de la Cámara de representantes del Congreso de la Unión* (México, 1831), sessions of Mar. 1 to May 16, 1831; also the Dictamen de la comisión de hacienda, ibid., session of Feb. 21, 1831.
31. Jesús Silva Herzog, *El pensamiento económico en Mexico* (Mexico: Fondo de Cultura Económica, 1947), p. 52.
32. For Alamán's explanation of the decision to form the companies, see the *Memoria de ... relaciones*, 1832, p. 18.
33. Circular de la secretaría de relaciones, Apr. 26, 1830, Dublán and Lozano, *Legislación mexicana*, 2:244.
34. The paid-in capital was much less, amounting to only $18,850 on Dec. 16, 1831; see "Razón de las cantidades que han pagado y están debiendo los Señores accionistas de la compañía Industrial Mejicana," MS in AGN, Ramo de Gobernación, leg. 118, exp. 35; for Alamán's role in promoting the company, see ibid., exps. 17 and 21.
35. The three were set up in Tlalnepantla, Tlaxcala, and Puebla. Ibid., exps. 30, 31, 37, 74; *RO*, Nov. 3, 4, 28, 1830; *Idea de la sociedad patriótica formada en este capital del estado de Puebla para fomento de las artes* (Puebla, 1831).
36. MSS in AGN, B/A, 1, exps. 48, 49, 56, 60, 65, 68, 69, 78.
37. The fourteen included the one formed in Mexico City in 1830; the others were located in Tlalnepantla, Tlaxcala, Puebla, San Andrés Tuxtla, Querétaro, Morelia, León, San Miguel Allende, Celaya, San Luis Potosí, Chihuahua, Parral, and Cuencamé. "Informe y cuentas," Jan. 1, 1832, p. 20.
38. These two were at Parral and Chihuahua; See J. Agustín Escudero to Dirección, Chihuahua, Oct. 18, 1831, MS in AGN, B/A, 1, exp. 72.
39. Gómez Linares to Lucas Alamán, Guanajuato, Feb. 4, 1831, MS in University of Texas Library, Hernández y Dávalos Papers, exp. 21, no. 4804.
40. Juan José de Zimavilla, "Esposición que manifiesta el establecimiento, progresos y estado de la compañía de industria de Celaya . . ," *RO*, Aug. 31, 1831; Gómez Linares to Dirección, Mar. 18, 1831, printed in *RO*, Mar. 24, 1831; see also the letter dated May 2 and printed ibid., July 13, 1831.
41. Twenty-nine officeholders pledged $4,050 of the total $15,350: twenty-one merchants pledged $2,950; see Zimavilla, "Exposición," *RO*, Aug. 31, 1831.
42. The Celaya company listed one cofradía and six priests as shareholders; the cabildo ecclesiástico of Mexico contributed to the local company, as did that of Puebla.
43. Clergy were prominent in the San Andrés Tuxtla, Puebla, León, and Celaya companies, and possibly in others. Father Zimavilla was board chairman at Celaya and Father Antonio de la Rosa at Puebla. For a description of the Puebla bishop's activities, see Francisco Pablo Vásquez to Lucas Alamán, Puebla, Dec. 22, 1831, MS in University of Texas Library, García Collection, Alamán Papers.

44. For the junta's inability to supply cost data on request, see Libro de Actas, June 23, 1831; see also its correspondence with the privately formed Chihuahua company, MSS in AGN, B/A, 1, exp. 72.

CHAPTER 6

1. "Invitación hecha al Gobierno político de Colima sobre fomento de diversos ramos de industria en aquel territorio," MS in AGN, B/A, 1, exp. 74.
2. Libro de Actas, Jan. 31, 1831.
3. Dirección to Tomás Illanes, Apr. 2, 1831, MS in AGN, B/A, 1, exp. 82; see also letter to same, dated Apr. 20, 1831, ibid., exp. 75.
4. Libro de Actas, June 10, 14, 1831. This reversal of policy inevitably produced hard feelings among the frustrated applicants. Most forthright was one Manuel Fernández Aguado, who had earlier been encouraged to lease a hacienda with the idea that the bank would provide funds and equipment to operate a cotton plantation: "If I had taken this finca on the basis of that expectation, I would now be looking for the highest tree on which to hang myself; such is the extremity to which pledges drive a man of honor."MS in AGN, B/A, 1, exp. 52.
5. Libro de Actas, Apr. 19, 1831. No iron smelters were in operation in Mexico at this time, although an attempt had been made since 1828 to erect one in the state of Durango.
6. Ibid., Dec. 3, 7, 1830; "Informe y cuentas que el Banco de Avío presenta," Jan. 1, 1832, Memoria de la secretaría . . . de relaciones interiores y esteriores (México, 1832), Doc. no. 2, pp. 18, 25.
7. Libro de Actas, Dec. 21, 1830; Jan. 31, 1831.
8. Ibid., Apr. 7, 19, 1831. For von Geroldt's role, see C. C. Becher, Mexico in den ereignissvollen Jahren 1832 und 1833 und die Reise hin und zurück. . . . (Hamburg: Perthes & Besser, 1834), p. 91.
9. Libro de Actas, Apr. 19, May 27, 1831.
10. MSS in AGN, B/A, 1, exps. 74, 86.
11. "Solicitud de D. Laureano de la Torre, vecino de Minatitlán, recomendada por el Supremo Gobierno, para que se le habilite con 10,000 pesos a efecto de poner allí una fábrica de papel," MS in AGN, B/A, 1, exp. 94.
12. Dirección to Secretario de Relaciones, Apr. 20, 1831; Dirección to de la Torre, June 15, 1831, ibid.
13. Strictly speaking, the $1,500 loan to Casarín was granted for a new project; the sawmill for which the previous loan had been granted had not been successful, due partly to the cutthroat competition that Casarín had to face. For details, see ibid., exp. 26.
14. See sources cited above in chap. 5, n. 34.
15. Valadés, Alamán, pp. 214, 226.
16. "Informe y cuentas," Jan. 1, 1832, p. 21.
17. Libro de Actas, Nov. 19, 1830; Dirección to López Pimental, Feb. 26, 1831, MS in AGN, B/A, 1, exp. 57.
18. Libro de Actas, Aug. 17 and Oct. 14, 1831.
19. Ibid., Nov. 11, 1831.
20. Ibid. The junta decided at the same time to assign a paper mill expected from the United States to the San Miguel Industrial Company.
21. Ibid., Dec. 20, 1831.

22. While the junta couldn't get the company even to reply to its letters, it learned that Antuñano had already purchased, as the site for his proposed factory, the Molino de Santo Domingo, which controlled valuable water rights on the Atoyac River. Libro de Actas, Oct. 14, Dec. 16, 1831. The shrewdness of this purchase was demonstrated in later years when the owner was able to sell water and sites for other factories. The interesting history of this property, and its transformation from a clerical possession to the site of several cotton and paper mills, is given in records which were generously made available by Sr. Enrique Villar of Puebla, who owned the Antuñano-built cotton mill, La Economía, in the 1940s.

23. *Idea de la sociedad patriótica formada en este capital del estado de Puebla para fomento de las artes* (Puebla, 1831); Francisco Pablo Vásquez to Lucas Alamán, Puebla, Dec. 26, 1831, MS in Alamán Papers, García Collection, University of Texas.

24. The details of the individual contracts can be examined at the Archivo de Notarías; for the names of the pertinent notaries, see Bibliography.

25. Libro de Actas, Feb. 7, 1832.

26. Ibid., June 14, Dec. 5, 1831. The necessity for precautions against misuse of bank funds was also revealed in the Sánchez loan. The borrower had received $5,000 on collateral provided by a *fiador* (bondsman), Col. Munuera of Tlaxcala; the latter soon suspected Sánchez of absconding with the money, and through legal action was able to recover $4,000 before Sánchez unexpectedly died. The junta moved to have the fiador repay the full amount at once, but Munuera, through legal maneuvers, persuaded it to accede to his request that he retain the loan for the original five years on the basis of fulfilling Sánchez's project, the construction of an apiary. Subsequent investigation revealed that Munuera, in violation of his contract, sold the property he had pledged as security to a Puebla prebendary, Antonio González Cruz. The latter had acted in good faith in purchasing the property, and was prepared to repay the loan as a simple mortgage, but the apiary, for which the money was advanced originally, was never developed. MSS in AGN, B/A, 1, exp. 40.

27. See tables 1 and 2 above.

28. In this category were the Vallarta, Sánchez, and Tlalnepantla loans; also $12,000 of the $50,000 given to the Zacualpa de Amilpas Co., $21,000 of the $30,000 given to Antuñano, and $20,000 of the $30,000 given to the Querétaro Industrial Co.

29. The provision applied to the Celaya Co. loan, and to $10,000 of the sum advanced to the Querétaro Co. The details of the contracts are given in Libro de Actas, Jan. 26, Feb. 21, 1832.

30. "Informe y cuentas," Jan. 1, 1832, p. 21.

31. Libro de Actas, Sept. 30, 1831.

32. Ibid., Sept. 30, 1831, Feb. 16, 1832.

CHAPTER 7

1. *RO*, June 14, 1832.

2. "Informe y cuentas que el Banco de Avío presenta," Dec. 31, 1832, *Memoria de la secretaria de . . . relaciones* (México, 1833), appendix 4, p. 8.

3. The annual salary bill for the woolen-mill technicians was $9,200, for the silk experts, $3,400; after the arrival of the latter group, the junta sent word abroad to cancel the departures of the other technicians. Ibid., p. 10.

4. Ibid., passim.

5. Ibid., p. 9

6. "Exposición hecha al Gobierno, solicitando inicie a las Cámaras se autorize al Banco p^a negociar un préstamo de 100,000 ps . . . ," Apr. 28, 1832, MS in AGN, B/A, 2, no. 80.

7. Law of May 25, 1832, Dublán and Lozano, *Legislación mexicana*, 2:437. This loan has been misinterpreted as an attempt by the Treasury to borrow from the bank. See Luis Chávez Orozco, *Historia de México*, p. 375.

8. "Informe y cuentas," Dec. 31, 1832, p. 7.

9. Art. 9, Law of Mar. 31, 1831, Dublán and Lozano, *Legislación mexicana*, 2:320.

10. Antuñano and the Tlálpam company each received $9,000 to complete loans approved on Dec. 16, 1831, and June 1, 1832, respectively. Ramón Rayón to Oficial Mayor Encargado de la Secretaría de Relaciones, Aug. 2, 1832, and Aug. 17, 1832, MSS in AGN, Ind. 1832 — 34, exp. 119.

11. The first reference to the new policy on *comisos* is found in a note to the Comisario General de Chiapas dated June 18; a general directive was issued on Aug. 17; the junta had sold the draft on the Sinaloa deposit on June 6. MSS in AGN, B/A, 2, Hacienda Cuadernos 1, 2.

12. Ramón Rayón to Oficial Mayor de Relaciones, Aug. 2, 1832; Rafael Mangino to Oficial Mayor de Relaciones, Aug. 10, 1832. MSS in AGN, Ind. 1832 — 34, exp. 119. The junta recovered the $9,000 from the Tlálpam company, but only $3,000 from Antuñano, who had already spent the balance.

13. "Informe y cuentas," Dec. 31, 1832, p. 7.

14. The fact that the first two men who were offered Aldazoro's post begged off on grounds of ill health suggests that membership on the junta was not regarded as a political plum. MSS in AGN, Ind. 1832 — 34, exps. 130 — 31.

15. MSS in AGN, Ind. 1832 — 34, exps. 95, 98; B/A, 2, Hacienda Cuadernos 3, 4.

16. González Angulo to Secretario de Hacienda, Feb. 15, 1833, MS in AGN, B/A, 2, Hacienda Cuaderno 4.

17. Sánchez to Secretario de Relaciones, Feb. 13, 1833; González Angulo to Secretario de Hacienda, Feb. 15, 1833(copy), MSS in AGN, Ind. 1832 — 34, exp. 129.

18. Secretario de Hacienda to Director General de Rentas, Mar. 1, 1833; Mar. 8, 1833, MSS in AGN, B/A, 2, Hacienda Cuaderno 4.

19. The Bustamante government had agreed to pay 5 percent monthly to place its hands on cash during its final struggle for existence. See Edgar Turlington, *Mexico and Her Foreign Creditors* (New York: Columbia University Press, 1930), p. 63.

20. Ibid., p. 69; Decrees of Jan 7, Feb. 12, 1833, Dublán and Lozano, *Legislación mexicana*, 2:475, 487 — 88.

21. See MSS cited in n. 18.

22. The contracts with foreign technicians involved the national credit, a fact that French minister Baron Deffandis was prompt to point out when payments of debts to individuals of his nationality lagged. See MSS in AGN, Ind. 1832 — 34, exps. 146, 148.

23. "Relación de las personas que han sido secretarios de . . . Hacienda," *Boletín Semanario del Ministerio de Hacienda* 1 (1853): 48 — 53; *Funcionarios de la secretaría de relaciones desde el año de 1821 a 1940* (México, 1940), p. 27.

24. *Informe presentado . . . por el contador major, gefe de la oficina de rezagos, Juan Antonio de Unzueta . . .* (México, 1833).

25. Roa to Vocales de la Junta, Oct. 1, 1833, MS in AGN, Ind. 1832 – 34, exp. 157.
26. Sánchez to Secretario de Relaciones, Oct. 22, 1833, ibid.
27. Secretario de Relaciones to Vicepresidente de la Junta, Nov. 13, 1833, ibid.
28. Francisco Lombardo, to Secretario de Hacienda, Jan. 20, 1834, MS in AGN, B/A, 2, Hacienda Cuaderno 6.
29. MSS in AGN, B/A, 2, Dirección General de Rentas, Año de 1833, exp. 758; B/A, 2, Hacienda Cuaderno 4, 6; Ind. 1832 – 34, exps. 95, 98.
30. See chap. 6.
31. Lombardo to Vicepresidente de la Junta, Jan. 17, 1834, Dirección del Banco de Avío to Secretario de Relaciones, Jan. 29, 1834, MSS in AGN, B/A, 1, exp. 40.
32. Lombardo to Vicepresidente de la Junta, Feb. 7, 1834, ibid.
33. Same to same, March 18, 1834, ibid.
34. Same to same, Aug. 14, 1834, ibid.
35. MSS in AGN, Ind. 1832 – 34, exps. 139, 155, 167; "Relación circunstanciada de las habilitaciones dadas por el Banco de Avío," *Memoria del ministerio de lo interior* (Mexico, 1838), pp. 56 – 59.
36. Gutiérrez Estrada to Secretario de Hacienda, Mar. 30, 1835, MS in AGN, B/A, 2, Hacienda Cuaderno 6.
37. *Memoria de la secretaría de . . . relaciones interiores y exteriores* (Mexico, 1831), p. 24.
38. Secretario de Relaciones (García) to Vicepresidente de la Junta, Nov. 2, 1833; Nov. 13, 1833; and Dec. 7, 1833, MSS in AGN, Ind. 1832 – 34, exps, 156, 157, 160.
39. Under the agreements, the purchaser promised to "pay the value of the machines with the sixth part of the profits obtained, one month after the factory is found to be in full operation." No special security was required and no time limit was fixed for full payment. See escrituras dated Nov. 23, 1833, Jan. 8, 1834, MSS in AN, Madariaga 1833, 939r – 941r, 1834, 24r – 26v.
40. Lombardo took over as acting minister on Dec. 16, and as minister on Jan. 10, 1834. For a complete list of the officials who served as chairman, ex-officio, of the junta, see Appendix D.
41. Lombardo announced that payments had to be made on a time schedule, rather than as a percentage of hypothetical profits; the entrepreneurs proposed a seven-year period with payments to begin in the third year, but this was cut down to four years, with payments to begin in the second. MSS in AGN, Ind. 1832 – 34, exp. 165.
42. Secretario de Relaciones (Lombardo) to Governor of the State of Puebla, Feb. 11, 1834, April 9, 1834. MSS in AGN, Ind. 1832 – 34, exp. 156.
43. Fifty thousand dollars were sent to the United States to pay debts on machinery. Lombardo to Secretario de Hacienda, June 2, 1834, MS in AGN, B/A, 2, Hacienda Cuaderno 6.
44. Secretario de Relaciones (Lombardo) to Vicepresidente de la Junta, Dec. 14, 1833, MS in AGN, Ind. 1832 – 34, exp. 162.
45. Lombardo to Secretario de Hacienda, Jan. 25, 1834, and Mar. 14, 1834. MSS in AGN, B/A, 2, Hacienda Cuaderno 6.
46. See MSS in AGN, B/A, 2, exps, 162, 163, for the handling of the requests of Bernardo González Angulo and Ignacio Leal; for the Antuñano loan, see Secretario de Relaciones to Vicepresidente de la Junta, Feb. 25, 1834, MS in AGN, Ind. 1832 – 34, exp. 98.
47. The Second Finance Committee of the Lower Chamber requested information on the bank's accumulated capital, but took no further action.

48. Exposition dated June 10, 1834, MS in AGN, Ind. 1832 – 34, exp. 136.
49. "Informe y cuentas que el Banco de Avío presenta," Jan. 1, 1835, *Memoria de la secretaría de . . . relaciones* (Mexico, 1835), p. 25.
50. Ibid., passim.
51. Ibid., p. 24.
52. This included $126,000 in loans and $37,916 in equipment. Only one wing of the factory was in operation; to complete the other wing, Antuñano requested, and promptly obtained, a new advance of $30,000; but since this was given in the form of Treasury *órdenes*, he had difficulty in discounting them, and subsequently returned part of them as useless. His net indebtedness to the bank was $184,000.

CHAPTER 8

1. Riva Palacio, *México a través de los siglos*, 4:358.
2. Sánchez y Mora to Secretario de Relaciones, Feb. 10, 1835, MS in AGN, Ind. 1832 – 34, exp. 136.
3. Esteban de Antuñano, *Manifiesto sobre el algodón manufacturado y en greña* (Puebla, 1833), pp. 9 – 12; see also his *Ampliación y corrección a los principales puntos del manifiesto sobre el algodón manufacturado y en greña* (Puebla, 1833), pp. 1 – 33.
4. See the action of the Jalisco and Guanajuato state legislatures in requesting the exclusion of foreign yarn. Senate session of Apr. 3, 1834, Chamber of Deputies session of Jan. 8, 1835, in *El Telégrafo*, Apr. 10, 1834, Feb. 3, 1835.
5. Puebla law of Feb. 19, 1834, *Decretos y acuerdos expedidos por la tercera [y cuarta] legislatura constitucional del estado libre y soberano de Puebla* (Puebla, 1850), 1:131.
6. Esteban de Antuñano, *Discurso analítico de algunos puntos de moral y economía política de Méjico . . .* (Puebla, 1834), p. 46.
7. Chamber of Deputies, sessions of Feb. 11, Mar. 2, 24, Apr. 10; Senate session of Apr. 7, *DG*, Feb. 13, Mar. 2, Apr. 5, 22, 25, 1835.
8. Esteban de Antuñano y Gumesindo Saviñon, *Esposición respetuosa que los que subscriben elevan a las soberanas cámaras de la unión sobre la prohibición de artefactos gordos de algodón estranjeros* (Puebla, 1835).
9. No directive to this effect has been found, but from other evidence, it is clear that by Apr. 1835, the junta was enjoying its former autonomy of action.
10. Iniciative no. 7, *Memoria de la secretaría de`. . . relaciones interiores y exteriores* (Mexico, 1835), appendix, p. 15. Gutiérrez de Estrada submitted this report as of Mar. 24, 1835; it was read in the Chamber of Deputies two days later.
11. *DG*, Apr. 3 – 6, 1835. These columns were also printed as a pamphlet, *Reflecciones sobre la prohibición de hilazas y mantas estranjeras de algodón* (México, 1835).
12. *Dictamen de la comisión de industria sobre prohibición de hilazas y tegidos de algodón del estrangero. Presentado en la cámara de diputados, el dia 27 de marzo de 1835* (Mexico, 1835), p. 12.
13. Chamber of Deputies, session of Apr. 11, 1835, in *DG*, Apr. 15, 1835.
14. *DG*, Apr. 16, 1835.
15. *DG*, Apr. 22, 1835.
16. The official gazette pointedly announced that the names of those voting for the measure would be kept in mind. Ibid.
17. The pattern of the voting reveals that this is essentially a measure desired by a small

number of states where cotton growing or processing was a significant activity. The twenty-five deputies from Puebla, Jalisco, México, Oaxaca, and Yucatán who voted in favor of prohibiting foreign yarn would have needed only one additional vote to carry the measure alone. The actual vote was 30 − 20. Juan Mateos, *Historia parlamentaria*, 10, sessions of May 12 − 14, 1835; *DG*, May 21, 1835.

18. Senate sessions of May 18 − 21, 1835, *DG*, May 28 − 30, June 13, 1835.

19. The six deputies included 3 from Oaxaca, 2 from Jalisco, and 1 from Puebla. Session of May 13, 1835, in *DG*, May 21, 1835.

20. Chamber session of May 22, Senate session of May 23, 1835, in *DG*, June 21, 1835; for the exact text of the law, see Mariano Galván, comp. *Colección de órdenes*, 7:353.

21. The loan for Alamán's paper mill had been granted originally on June 1, 1832, a few days after he had resigned from the ministry. Political and financial circumstances postponed the loan's consummation. Alamán to Dirección, Mar. 13, 1835, MS in AGN, B/A, 2, exp. 146; for the other loans, see AGN, B/A, 2, Hacienda Cuaderno 6.

22. Sánchez y Mora to Secretario de Relaciones, June 3, 1835, MS in AGN, Ind. 1832 − 34, exp. 160.

23. S. Aldazoro, *Exposición presentada a la Cámara de diputados . . .* (México, 1841), pp. 5 − 7; "Relación circunstanciada de las habilitaciones dadas por el Banco de Avío," *Memoria del ministerio de lo interior* (México, 1838), pp. 40 − 42.

24. Sánchez y Mora to Secretario de Relaciones, May 30, 1833, MS in AGN, Ind. 1832 − 34, exp. 143.

25. Alamán to Dirección, June 23, 1835; Dirección to Alamán, June 30, 1835, MSS in AGN, B/A, 2, exp. 146.

26. Dirección to Agustín Vicente de Eguía, Feb. 20, 1835, MS in AGN, B/A, 1, exp. 109.

27. It was promulgated by the junta on Sept. 25, and approved by the Supreme Government on Oct. 5, 1835. The full text can be found in Dublán and Lozana, *Legislación mexicana*, 3:78 − 84.

28. For example, listed among the powers of the junta was that of promoting the establishment of industrial companies in the towns of the republic (art. 7, par. 3). Yet the junta itself, only three months before, had admitted that such companies were a failure. See Dirección to Alamán, June 30, 1835, MS in AGN, B/A, 2, exp. 146.

29. Art. 9.

30. Art. 8, par. 9; arts. 10 − 13.

31. Art. 15.

32. These were the loans to the Puebla Hospicio, Ignacio Leal, the Tlálpam Co., and General Barrera; each loan involved the development of equipment previously supplied by the bank.

33. Díaz de Bonilla to Secretario de Hacienda, Aug. 27, 1835, MS in AGN, B/A, 2, Hacienda Cuaderno 6; Sánchez y Mora to Secretario de Relaciones, Oct. 16, 1835, MS in AGN, Ind. 1832 − 34, exp. 129. The junta did try to have the Treasury assume the $91,000 debt in order to free bank funds for loans, but the debt remained unpaid.

34. Bank income from customs duties in the period Oct. 16, 1830 − Nov. 30, 1831, was only $459,393, and cotton-textile imports were higher than in any succeeding year.

35. Merchants offered only $24,000 for the $40,000 in drafts issued to the Puebla Hospicio. Manuel Rincón to Oficial Mayor Encargado de Relaciones, Nov. 14, 1835, MS in AGN, Ind. 1832 − 34, exp. 156.

36. See Appendix D.

37. For the Bracho, Sodi, and Tornel-Escandón loans, see "Relación circunstanciada," pp. 54 – 56; for the suspension of the Miranda-Padilla loans, see *DG*, Dec. 13, 1838.

38. "Relación circunstanciada," pp. 51 – 52.

39. Ibid., pp. 49 – 51, 64. Victoria's proposed project was to develop his Veracruz haciendas to produce cacao, cotton, and coffee for both domestic use and export.

40. Decree of Jan. 20, 1836, art. 15, Mariano Galván, *Colección*, 8:5. This law reorganized the assignment of all customs revenues; previously, a forced loan and a special war tax on urban property had been voted.

41. Ibid.; Congress session, Jan. 16, 1836, in *DG*, Jan. 20, 1836. The bicameral legislature had been converted into a unicameral body on Sept. 14, 1835.

42. Decrees of Mar. 7 and June 8, 1836, in Mariano Galván, *Colección*, 8:14, 47. The latter measure also provided that bank obligations other than drafts would be paid from the $15,000 installments.

43. Liquidación que presenta la contaduría de la dirección del Banco del Avío, Sept. 15, 1839, MS in AGN, B/A, 3, no. 68.

44. Ramón Pardo claimed that he had to make a contribution of $4,000 as a gift to the Treasury to get $40,000 in drafts exchanged for Treasury orders, and that he ultimately realized only $22,000. Statement of Ramón Pardo, Jan. 14, 1839, MS in AGN, B/A, 3, Pardo Papers, no. 3.

45. "Relación circunstanciada," pp. 64 – 65; Decree of Aug. 11, 1836, Mariano Galván, *Colección*, 8:75.

46. Congress sessions of Aug. 22, 24, Oct. 22, 1836, Jan. 31, 1837, *DG*, Aug. 26, 29, Oct. 30, 1836; Feb. 7, 1837.

47. Congress sessions of Oct. 29, 1836, in *DG*, Nov. 3, 1836. The requests of Aldazoro, Ruiz, and Roa were shelved in 1838, but the Tlálpam Co. kept the issue alive until 1842.

48. Alamán to Dirección, Dec. 14, 1836, MS in AGN, B/A, 2, exp. 146.

49. Ibid. The sum Alamán requested in Treasury orders was $60,000, or $10,000 more than the $50,000 he was committed to invest in the spinning mill.

50. Ibid.

51. This condition was included in the *dictamen* presented by the junta's vice-chairman, José Delmotte, on Dec. 20, and was approved on Dec. 23. Noteworthy among the other conditions was one obligating Alamán "never to request an exemption from the interest due on the capital . . ." and another whereby he agreed not to protest any loss that might be incurred through discounting the credits at Alvarado. MSS in AGN, B/A, 2, exp. 146.

52. This was a private contract that was formalized as an "escritura de compañía en comandita" on Sept. 20, 1837. MS in AN, Madariaga 1837, 1001v – 1005v.

53. Alamán to Vicepresidente de la Junta, Apr. 15, 1837 and May 2, 1837; Alamán to Ministro de lo Interior, Presidente del Banco de Avío, June 19, 1837. MSS in AGN, B/A, 2, exp. 146.

54. Manuel de Segura, "Apuntes estadísticas del distrito de Orizava formados el año de 1839," *Boletín del Instituto Nacional de Geografía y Estadística*, Época 1ª, 4 (1854): 24 ff.

CHAPTER 9

1. Newspapers consulted were the profederalist *La Oposición* and *El Cosmopolita*, the conservative *La Lima* and *El Mosquito Mexicano*, and the official *Diario del Gobierno*.

2. Including machinery valued at $22,320, and $50,000 in customs bills. "Relación circunstanciada," p. 42.

3. "Informe y cuentas que el Banco de Avío presenta . . . ," *Memoria de la secretaría . . . de relaciones interiores y exteriores* (México, 1832 — 1833, 1835). A report dated Dec. 31, 1833, was not published.

4. *El Cardillo de los Agiotistas* (Mexico, Apr.— May, 1837), nos. 1 — 5.

5. Ibid., no. 4.

6. MSS in AN, Madariaga, 1835, 90v — 94r, 534r — 537r; Gutiérrez Estrada to the Minister of Finance, Mexico, June 3, 1835, MS in AGN, B/A, 2, cuaderno 6; "Relación circunstanciada," p. 41.

7. The first legislature elected under the centralist constitution; it assembled on June 1, 1837.

8. Manuel de la Peña to Luis Ruiz, México, June 20, 1837, *DG*, Nov. 4, 1838.

9. "Relación circunstanciada," p. 72.

10. For Illanes's activity, see chap. 4; Chamber sessions, June 26, 29, 1837; Senate session, July 24, 1837, reported in *DG*, July 1, 8, 26, 1837.

11. *El Cosmopolita*, Feb. 17, 1838.

12. *DG*, Oct. 31, 1837.

13. *DG*, June 5, 1839. A good sketch of Cortina's manifold activities is given in García Cubas, *Diccionario geográfico*, 2:356 — 59.

14. Originally subordinate to the Relaciones Ministry, the Banco de Avío was placed under the newly created Interior Ministry in Jan. 1837.

15. "Actas de la Junta directiva del Banco de Avío," Mar. 30, 1838, *DG*, Apr. 26, 1838.

16. *El Cosmopolita* facetiously ascribed the source of its figures to a "hobgoblin" but their accuracy suggests that they were provided by someone who had access to the bank's files.

17. "Actas," Mar. 30, Apr. 2 and 5, 1838, *DG*, Apr. 26, May 18, 1838.

18. Santa Anna intervened at the request of the former employee's father, José María Icaza, then prefect of Mexico City. MSS in AGN, B/A, 3, exp. 89.

19. "Actas," May 2, 1838, *DG*, May 19, 1838; "Informe a los Srs. Vice Presidente y Vocales de la Dirección del Banco de Avío," July 11, 1840, MS in AGN, Tribunal de Cuentas, 77.

20. "Actas," May 7, June 25, July 2, 1838, *DG*, May 31, July 17, Nov. 4, 1838.

21. Mariano Marín to the Minister of the Interior, Mexico, July 19, 1839, MS in AGN, B/A, 3, exp. 68; "Informe a los Srs. Vice Presidente y Vocales," pp. 1 — 2.

22. Chamber of Deputies, sessions of Jan. 2, 9, 12, 1838; Feb. 18, 19, 20, 1839; reported in *DG*, Jan. 8, 23, 25, 1838, Mar. 2, 3, and 4, 1839.

23. "Informe a los Srs. Vice Presidente y Vocales," passim.

24. See n. 3.

25. Madrid himself described his duties as "encargado de cuenta y razón" when he asked for a salary increase on Dec. 16, 1831. "Solicitud de los empleados de esta Sría. para que se les aumente el sueldo que disfrutan en ella," MS in AGN, B/A, 1, exp. 137.

26. "Informe a los Srs Vice Presidente y Vocales," passim; *Informe y cuentas que el Banco de Avío presenta . . . 30 de enero de 1841* (Mexico, 1841), pp. 1 — 18; Viya y Cosío to the Minister of Justice, Mexico, Jan. 15, 1842, MS in AGN, B/A, 3, exp. 68.

27. "Actas," Mar. 30, Apr. 2, May 17, 1838, *DG*, Apr. 26, May 31, 1838.

28. "Actas," May 25, June 18, 1838, *DG*, June 29, July 6, 1838; also advertisement section, *DG*, July 6 — 13, 1838.

29. "Actas," Aug. 9, 1838, *DG*, Dec. 13, 1838.

30. "Actas," June 18, 1838, *DG*, July 6, 1838; Interior Ministry circular dated June 26, 1838, in Galván Rivera, 2:28.

31. *Informe y cuentas* . . . , 1841.

32. Ibid.

33. Ibid. The following sums were recovered:

Borrower	In cash or commercial paper	In bank-issued paper
E. Antuñano	$146,000	$ 30,000
A. González Cruz	1,500	—
Carlos Sodi	150	—
Luis Bracho	—	40,000
Tlálpam Textile Co.	—	40,000
Juan Icaza	—	50,000
M. Escandón	—	20,000
M. Barrera	—	16,000
Totals	$147,650	$196,000
Grand total	$343,650	

34. "Actas," Mar. 30, May 17, June 25, 1838, *DG*, Apr. 26, May 31, July 17, 1838; *Informe y cuentas* . . . , 1841.

35. "Actas," July 24, 1838, *DG*, Nov. 19, 1838; *Informe y cuentas* . . . , 1841. In 1847 the Treasury recovered $8,000 of the loan through the forced sale of a house belonging to Pardo's estate. MSS in AN, A badiano, 1847, 35v–44v.

36. Eduardo Gorostiza, Minister of Finance, to the Minister of the Interior, Mexico, July 27, and Aug. 14, 1838, MSS in AGN, Ramo de Justicia, 157, exp. 41.

37. Mariano Marín to the Minister of the Interior, Mexico, June 8, 1839, MS in AGN, B/A, 3, exp. 68.

38. Ibid.

39. Mariano Marín to the Minister of the Interior, Mexico, Oct. 25, 1839, published in *DG*, Nov. 10, 1839.

40. *Informe y cuentas* . . . , 1841, p. 11. The bank had $188,000 involved in the four cases before the court.

41. "Informe y cuentas que el Banco de Avío presenta . . . 1835," appendix, p. 27.

42. "Actas," Apr. 2, May 2, 1838, *DG*, Apr. 26, May 19, 1838; advertisement dated Sept. 28, 1840, *DG*, Oct. 5, 1840. Ironically, the year after the bank was dissolved, the animals it had introduced became much in demand because of the erection of two wool-textile factories. *MDG*, 1843, p. 34.

43. See chap. 10.

44. "Actas," June 25, 1838, *DG*, July 17, 1838; advertisement dated June 26, 1838, in *DG*, July 16, 1838.

45. *El Cosmopolita*, Mar. 24, 1838. The junta subsequently gave looms to bank employees

in lieu of unpaid salaries. "Actas," July 2, 1838, *DG*, Nov. 4, 1838; "Puntos de la sesión de 21 de octubre de 1838," MS in AGN, B/A, 3, Borradores de sesiones.

46. Minister of the Interior to the Vice-chairman of the Banco de Avío, Mexico, Aug. 11, 1839, MS in AGN, B/A, 3, Fauré Papers.

47. Vice-chairman of the Banco de Avío to the Minister of the Interior, Mexico, Aug. 17, 1839; "Liquidación que forma la Contaduría de este establecimiento a Don José Fauré," MSS AGN, B/A, Fauré Papers.

48. José Fauré to the Chairman and Members of the Junta, Mexico, Sept. 5, Oct. 19, 1839, MSS AGN, B/A, Fauré Papers. The appraisers fixed the current value of the woolen equipment at $9,150; it had cost the bank $40,240 delivered to Mexico City.

49. See chap. 8.

50. The finance minister obtained $45,000 in cash on the $83,000 in drafts. M. E. Gorostiza, *Gorostiza á sus conciudadanos o breve reseña de las operaciones del ministerio de hacienda* (Mexico, 1838), p. 21.

51. Board of Directors of the Banco de Avío to the Minister of Interior, Mexico, Nov. 13, 1839, MS file copy, in AGN, B/A, 3, exp. 90.

52. The background of this law will be discussed in detail in chap. 11.

53. Esteban de Antuñano, *Pensamientos para la regeneración industrial de México* (Puebla, 1837), p. 17.

54. "Actas," May 2, 25, 28, June 18, 1838, *DG*, May 19, June 29, July 6, 1838; advertisement of the Ferrería de Miraflores, *DG*, July 20, 1838.

55. MSS in AGN, B/A, 3, exp. 64 and 65.

56. Bernardo Mier and Francisco Villegas to the President of the Mexican Republic, Puebla, Nov. 25, 1841, MS in AGN, B/A, 3, exp. 65.

57. Legal advice was provided by the Promotor Fiscal, Lic. Mier y Altamirano, and for a short time by a specially hired attorney, Lic. Francisco Molinos del Campo. Molinos was engaged at a $1,500 annual stipend in June 1838; two months later, the junta, realizing it had no authority to create such a position, revoked the appointment, but, curiously enough, neglected to inform him until the following May, meanwhile calling on his services. When finally informed, Molinos, though much surprised, generously renounced his fees in favor of the funds of the bank. MSS in AGN, B/A, 3, exp. 72.

58. Statement of Contaduría of the Banco de Avío, Sept. 15, 1839, MS in AGN, B/A, 3, exp. 68.

59. The essentials of these loans were as follows:

Borrower	Purpose	Amount
Lucas Alamán	Expansion of Cocolapam spinning factory at Orizaba	$60,000
José Fauré	Expansion of Hospital de Naturales weaving factory at Mexico City	20,000
George Ainslee	Conversion of hand-weaving shop to power spinning and weaving in Mexico City	20,000
Agustín Montiel	Completion of glass factory in Puebla	10,000

MSS in AGN, B/A, 2, exp. 146; 3, 64; 3, Fauré Papers, MS in AN, Madariaga, 1839, 751v—760r.

60. MSS in AGN, B/A, 3, exp. 68.

61. Board of Directors to the Minister of the Interior, Mexico, Oct. 30, 1840, MS copy, AGN, B/A, 3, exp. 68.

62. In almost every case, the sums provided were less than those requested. In addition to $4,167 provided in cash to the Montiel glass works (see n. 59), the loans included: $1,000 to Jacinto Font to convert from cotton to wool weaving; $500 to José Faustino Samudio for tools for his iron foundry in Tlascala; and $6,000 to José Ignacio Guerrero to develop a cloth-printing factory at Puebla. *Informe y cuentas . . .*, 1841.

63. The available evidence indicates that the only sum loaned after Dec. 1840 was $1,167, given in cash to Agustín Montiel of the Puebla glass works. This sum and $3,000 in cash provided prior to that date were given to replace drafts issued to the company in 1839, and subsequently returned unused. MS in AN, Madariaga, 1839, 762r, marginal notation dated Nov. 18, 1842. The possibility that other small sums were advanced must be admitted, though no trace of them has been found.

CHAPTER 10

1. Chamber of Deputies session of Feb. 8, 1841, reported in *DG*, Feb. 20, 1841.

2. Documents detailing the founding of the association were published in *DG*, June 15, 1839; the official charter is given in Dublán and Lozano, *Legislación mexicana*, 3:632 – 34.

3. For example, Lucas Alamán, Santiago Aldazoro, and the principal owners of the Tlalpam cotton mill: Andrés Pizarro, Felipe Neri del Barrio, Manuel Portú, Estanislao Flores, and Joaquín Flores.

4. "Proyecto de ley de los Sres. Chico y otros tres sres. sobre nueva organización y denominación de la junta de industria establecida en esta capital," Mar. 23, 1841, MS in AGN, Ind. 1841 – 1843, exp. 9.

5. "Dictamen de la comisión de industria y primera de hacienda," July 14, 1841, ibid.

6. Andrés Pizarro, vice-president of the Junta de Industria, was director of the Tlalpam Co., which had been refusing since 1837 to pay interest to the bank; Santiago Aldazoro was likewise trying to avoid interest payments. *Informe y cuentas que el Banco de Avío presenta . . .*, Jan. 30, 1841 (Mexico, 1841); Santiago Aldazoro, *Exposición presentada a la cámara de Diputados solicitando dispensa del pago de réditos . . .* (Mexico, 1841), p. 10.

7. Lucas Alamán, president of the Junta de Industria, to the minister of justice, Dec. 18, 1841, MS in AGN, Ind. 1841 – 1843, exp. 7.

8. The sole exception was the $83,000 borrowed from the bank's portfolio during the French blockade in 1838. See chap. 9.

9. The loans were: $43,000 of principal and interest owed by Saracho Mier &. Co.; $4,167 owed by the Puebla Glass Co.; $1,000 owed by Jacinto Font. See MSS in AN, Madariaga, 1838, 1238r – 1245v; 1839, 726r; 1840, 308v.

10. Libro común de cargo de la Tesorería General de la Nación, 1843, 2: 706r, MS in AGN.

11. Dublán and Lozano, *Legislación mexicana*, 4:267.

12. See Lobato López, *El Crédito en México*, pp. 139 – 40; also Henry Aubrey, "Deliberate Industrialization," *Social Research* 16 (1949): 162, 172. Barbara Tenenbaum's "Straightening out Some of the Lumpen in Development," *Latin American Perspectives* 2, no. 2 (Summer 1975): 7, n. 4, perpetuates this myth.

13. The figures for the fiscal years 1833 — 34, 1835 — 36, 1836 — 37, 1841, and 1842 are given in the Secretaría de Hacienda, *Memorias* (México, 1835, 1837, 1838, 1844); the 1834 — 35 outlay is listed in the Libro común de data de la Tesorería General de la Nación, 1834 — 35, MS in AGN; the outlays for 1837 — 38 (18 months) and 1839 are given in Tomo 77, Ramo del Tribunal de Cuentas, MSS in AGN.

14. Drafts for $73,572 issued by the Treasury in the years 1835 — 1840 were canceled and destroyed in August 1843; other useless drafts that had been issued by the Banco de Avío were destroyed at the same time. See Libro común de cargo de la Tesorería General de la Nación, 1843, 2, 707v, MS in AGN; also *DG*, Oct. 31, 1843.

15. "Informe y cuentas," 1835, pp. 26 — 27.

16. *Informe y cuentas*, 1841, appendix.

17. Ibid. The figures cited do not include the sums spent for cotton gins, farm tools, handlooms, and spindles.

18. *Consideraciones sobre la situación política y social de la república mexicana en el año 1847* (Mexico, 1848), p. 15.

19. Juan Suárez y Navarro, *Historia de México y del General Antonio López de Santa Anna* (Mexico: I. Complido, 1850 — 1851), 1:326; Carlos Díaz Dufoo, *México y los capitales extranjeros* (Paris: La Vda de C. Bouret, 1918), pp. 213 — 14. See also Bocanegra, *Memorias para la historia de México independiente*, 2:163. For a nearly verbatim reproduction of the paragraph quoted in the text, see Felix Lavallée, "Études historiques sur Le Mexique . . . ," in *Revue des Races Latines* (Paris, 1959), p. 76.

20. These two were paper-mill projects for which the bank issued drafts that could not be cashed; one recipient, the Hospicio de Pobres de Puebla, returned the drafts but retained the machinery, which it later put into operation; the other, Alamán, eventually returned the machinery as well as the drafts. *Informe y cuentas*, 1841, appendix.

21. In both instances, the machinery was never withdrawn from the bank's warehouse. Ibid.

22. *MDG*, 1843, pp. 32 — 33; *MDG*, 1845, p. 64.

23. See above, table 4; Antuñano & Co., the largest single borrower, repaid its debt in full before the bank was dissolved.

CHAPTER 11

1. Laws of May 23, 1837, Oct. 26, 1842, Mar. 4, 1843, Dublán and Lozano, *Legislación mexicana*, 3:407; 4:315, 364. Law of Dec. 22, 1843, in *Memoria del secretario . . . de Justicia e instrucción pública, leida . . . en enero de 1844* (Mexico, 1844), p. 81.

2. See chap. 2.

3. Antuñano, *Breve memoria del estado que guarda la fábrica. . . . Constancia Mexicana y la industria de este ramo* (Puebla, 1837), pp. 12 ff.

4. Law of May 23, 1837, art. 2, Dublán and Lozano, *Legislación mexicana*, 3:407.

5. Finance Ministry regulations, May 23, 1837, in *DG*, June 13, 1837.

6. MSS in AGN, Ind. 1841 — 1843, exps. 94, 103.

7. MSS in Archivo de la Cámara de Senadores, 48, exp. 601.

8. *Memoria de la Dirección de colonización e industria: Año de 1849* (Mexico, 1950), p. 13. Pablo Macedo in *La evolución mercantil. Comunicación y obras públicas. La hacienda pública; tres monografías que dan idea de una parte de la evolución económica de*

México (Mexico: J. Ballescá, 1905), p. 70, points out that interstate economic discrimination persisted right through the nineteenth century.

9. See chaps. 2 – 4, 7.

10. Algodón en rama, permitted to enter by the tariff of 1827, was excluded by the prohibition law of May 22, 1829; but parts of this law had been suspended by the laws of Apr. 6 and Oct. 16, 1830.

11. Session of Apr. 16, 1836, reported in *DG*, Apr. 26, 1836; Law of Aug. 9, 1836, in Dublán and Lozano, *Legislación mexicana*, 3:191. Among the seven deputies who sponsored the bill was Luis Ruiz of Veracruz, proprietor of a cotton-ginning business that had received a loan from the Banco de Avío.

12. See the views of Estevan de Antuñano y Gumesindo Saviñón, *Esposición respetuosa que los que subscriben elevan a las soberanas cámaras de la unión sobre la prohibición de artefactos gordos de algodón estranjeros* (Puebla, 1835), pp. 10 – 11.

13. Law of Mar. 11, 1837, Dublán and Lozano, *Legislación mexicana*, 3:303 – 22. Tejidos ordinarios de algodón were subsequently defined as cotton stuffs, plain or figured, white or gray, printed or dyed, which had less than 30 threads to the quarter inch (Mexican) on both sides.

14. Estevan de Antuñano to Carlos María Bustamante, Puebla, Dec. 4, 1836, printed in Antuñano, *Breve memoria*, pp. 1 – 10; session of the unicameral legislature Nov. 19, 1836, reported in *DG*, Nov. 26, 1836.

15. Sessions of Dec. 16, 27, 1836, in *DG*, Dec. 24, 1836, Jan. 2, 1837.

16. This is the view advanced by Miguel Lerdo de Tejada, *Comercio esterior*, p. 34. That the tariff act of 1837 had its inspiration in a British plot to destroy United States textile markets in Mexico is the theory advanced by Franklin Chase, American consul at Tampico. See his letter to the department of state dated Dec. 31, 1854, quoted in Carlos Butterfield, *United States and Mexican Mail Steamship Line and Statistics of Mexico* (New York: J. A. H. Hasbrouck & Co., 1859), pp. 53 – 54.

17. For his views on prohibition, see his *Memoria de la secretaría de estado y del despacho de relaciones interiores y exteriores* (Mexico, 1832), p. 21. Alamán on Dec. 24, 1836, had become a special partner of Legrand and Co., who were building the Cocolapam textile factory near Orizaba. "Escritura de compañia en comandita," Sept. 20, 1837, MS in AN, Madariaga, 1837, 1001 v.

18. "Relación de las personas que han sido secretarios de estado y del despacho de hacienda o han estado encargadas de esa secretaría," *Boletín Semanario del Ministerio de Hacienda* 1, no. 2 (1853): 48 – 53.

19. The following is a comparison of the duties established in the 1827 and 1837 tariff acts for the principal articles involved:

Item	1827	1837
Twist, white or grey, no. 21 and up	—	.19
Twist, colored, no. 21 and up	—	.50
Thread, white, no. 21 and up	1.25	1.00
Thread, colored, no. 21 and up	1.25	1.50
Cotton stuffs, white or grey, plain, per vara	.18 3/4	.12 1/2
Cotton stuffs, white or grey, figured, per vara	.18 3/4	.14

The considerable reduction noted in the duty on yard goods—33 1/3 percent in one case—was practically eliminated after Nov. 23, 1837, when a special duty of 4 centavos per vara was collected on all ordinary cotton textiles entering during the balance of the grace period.

20. "Quantities and Declared Value of British and Irish Produce and Manufactures Exported from the United Kingdom to Mexico," Great Britain, *Parliamentary Papers*, vol. 39 (1842).

21. Customs duties collected on cotton goods from 1830 – 1838 were as follows:

1830 – 31 1,588,266	1833 – 34 615,367	1836 – 37 393,924
1831 – 32 1,166,307	1834 – 35 715,109	1837 – 38 134,065
		(18 months)
1832 – 33 829,536	1835 – 36 473,021	

Memoria que sobre el estado de la hacienda nacional . . . presentó . . . el ministro del ramo en julio de 1845 (Mexico, 1846), pp. 120 ff.

22. Petitions were submitted by at least ten departmental assemblies. Chamber of Deputies, sessions of June 9, 23, July 11, 1837, in *DG*, June 12, 29, July 15, 1837; also MSS in AGN, Ramo de Justicia, 53, exp. 49. The official position of the government was given by Finance Minister Lebrija in a letter to the interior minister, July 26, 1837, MS , ibid.

23. Chamber sessions, Aug. 14, 18, 1838, reported in *DG*, Aug. 30, Sept. 4, 1838; Law of Oct. 20, 1838, Dublán and Lozano, *Legislación mexicana*, 3:556.

24. Estevan de Antuñano, *Economía política en México. Exposición respetuosa que el que subscribe dirige a las augustas Cámaras de la Nación* (Puebla, 1839), p. 3; *DG*, Mar. 13, 1841; *Niles' Register* 56 (1839): 50.

25. The earlier instance is described in Manuel Piña y Cuevas, *Satisfacción al público del administrador de la aduana marítima de Matamoros* (Matamoros, 1841).

26. Mariano Arista to the Minister of War, Matamoros, Sept. 11, 1840; Juan N. Almonte to Gen. Mariano Arista, Mexico, Sept. 30, 1840. Printed in *DG*, Nov. 11, 1840.

27. For the exact amount of yarn involved in the contracts, see *DG*, June 7, 1842; yarn production in Mexico in 1841 was reported to be 1,014,000 pounds. *MDG*, 1843, appendix, table 6.

28. Carlos María Bustamante, *El gabinete mexicano durante el segundo período de la administración del exmo. Señor Presidente D. Anastasio Bustamante* (Mexico: J. M. Lara, 1842) 2:93 – 94; *El Monitor* (Veracruz), Nov. 3, 1840, editorial reprinted in *DG*, Nov. 13, 1840.

29. Bustamante, *El gabinete mexicano*, 1:13; 2:93; *Colección de leyes y decretos publicados en el año de 1839 y de 1840* (Mexico: Edición del Constitucional, 1851), p. 836. For a defense of the Almonte-Arista affair as a patriotic action that would have led to the recovery of Texas, see M. Payno, "Un viaje a Veracruz en el invierno de 1843," *El Museo Mexicano* 3 (1843): 163 – 64.

30. Statement signed by Francisco Morphy, Jan. 6, 1842, published in *DG*, Jan. 25, 1842.

31. Bustamante, *El gabinete mexicano*, 2:104.

32. Many came from interested farmer and manufacturer groups; others from municipal and departmental authorities. The departmental assemblies of Durango, Jalisco, Mexico, Puebla, Querétaro, and Veracruz all sent protests.

33. *El Cosmopolita*, Jan. 30, Feb. 13, Mar. 13, 1841.

34. Justo Corro, a Jaliscan, had himself become a cotton-manufacturer in 1843; Álvarez came from the cotton-growing regions near Acapulco.

35. Decree of Feb. 20, 1841, *Colección de leyes y decretos publicados en el año de 1841*, p. 11.

36. "Representación al supremo gobierno de los empresarios de fábricas nacionales de hilados y tegidos de algodón," Sept. 5, 1840, in *DG*, Oct. 15, 1840; "Representación de la Junta de Industria al Supremo Gobierno," May 19, 1841, *Semanario de la industria mexicana* 1, no. 2 (1841): 1−2.

37. *Informe y cuentas*, 1841.

38. Some of their bitterest critics agree with them in this interpretation. See M. Payno, "Un viage a Veracruz en el invierno de 1843," 162 − 63; Emil Richthofen, *Die Aüsseren und Inneren Politischen Zustände der Republik Mexico* (Berlin: W. Hertz, 1859), p. 27; Felix Lavallée, "Études historiques sur Le Mexique," p. 76.

39. See the correspondence between the Junta de Industria and the government published in *DG*, June 28, 1842.

40. Ibid., editorial.

41. The desirability of such a step was voiced in the official organ of the Junta de Industria. *Semanario de la Industria Mexicana* 1, no. 17 (1841). The idea had been put forth earlier by Estevan de Antuñano, *Economía política en México* (Puebla, 1839), pp. 4 − 5.

42. Decree of Oct. 21, 1841, Dublán and Lozano, *Legislación mexicana*, 4:41.

43. Ibid., 4:135.

44. See n. 39.

45. Decree of July 11, 1842, Dublán and Lozano, *Legislación mexicana*, 4:240.

46. "Proposal submitted to the Supreme Government by some members of this commerce," Jan. 6, 1842, printed in *DG*, Jan. 25, 1842.

47. Ignacio Trigueros, Minister of Finance, to Lucas Alamán, Jan. 7, 1842, ibid.

48. Lucas Alamán, president of the *Junta de fomento de Industria*, to the minister of finance, Jan. 14, 1842, and Jan. 26, 1842, ibid.

49. Ignacio Trigueros to Lucas Alamán, Jan. 15, 1842, ibid. Carlos Bustamante in his *Apuntes para la historia del gobierno del General D. Antonio López de Santa Anna desde principios de Octubre de 1841 hasta 6 de diciembre de 1844* (Mexico: J. M. Lara, 1845), p. 37, says that it was General Valencia's opposition that caused Santa Anna to reject the offer. Valencia, commander of the garrison in the capital, was apparently the strong right arm of the industrialists. His intervention had been instrumental in preventing President Bustamante from going through with the contracts the year before.

50. *DG*, June 7, 1842.

51. See chap. 10.

52. MSS in AGN, Ind. 1841 − 1843, exp. 112; Decree of Dec. 2, 1842, Dublán and Lozano, *Legislación mexicana*, 4:338 − 46.

53. Ibid., arts. 38 − 39.

54. Ibid., arts. 37, 42 − 44, 53.

55. Ibid., arts. 4 − 6, 8.

56. Ibid., arts. 14 − 29.

57. The other two-thirds were assigned to the *Junta de Minería*. Decree of Dec. 2, 1842 (a decree distinct from the one previously cited), *El Observador judicial y de legislación* (Mexico, 1842 − 1843), 2:510. In practice, this fund was never established; instead, the entire spindle tax, plus a fixed sum of $65,000, was assigned to the Dirección. MSS in AGN, Ind. 1841 − 1843, exp. 58.

58. Decree of Dec. 2, 1842, Dublán and Lozano, *Legislación mexicana*, 4:338–46, arts. 30–31.

59. Ibid., art. 7.

60. Minister of Justice to Luis Vieyra, Governor of the Department of Mexico, Dec. 16, 1842, MS in AGN, Ind. 1841–1843, exp. 12.

61. For background of these schools, see AGN, Ind. 1841–1843, exp. 57; the results of the statistical work are to be found in its annual publication, *MDG*, 1843–1845.

62. Law of Sept. 17, 1846, Dublán and Lozano, *Legislación mexicana*, 5:169–70; also *Biografía necrológica del Exmo. Señor D. Lucas Alamán* (Mexico, 1853), p. 20.

63. Decree of Nov. 27, 1846, Dublán and Lozano, *Legislación mexicana*, 5:217.

64. Annita M. Ker, *Mexican Government Publications* (Washington: Library of Congress, 1940), pp. 121–22.

65. *Memoria que el secretario de estado y del despacho de Hacienda . . . presentó . . . en los dias 3 y 6 de febero . . .* (Mexico, 1844), pp. 29–30; Decree of Apr. 30, 1842, Dublán and Lozano, *Legislación mexicana*, 4:160–88.

66. *DG*, May 29, 1843.

67. "La Dirección de industria pide se reforme el arancel vigente . . . ," July 26, 1843, MS in AGN, Ind. 1841–1843, exp. 101.

68. Dublán and Lozano, *Legislación mexicana*, 4:576–78.

69. *Memoria que el secretario . . . de Hacienda presentó*, 1844, p. 31.

70. Dublán and Lozano, *Legislación mexicana*, 4:510–11, 576–78.

71. *MDG*, 1844, pp. 25–26.

72. The tariff decrees issued by Santa Anna were an exception in that they were issued dictatorially without legislative authorization; the resumption of constitutional forms in 1843 restored legislative control over tariff making.

73. *Bases de organización política de la república mexicana* (Mexico, 1843), p. 15.

74. Justo Sierra, *Evolución política*, pp. 252–53, 254.

75. *Proyecto de constitución que presenta al soberano congreso la mayoría de su comisión especial. Voto particular de la minoría* (Mexico, 1842), p. 96.

76. Ibid., p. 29. The same article also placed restrictions on the power of Congress to authorize foreign loans, approve the farming of revenues, or decree the cession of any territory.

77. See Carlos de Landa, *Sobre el sistema prohibitivo como contrario al interés nacional bien entendido o sea refutación de las ideas del Siglo Diez y Nueve* (Mexico, 1843); M. Payno, "Un viage a Veracruz en el invierno de 1843," p. 164; Robert Crichton Willie, *México. Noticia sobre su hacienda pública bajo el gobierno español y después de la independencia* (Mexico: Ignacio Cumplido, 1845). Landa was the editor of a mercantile journal, Payno a permanent official of the Finance Ministry; Willie appears to have been an agent of English bondholders.

78. *MDG*, 1845, pp. 49, 47.

79. For the expansion of manufacturing, see chap. 12. Price data is scarce and frequently unreliable, but there can be no doubt of the sharp rise that took place in 1840. According to figures drawn up by the secretary of the Veracruz merchants association and reproduced by Estevan de Antuñano in *El Mercurio Poblano*. Supplement to no. 31, Oct. 12, 1843, the spot price paid for one quintal of ginned cotton rose from $25 in 1839 to $40 the following year; it remained at that figure until 1842 when it dropped to $36. For the prices paid by manufacturers in 1843, see *MDG*, 1843, table 5.

80. *Representación al supremo gobierno de los empresarios de fábricas nacionales de hilados y tejidos de algodón* (Mexico, 1840); E. Antuñano, *Teoría fundamental de la industria de algodones en México* (Puebla, 1840); also his *Economía política. Refutación que el que subscribe hace . . . del artículo editorial del Monitor de Veracruz . . .* (Puebla, 1840); and his *Raciocinios para un plan para repeler noblemente la importación de algodones extranjeros . . .* (Puebla, 1840).

81. Sessions of Chamber of Deputies, Oct. 2, 20, 26, 30, Nov. 22, 1840, in *DG,* Oct. 11, 21, Nov. 2, 8, Dec. 4, 1840; *El Cosmopolita,* Sept. 30, Oct. 3, 1840; also *DG,* July 10, 13, 14, Nov. 27, 1841.

82. *Representación dirigida al escmo. señor presidente de la república por la Junta de industria de Puebla a fin de que se queme el algodón introducido clandestinamente* (Puebla, 1843), p. 11.

83. "Representación dirigida al supremo gobierno por la dirección general . . . ," Mar. 29, 1843, *DG,* Apr. 17, 1843; "Representación dirigida al supremo gobierno por la dirección general . . . ," Apr. 27, 1843, *DG,* May 4, 1843.

84. The concession was given to Sres. Agüero González y compañía who subsequently transferred it to Cayetano Rubio to whom the second concession was also given. Rubio was a textile manufacturer as well as a merchant. Decree of Apr. 12, 1843, *El Observador judicial y de legislación,* 3:366 – 67; *Memoria que el secretario de hacienda . . . presentó,* 1844, p. 15.

85. *MDG,* 1843, p. 24.

86. Ex-President Justo Corro was one of those who changed his mind. See his letter to Antuñano, printed in *El Mercurio Poblano.* Supplement to no. 51, Dec. 16, 1843; see also the statement signed by sixteen Puebla manufacturers dated Aug. 24, 1844, in *El Mercurio Poblano,* Sept. 14, 1844.

87. *MDG,* 1844, appendix, pp. 22 – 23.

88. *MDG,* 1845, pp. 40 – 41.

89. *Exposición con que la comisión nombrada para la reforma del arancel de las aduanas marítimas y fronterizas dió cuenta al gobierno supremo del plan que siguió en el cumplimiento de su encargo* (Mexico, 1845); law of Oct. 4, 1845, Dublán and Lozano, *Legislación mexicana,* 5:42 – 44.

90. *MDG,* 1845, p. 42.

91. Ibid., p. 47.

92. *El Mercurio Poblano,* Mar. 2, 1844, Supplement to no. 26, Feb. 22, 1845. A move was undertaken to exclude cotton textiles with up to 40 threads in the quarter inch. Under existing laws, goods having over 30 threads entered on payment of duties.

93. See the balanced comments of Minister J. M. Lafragua. *Memoria de la primera secretaría de . . . relaciones interiores y esteriores . . . 1846* (Mexico, 1847), pp. 71 – 72.

94. Ibid., appendix 54, p. 159. Garay was an industrialist himself, with interests in two cotton-textile factories in Mexico City.

CHAPTER 12

1. These were Antuñano's La Constancia in Puebla, the Tlálpam factory in Tlálpam, and the mills owned by Aldazoro and Roa in Mexico City. Roa's factory subsequently closed.

2. The Cocolapam spinning factory near Orizaba owned by the Legrand brothers and Lucas Alamán.

3. Antuñano in his *Breve memoria del Estado que guarda la fábrica de hilados de algodón Constancia Mexicana* (Puebla, 1837) asserted that he had obligated himself to assist and direct three other spinning factories, all presumably in the Puebla area; but a petition signed by Puebla weavers and spinners on July 27, 1837, lists only two proprietors of spinning factories in addition to Antuñano. *Representación que los artesanos de algodón . . . dirigen al exmo. sr. Presidente* (Puebla, 1837).

4. Although Baranda's factory was begun before 1833, it did not reach full production until about 1839. For an illuminating account of this factory and of its founder, see Howard F. Cline, "The 'Aurora Yucateca' and the Spirit of Enterprise in Yucatan, 1821 – 1847," *Hispanic American Historical Review* 27 (1947): 30 – 46.

5. *MDG*, 1843, table 6; *MDG*, 1845, table 4. Apparently because of the confused political status of Yucatán, the Dirección consistently omitted reference to the Baranda mill. The figures cited in the text include this mill with its 432 spindles and 20 looms for the years 1840 through 1844. Baranda's factory closed on his death in 1845.

6. Gumesindo Saviñón to the Minister of the Interior, Puebla, Nov. 25, 1838, printed in *DG*, Feb. 12, 1839.

7. *MDG*, 1843, table 5.

8. Ibid.; "Circular a los Gobiernos de los departamentos pidiendo noticia de número de telares de algodón y lana," Aug. 22, 1843, MS in AGN, Ind. 1841 – 1843, exp. 97.

9. Ibid.

10. *MDG*, 1843, table 5; *Semanario de la Industria Mexicana* 1, no. 21 (Nov. 1841).

11. Decree of Sept. 28, 1842, Dublán and Lozano, *Legislación mexicana*, 4:274.

12. Decree of Feb. 17, 1843, ibid., 4:365. A request supported by the governor of Tamaulipas to establish a factory at Matamoros was denied for this reason. "La Junta de Fomento de Matamoros sobre que se establezca en esa ciudad una fábrica de hilados y tegidos," Nov. 16, 1843, MS in AGN, Ind 1841 – 1843, exp. 90.

13. For Orizaba's subsequent rise as a textile city, see Alice Foster, "Orizaba—a community in the Sierra Madre Oriental," *Economic Geography* 1 (Oct. 1925): 356 – 72.

14. *MDG*, 1843, table 5.

15. The factory was located in Durango. *Memoria en que el gobierno del estado de Durango da cuenta . . . de la marcha de la administración pública*, Mar. 1, 1848 (Victoria, 1848), p. 33.

16. See rates quoted for mule loads between Veracruz, Puebla, and Mexico in *El Censor* (Veracruz), May 30, 1830, Feb. 16, 1831, July 17, 1835. The cost of a *cargo de ropa* usually was $4 – 5 greater than a *carga de abarrotes*.

17. *MDG*, 1843, table 5.

18. Of the three, one was in Mexico, one at Alvarado, Veracruz, and the other in Yucatán. Wood was used as the fuel. Ibid.; Cline, "The Aurora Yucateca," p. 40.

19. Waddy Thompson, *Recollections of Mexico* (New York: Wiley and Putnam, 1846), p. 210.

20. Brantz Mayer, *Mexico As It Was and As It Is*, 3d ed. (Baltimore: W. Taylor & Co., 1846), p. 315.

21. Jan Bazant, "Estudio sobre la productividad de la industria algodonera mexicana en 1843 – 1845," in *La Industria nacional y el comercio exterior (1842 – 1851)* (Mexico: Banco Nacional de Comercio Exterior, 1962), pp. 60 – 64.

22. This is somewhat lower than the official estimate of $16 million given for the value of 62 cotton and 5 woolen mills as of the close of 1846 in "Informe del Sr. Presidente de la Junta de colonización e industria," *Memoria de la primera secretaría . . . de relaciones interiores e esteriores, 1846* (Mexico, 1847), p. 158.

23. See chap. 10.

24. Dufoo's words were: "El Banco se liquidó con grandes pérdidas, dando de esta suerte término a un intento que, en el fondo, estaba inspirado por un sentimiento de mala voluntad al capital extranjero, ya que—como dice el doctor Mora—el propósito era nacionalizar las industrias fundadas y sostenidas por esa capital." Carlos Díaz Dufoo, *México y los capitales extranjeros* (París: La Vda. de C. Bouret, 1918), pp. 213 – 14.

25. These were the factories "Industria Jalapeña," owned by Joseph Welsh and John Maurice Jones, and the Cocolapam Spinning Factory, owned by Prospère and Auguste Legrand with Lucas Alamán as a special partner.

26. Including two of the foreign technicians hired at great expense by the Banco de Avío in 1831, Carlos Saulnier and Tomás MacCormick. They established a power-loom weaving shop and a spinning mill respectively.

27. The Cocolapam mill at Orizaba had 11,500 spindles; the Magdalena mill in Mexico, set up in partnership with Mexican capitalists, had 8,400. French interest in the former ended in 1841 as a result of bankruptcy proceedings.

28. As far as can be deduced from the names of spinning-mill proprietors published by the Dirección de Industria in *DG*, Mar. 28, 1843.

29. For such charges, see *Semanario de la Industria Mexicana* 1, no. 23 (1841); editorial in *El Nacional* (Jalapa), Oct. 27, 1842, reprinted in *DG*, Nov. 3, 1842.

30. See the open letter of James Barlow to Minister Packenham printed in *El Cosmopolita*, Feb. 27, 1841; also Bustamante, *El Gabinete mexicano*, 2:104.

31. See Estevan de Antuñano y Gumesindo Saviñón, *Exposición respetuosa que los que subscriben elevan a las soberanas cámaras de la unión*, pp. 1 – 5; Santiago Aldazoro, *Exposición presentada a la Cámara de Diputados*, pp. 11 – 12.

32. See, for example, Chávez Orozco, *Historia de México*, p. 372; Lobato López, *El Crédito en México*, p. 137.

33. Antonio de Raso, "Notas estadísticas del departamento de Querétaro," June 26, 1845, *Boletín del Instituto Nacional de Geografía y Estadística de la Repúblicá Mexicana* 3 (1852): 201. Rubio also owned a woolen factory in Celaya. *MDG*, 1845, p. 76.

34. "Informe del Sr. Presidente de la Junta de colonización e industria," p. 158.

35. Waddy Thompson believed that the same machinery could have been set up in the United States at one-third the cost. *Recollections of Mexico*, p. 210.

36. Eventually, for some factories, parts were cast in Mexico. See José F. Ramírez, *Noticias históricas y estadísticas de Durango* (Mexico, 1851), p. 54. The historian, Ramírez, was a partner in the Durango factory, El Tunal.

37. "Patente para el primer camino de fierro en esta república," Aug. 22, 1837, in *DG*, Sept. 4, 1837. For the subsequent history of this concession, see D. M. Fletcher, "The Building of the Mexican Railway," *Hispanic American Historical Review* 30 (1950): 26 – 62.

38. For the disastrous effects of the 1832 revolt, see chap. 6; the French blockade of 1838 – 39 delayed the completion of three factories for over a year.

39. *Calendario de Galván* (Mexico, 1842), pp. 61 – 64.

40. The luxuriousness of the factories was noted by a Spanish visitor, Luis Manuel del Ri-vero, *Méjico en 1842* (Madrid: D. E. Aguado, 1844), p. 251.

41. *Life in Mexico*, 2:305.

42. José María Naredo, *Estudio geográfico, histórico y estadístico del cantón y de la ciudad de Orizaba* (Orizaba: Imprenta del Hospicio, 1898), 2, bk. 3, 16.

43. See table 9.

44. "El Ayuntamiento de Orizava sobre que se lleve al cabo la sub-hasta del arrendamiento de la fábrica de hilados de Cocolapam," Sept. 27, 1843, MS in AGN, Ind. 1841 – 1843, exp. 108.

45. "Cocolapam," *El Mosaico Mexicano* 5 (1841): 437 – 40.

46. *Memoria en que el gobierno del estado de Durango da cuenta*, p. 32.

47. Calderón de la Barca, *Life in Mexico*, 2:102.

48. Mayer, *Mexico As It Was*, p. 315.

49. *Semanario de la Industria Mexicana* 1, no. 21 (1841); 2, nos. 4, 6 (1842).

50. *MDG*, 1843, table 5.

51. See n. 48. The most efficient power-weaving shop had 10 workers for each 9 looms; the least efficient had 8 workers for every 5.

52. Jan Bazant, "Industria algodonera poblana de 1800 – 1843 en números," *Historia Mexicana* 14, no. 1 (1964): 136 – 37.

53. This assumes the validity of the weaving efficiency ratio of 1.05 looms per worker. The labor force, on this assumption, consisted of 4,183 in weaving and 6,133 in spinning. Dividing the 161,860 spindles by the latter number yields the spindle : worker efficiency ratio of 26 to 1. For the 1854 statistics on spindles, looms, and total employment, see Guillermo Beato, "La Casa Martínez del Rio," in *Formación y desarrollo de la burguesía en México sigle XIX*, Margarita Urías et al. (Mexico: Siglo Veintiuno Editores, 1978), pp. 74 – 75 and n. 25.

54. Estevan de Antuñano, *Ventajas políticas, civiles, fabriles y domésticas que, por dar ocupación también a las mujeres en las fábricas de maquinaria moderna que se está levantando en México, deben recibirse* (Puebla, 1837); Bazant, "Industria algodonera," p. 136.

55. In Durango, German Stalknecht employed 150 women and 100 men at El Tunal; the Ojo de Agua factory at Peñon Blanco had a work force of 61 men, 40 boys, 50 women, and 32 girls; Manuel Iñigo's Los Angeles plant in Sonora planned a labor force of 54 women and 34 men and boys (see his detailed report of Apr. 16, 1843, published in *DG*, June 12, 1843); Cayetano Rubio's Hercules plant in Querétaro was said to employ 584 women and 292 men. For references to the presence of women in the Cocolapam work force, see letters of Francisco Pablo, Obispo de Puebla, to Lucas Alamán, Mar. 4, 27, 1839 in AGN, Ramo Hospital de Jesús, Leg. 420, Exp. 10 and 11.

56. *MDG*, 1844, p. 33.

57. The schools were founded by Alamán at the Cocolapam plant and by Antuñano at La Constancia, which also had the medical arrangements. Valadés, *Alamán, estadista e historiador*, p. 375; Antuñano, *Documentos para la historia de la industria algodonera de Mégico* (Puebla, 1843), p. 14.

58. *MDG*, 1843, table 5.

59. Antuñano, *Breve memoria*, p. 10.

60. *La Lima*, Sept. 28, 1839; Riva Palacio, ed., *México a través de los siglos*, 4:452. The issue, however, of whether workers could be employed on a night shift from Saturday to Sun-

day still remained open. For Alamán's successful effort to secure episcopal permission to allow workers at the Cocolapam mill to remain at their tasks until Sunday mornings, see AGN, Ramo Hospital de Jesús, Leg. 420, Exp. 11, Alamán to Francisco Pablo, Obispo de Puebla, Mar. 23, 1839, and the latter's reply of Mar. 27, 1839.

61. For an ingenious effort to calculate wages, productivity, and profits in the new cotton factories, see Jan Bazant's "Estudio sobre la productividad," pp. 29–85, and his "Industria algodonera," pp. 135–43.

62. Manta woven in 1838 consumed 10 pounds of yarn per piece; as of 1845, with the use of finer yarns, the average weight was said to be 8 pounds. See report of Gumesindo Saviñón, Nov. 25, 1838, in DG, Feb. 12, 1839, and MDG, 1845, p. 41.

63. MDG, 1845, p. 52.

64. MDG, 1844, p. 18.

65. "Informe del Sr. Presidente de la Junta de colonización e industria," p. 158.

66. The average annual mintage in the period 1830–1844 was $12,350,000. "Razón que resume . . . el importe de lo amonedado en oro y plata en las casas de moneda de la república en los quince años contados de 1830 a 1844," Memoria que sobre el estado de la hacienda nacional . . . presentó el ministro del ramo en julio de 1845 (Mexico, 1846), p. 114.

67. Henry G. Aubrey, in "Deliberate Industrialization," Social Research 16 (June 1949): 165, contended that the reduction in the price of manta from around 1820 to 1843 was nearly 60 percent. He based this on the belief that manta of 22-inch width sold for 3 reales in the earlier year. Aubrey relied on the statements in the 1843 Memoria, p. 25, of the Dirección de Industria, which gave 3 reales as the price of manta in colonial times. This figure, however, was certainly not the normal price before 1810 in Mexico City, where guild officials asserted that "from time immemorial" the customary price had been only 2 reales. "Reformación de las ordenansas del Gremio de Tejedores . . . nuebamente instruidas . . . ," June 2, 1809, MS in AGN, Com., exp. 10.

68. Keremitsis, La industria textil mexicana en el siglo xix, pp. 41–98; for growth of the industry in the early 1850s, see also Guillermo Beato, "La Casa Martínez del Rio," pp. 73–78.

POSTSCRIPT

1. Enrique Florescano, "Mexico," in Latin America: A Guide to Economic History 1830–1930, ed. Roberto Cortés Conde and Stanley Stein (Berkeley and Los Angeles: University of California Press, 1977), p. 436.

2. Luis Chávez Orozco, ed., El Banco de Avío y el fomento de la industria nacional, Colección de documentos para la historia del comercio exterior de México, segunda serie, no. 3 (Mexico: Banco Nacional de Comercio Exterior, 1966).

3. Jesús Silva Herzog, El pensamiento económico y político de México 1810–1964 (Mexico: Instituto Mexicano de Investigaciones Económicas, 1967); Diego G. López Rosado, Historia y pensamiento económico de México, 4 vols. (Mexico: Universidad Nacional Autónoma de México, 1968–1971); Jesús Reyes Heroles, El liberalismo mexicano, 3 vols. (Mexico: Universidad Nacional Autónoma de México, 1957–1961).

4. Charles A. Hale, Mexican Liberalism in the Age of Mora 1821–1853 (New Haven: Yale University Press, 1968); see also his "Alamán, Antuñano y la continuidad del liberalismo," Historia Mexicana 11, no. 2 (Oct.–Dec. 1961): 224–45.

5. See for example Carl Dale Donathan, "Lucas Alamán and Mexican Foreign Affairs" (Ph.D. diss., Duke University, 1968); Stanley C. Green, "Lucas Alamán: Domestic Activities 1823 – 1835" (Ph.D. diss., Texas Christian University, 1970); and Jane Ellen Dysart, "Against the Tide: Lucas Alamán and the Hispanic Past" (Ph.D. diss., Texas Christian University, 1972).

6. Michael Costeloe, "The Administration, Collection and Distribution of Tithes in the Archbishropic of Mexico, 1810 – 1860," *The Americas* 23 (July 1966): 3 – 27.

7. Costeloe, *Church Wealth*, p. 29.

8. Asunción Lavrín, "Problems and Policies in the Administration of Nunneries, 1800 – 1835," *The Americas* 27 (July 1971): 57 – 77.

9. Bazant, *Los bienes de la Iglesia*, pp. 13 – 14.

10. Romeo Flores Caballero, *La contrarevolución en la independencia. Los españoles en la vida política, social y económica de México (1804 – 1838)* (Mexico: El Colegio de México, 1969).

11. Barbara A. Tenenbaum, "Merchants, Money and Mischief," *The Americas* 35 (Jan. 1979): 333.

12. Miguel Lerdo de Tejada, *Comercio exterior de México* (1853; reprint ed. with a preliminary note by Luis Córdova, Mexico: Banco Nacional de Comercio Exterior, 1967).

13. Harold Sims, "Las clases económicas y la dicotomía criollo-peninsular en Durango, 1827," *Historia Mexicana* 20 (Apr. – June 1971): 539 – 62.

14. For references to the penetration of Veracruz merchants into interior markets, see Guillermo Beato, "La Casa Martínez del Rio: del comercio colonial a la industria fabril, 1829 – 1864," in *Formación y desarrollo de la burguesía en México siglo XIX*, Margarita Urías et al. (Mexico: Siglo Veintiuno Editores, 1978), p. 63, n. 13.

15. Jan Bazant, *Cinco haciendas mexicanos. Tres siglos de vida rural en San Luis Potosí (1600 – 1910)* (Mexico: El Colegio de México, 1975); David A. Brading, *Haciendas and Ranchos in the Mexican Bajío. Leon, 1700 – 1860* (Cambridge: Cambridge University Press, 1978); Ward Barrett, *The Sugar Hacienda of the Marqueses del Valle* (Minneapolis: University of Minnesota Press, 1970); Charles Harris III, *A Mexican Family Empire: The Latifundio of the Sánchez Navarro Family 1765 – 1867* (Austin: University of Texas Press, 1975).

16. David A. Brading, "La estructura de la producción agrícola en el Bajió de 1700 a 1850," *Historia Mexicana* 23 (Oct. – Dec. 1973): 197 – 237; John Tutino, "Hacienda Social Relations in Mexico: The Chalco Region in the Era of Independence," *Hispanic American Historical Review* 55 (Aug. 1975): 496 – 528.

17. México, D. F. Archivo General de Notarías, Protocolos de José V. Maciel, Apr. 4, 1829; May 2, 12, 1829.

18. For example, Andrés Lira González, "Aspecto fiscal de la Nueva España en la segunda mitad del siglo xviii," *Historia Mexicana* 17 (Mar. 1968): 361 – 94; Masae Sugawarah, "Los antecedentes coloniales de la deuda pública de México. Introducción, apéndice notas y selección," *Boletín del Archivo General de la Nación*, n.s. 8 (1967): 129 – 402; Richard L. Garner, "Reformas Borbónicas y operaciones hacendarias – la Real Caja de Zacatecas 1750 – 1821," *Historia Mexicana* 27, no. 4 (Apr. – June 1978): 542 – 87; Bernardo García Martínez, "El sistema monetario de los últimos años de período novohispano," *Historia Mexicana* 17, no. 3 (1968): 349 – 60; John J. Te Paske, *La Real Hacienda de Nueva España: La Real Caja de México*, Colección Científica Fuentes no. 41 (Mexico: Sep-INAH, Departamento de Investigaciones Históricas, 1976).

19. *Historia de la administración hacendaria en México*, 2 vols. (Mexico: Secretaría de Hacienda y Crédito Público, 1970 – 1971); *Historia de la Tesorería de la Federación* (Mexico: Secretaría de Hacienda y Crédito Público, 1972); *Historia y legislación aduanera de México* (México: Secretaría de Hacienda y Crédito Público, 1973); *El papel sellado y la ley del timbre 1821 – 1871 – 1971, Relación documental* (Mexico: Secretaría de Hacienda y Crédito Público, 1970).

20. I am indebted to Dr. Tenenbaum for providing me with a copy of this manuscript.

21. Beato, "La Casa Martínez del Rio," pp. 70 – 84.

22. "Estudio sobre la productividad de la industria algodonera mexicano en 1843 – 1845 (Lucas Alamán y la revolución industrial en Mexico)," in *La industria nacional y el comercio exterior (1842 – 1851)* (Mexico: Banco Nacional de Comercio Exterior, 1962), 29 – 85; "Evolución la industria textil poblana (1554 – 1845)," *Historia Mexicana* 13 (Apr. – June 1964): 473 – 516; "Industria algodonera poblana de 1800 – 1843 en números," *Historia Mexicana* 14 (July – Sept. 1964): 131 – 43.

23. Beato, "La Casa Martínez del Rio," pp. 73 – 78.

24. "The Dangerous Classes in Early Nineteenth-Century Mexico," *Journal of Latin American Studies* 5 (May 1973): 79 – 105.

25. "The Artisan in Mexico City (1824 – 1853)," in *El trabajo y los trabajadores en la historia de México*, comps. Elsa Frost, Michael C. Meyer, and Josefina Z. Vázquez (Mexico: El Colegio de México and University of Arizona Press, 1979), pp. 399 – 418. A valuable treatment of selected aspects of working-class life is presented by Alejandra Moreno Toscano, "Los trabajadores y el proyecto de industrialización, 1810 – 1867," in Enrique Florescano et al., *De la colonia al imperio*, La clase obrera en la historia de México, vol. 1, 2d ed. (Mexico: Siglo Veintiuno Editores, 1981).

26. "Obstacles to Economic Growth in Nineteenth-Century Mexico," *American Historical Review* 83, no. 1 (Feb. 1978): 80 – 100; *Growth against Development: The Economic Impact of Railroads in Porfirian Mexico* (DeKalb, Ill.: Northern Illinois University Press, 1981).

27. See Barbara Tenenbaum's "Straightening out Some of the Lumpen in Development: An Examination of André Gunder Frank's Explanation of Latin American History in Terms of Mexico, 1821 – 1856," *Latin American Perspectives* 2, no. 2 (Summer 1975): 316.

28. Ciro Cardoso, coordinator, *México en el siglo xix (1821 – 1910). Historia económica y de la estructura social* (Mexico: Nueva Imagen, 1980). The eleven authors were participants in a seminar sponsored by the Department of Historical Investigations of the National Institute of Anthropology and History.

29. The Casa Amarilla was an archival depository in Tacubaya. Originally a chapel, but located next to a reform school, its broken windows had allowed pigeons to drop a layer of guano over the documents when this writer first visited the building in 1949. Scholars owe a debt of gratitude to the dynamic director of the Archivo General de la Nación, Dr. Alejandra Moreno Toscano, for modernizing its services and arranging for its relocation.

30. Robert A. Potash, "Pilot Project for a Computerized Guide to the Archivo General de Notarías. A report to the 6th Conference of Mexican and United States Historians" (unpublished).

31. Enrique Florescano, coordinator, *Bibliografía general del desarrollo económico de México 1500 – 1976*, 3 vols. (Mexico: Secretaría de Educación Pública, 1980). This is an updated and expanded version of the work cited above in n. 1.

BIBLIOGRAPHY

Outline of Contents

I. Primary sources

A. Manuscript materials

The principal archives utilized for this study were the Archivo General de la Nación, the Archivo General de Notarías del Distrito Federal, and the Archivo de la Secretaría Municipal of Puebla.

The Archivo General de la Nación (AGN) furnished the most valuable materials, especially the papers of the Banco de Avío. These consisted of the Libro de Actas, or minute book, of its board of directors for the period 1830 – 1832, the bank's account books, and its correspondence files. Also used in the AGN were the records of the Office of Industry (Sección de Industria) which was originally within the Ministry of Foreign and Domestic Affairs (Relaciones) and later attached to the Interior Ministry, and then to the Justice Ministry. The Office of Industry papers consisted of four bundles (legajos), two covering the period 1822 – 1834, and two, the period 1840 – 1843. Apart from the Banco de Avío and Office of Industry papers, useful materials were found in the following divisions (ramos) of the AGN: Industria y Comercio, Historia, Bandos, Tribunal de Cuentas, Justicia, and Hospital de Jesús. It might be noted that at the time the research was conducted, the Banco de Avío and Office of Industry materials were scattered in various parts of the AGN, including its Tacubaya annex known as the Casa Amarilla. These papers have since been consolidated into the main collection.

The Archivo General de Notarías del Distrito Federal, although not well organized for research, contains what is probably the richest single depository of materials for Mexico's economic history. For the present study, it furnished copies of the contracts entered into between the Banco de Avío and its borrowers, foreign artisans, freight handlers, and so forth. These records are filed by the name of the attesting notary, and are bound chronologically, the papers for one year ordinarily constituting a volume. The notaries most frequently employed by the Banco de Avío were: Mariano García Romero, who was its official notary for a time; Ramón de la Cueva; Mariano Flores; Francisco Madariaga; Ignacio Peña; and Manuel Pinzón.

The Archivo de la Secretaría Municipal de Puebla provided data on colonial industrial activity. Most useful were the bound volumes of expedientes numbered 220 – 34, which dealt with the craft guilds and the obrajes.

Manuscript materials of varying value were also found in archives other than the three discussed above. These included: Archivo de la Cámara de Senadores, Mexico; Archivo Histórico de Hacienda, Mexico; Biblioteca de la Sociedad Mexicana de Geografía y Estadística, Mexico; University of Texas (Austin) Library; Román Beltrán, Mexico (private archives); Enrique Villar, Puebla (private archives).

B. Printed documents

1. Legislative branch

a. Compilations of laws

(1) National laws

Arrillaga, Basilio José, comp. Recopilación de leyes, decretos bandos, reglamentos, circulares y providencias de los supremos poderes y otras autoridades de la república mexicana. 1828 – 1839, 1849 – abril de 1850. 17 vols. in 16. Mexico, 1834 – 1850.

Brito, José. *Índice alfabético razonado de las leyes, decretos. reglamentos, órdenes y circulares que se han expedido desde el año de 1821 hasta el de 1869.* 3 vols. Mexico, 1872 – 1873.

Colección de las leyes, decretos y providencias importantes espedidos por las supremas autoridades de la república mexicana formada y publicada en obsequio de los suscritores del Republicano. Años de 1838 y 1839. Mexico, 1846 – 1847.

Colección de leyes y decretos publicados en el año de 1839 – 1841, enero de 1844 – diciembre de 1846 (Edición del Constitucional). 3 vols. Mexico, 1851 – 1852.

Colección de leyes y disposiciones relativas al crédito público desde el año de 1821, primero de la independencia. 2 vols. Mexico, 1883.

Dublán, Manuel and Lozano, José María. *Legislación mexicana. Colección completa de las disposiciones legislativas expedidas desde la independencia de la república* (Edición oficial). 34 vols. Mexico, 1876 – 1904.

Galván Rivera, Mariano, comp. *Colección de los decretos y órdenes de las cortes de España que se reputan vigentes en la república de los Estados-Unidos Mexicanos.* Mexico, 1829.

———. *Colección de órdenes y decretos de la soberana junta provisional gubernativa y soberanos congresos generales de la nación mexicana.* 8 vols. Mexico, 1829 – 1840.

———. *Decretos del Rey Fernando VII expedidos desde su restitución al trono español hasta el establecimiento de la constitución de 1812.* Mexico, 1836.

———. *Repertorio de legislación o índice alfabético y cronológico de las materias más notables contenidas en la colección de leyes . . . que se han espedido en la república desde el año de 1821 hasta el de 1837, inclusos los dos volúmenes en que se refundieron últimamente las leyes y decretos de las cortes españolas y las espedidas por el Rey d. Fernando VII, que se reputan vigentes. . . .* Mexico, 1840.

The most generally useful of these compilations was that of Dublán and Lozano, the standard work; the volumes of Galván Rivera contained additional material for the years prior to 1838. The unique value of Arrillaga's work is its inclusion of administrative as well as legislative directives.

(2) State laws

Chiapas:

Velasco, José A., comp. *Colección de leyes del estado de Chiapas.* Tomo 1, 1825 – 1844. N.p., 1892.

Coahuila:

Garza García, Cosme, comp. *Prontuario de leyes y decretos del estado de Coahuila de Zaragoza.* Saltillo, 1902.

Guanajuato:

Decretos del congreso constituyente y del primero constitucional del estado de Guanajuato. Mexico, 1834.

Decretos del segundo y tercer congresos constitucionales del estado de Guanajuato. Mexico, 1834.

Decretos del cuarto congreso del estado de Guanajuato expedidos desde el mes de enero de 1833 hasta mayo de 1835. Guanajuato, 1849.

Decretos expedidos por las asambleas constitucionales del departamento de Guanajuato en los años de 1844 – 1846. Guanajuato, 1851.

Jalisco:

Colección de los decretos, circulares y órdenes de los poderes legislativo y ejecutivo del estado de Jalisco. Tomos 1 – 9. Guadalajara, 1874 – 1877.

Colección de los decretos y órdenes del honorable congreso constituyente del estado libre de Jalisco desde su instalación en 14 de septiembre de 1823 hasta 24 de enero de 1824 que cesó. Guadalajara, 1826.

México:

Colección de decretos y órdenes del congreso constituyente del estado libre y soberano de México. Tomo 1. Toluca, 1848.

Colección de decretos de los congresos constitucionales del estado libre y soberano de México. Tomo 2. Toluca, 1850.

Colección de decretos y órdenes del primer congreso constitucional de México. 8 vols. in 6. Tlálpam and Toluca, 1827 – 1832.

Colección de leyes y disposiciones relativas al ramo de hacienda. Toluca, 1876.

Michoacán:

Coromina, Amador, comp. *Recopilación de leyes, decretos, reglamentos y circulares expedidos en el estado de Michoacán.* Tomos 1 – 9. Morelia, 1886 – 1913.

Nuevo León:

Colección de leyes, decretos, y circulares espedidos por el gobierno del estado desde el 1 de agosto de 1824 hasta el 30 de diciembre de 1830. Monterrey, 1895.

Oaxaca:

Colección de leyes y decretos del estado libre de Oaxaca. Tomo 1. Oaxaca, 1879.

Puebla:

Colección de los decretos y órdenes más importantes que espidió el congreso constitu-yente del estado de Puebla en los años de 1824 – 1825, 1826 – 1828, 1830 – 1831. 3 vols. Puebla, 1827 – 1832.

Colección de leyes y decretos de la autoridad legislativa del estado de Puebla correspon-diente a la segunda época del sistema federal. Tomo 2, Puebla, 1850.

Decretos y acuerdos expedidos por la tercera (y cuarta) legislatura constitucional del estado libre y soberano de Puebla. Tomo 1. Años de 1832 – 1835. Puebla, 1850.

Querétaro:

Colección de los decretos y órdenes del congreso constituyente del estado de Querétaro. N.p., 1826.

Colección de los decretos y órdenes del primer congreso constitucional del estado de Querétaro. N.p., n.d.

San Luis Potosí:

Colección de leyes y decretos de la legislatura constituyente expedidos desde 21 de abril de 1824 hasta 1835. 10 vols. San Luis Potosí, 1835 – 1924. Vol. 1.

Tabasco:

Compilación de los decretos expedidos por la legislatura del estado de Tabasco desde el congreso de 1824 hasta 1850. San Juan Bautista, 1901.

Veracruz:

Colección de decretos correspondientes a los años de 1824 – 1831. 4 vols. Xalapa, 1901 – 1904.
Colección de leyes, decretos y circulares correspondientes a los años de 1832 – 1834. Jalapa, 1921.
Legislación del estado de Veracruz desde el año de 1824 hasta la presente época. Tomos 1 – 3. Jalapa, 1881 – 1882.
Recopilación de los decretos y órdenes expedidos en el estado de Vera Cruz desde el 4 de diciembre de 1840 al 24 de diciembre de 1852. 2 vols. Xalapa, 1907.

b. Legislative debates (chronologically arranged)

Diario de las sesiones de la soberana junta provisional gubernativa del imperio mexicano. Mexico, 1821 – 1822.
Actas del congreso constituyente mexicano. 3 vols. Mexico, 1822.
Diario de la junta nacional instituyente del imperio mexicano. Mexico, 1822 – 1823.
Diario de las sesiones del congreso constituyente de México. Mexico, 1823.
Diario de las sesiones del congreso constituyente de la federación mexicana. 3 vols. Mexico, 1824.
Estracto de las sesiones de la cámara de representantes del congreso de la unión. Mexico, 1830.
Estracto de las sesiones de la cámara de senadores del congreso de la unión. Mexico, 1830.
Estracto de las sesiones de la cámara de representantes del congreso de la unión, correspondiente al año de 1831. Mexico, 1831.
Estracto de las sesiones de la cámara del senado del congreso de la unión correspondiente al año de 1831. Mexico, 1831.
Mateos, Juan A. *Historia parlamentaria de los congresos mexicanos de 1821 a 1857.* 10 vols. Mexico, 1877 – 1886.

These documents furnished a valuable key for understanding the origin and intent of important legislation. The volumes devoted to the work of a single legislative body or session are more complete than the general work of Mateos, which suffers from omissions and provides little more than a bare summary. Better coverage of congressional proceedings is given in the official gazettes and the larger newspapers. See section D.

c. Legislative committee reports (chronologically arranged)

Arancel general interino e instrucción para gobierno de las aduanas marítimas en el comercio libre del imperio mexicano. Mexico, 1821.
Despite its title, this is the report of the Tariff Committee of the Soberana Junta Provisional.
Dictamen de las comisiones unidas de hacienda y comercio sobre prohibiciones de efectos. Mexico, 1824.
Dictamen sobre reformas del arancel general presentado al congreso por sus comisiones de hacienda y comercio unidas. Mexico, 1824.
Dictamen de la comisión de hacienda [del senado] sobre reforma del arancel provisional de aduanas marítimas. Mexico, 1826.
Dictamen de la comisión primera de hacienda de la cámara de representantes del congreso general de la federación mexicana sobre arreglo de aranceles para las aduanas marítimas. Mexico, 1827.

Dictamen de la comisión primera de hacienda de la cámara de diputados sobre prohibición de géneros toscos de algodón y lana. Mexico, 1829.

Dictamen de la comisión de industria de la cámara de diputados sobre el nuevo arbitrio
para dar un grande aumento a la hacienda federal, para proporcionar al mismo
tiempo ocupación y medios de subsistir a la clase de gentes pobres de la república
mexicana. Mexico, 1829.

Dictamen de las comisiones unidas de hacienda, comercio, agricultura, y artes de la
honorable legislatura de Puebla sobre el nuevo arbitrio que proponen el C. José María
Godoy, Guillermo Dollar, y Jorge Winterton. Mexico, 1829.

Segundo dictamen de la comisión de industria sobre el proyecto de Godoy y compañía.
Mexico, 1829.

Dictamen de la comisión de industria sobre prohibición de hilazas y tejidos de algodón del
estrangero. Presentado en la cámara de diputados el día 27 de marzo de 1835. Mexico,
1835.

Dictamen de las comisiones primera de hacienda, de comercio, y de industria de la cámara
de diputados sobre formación de nuevo arancel para las aduanas marítimas y fronterizas. Mexico, 1845.

Dictamen de la comisión especial de aranceles del senado sobre las reformas acordadas
por la cámara de diputados. Mexico, 1849.

2. Executive branch

a. National authorities

(1) Presidential papers

Informes y manifiestos de los poderes ejecutivo y legislativo de 1821 a 1904. 3 vols. Mexico,
1905.

A collection of addresses made at the opening and closing sessions of the legislature
by the president of the Republic and the spokesman of the Congress. Occasionally useful
for indicating the chief executive's attitude on such matters as tariffs, laissez-faire, and
manufacturing industry.

(2) Ministry reports

Ministerio de lo Interior. Memoria. Mexico, 1838.
Ministerio de Justicia e Instrucción Pública. Memorias. 2 vols. Mexico, 1844 — 1845.
Secretaría de Hacienda. Memorias. 28 vols. Mexico, 1822 — 1846, 1913.
Secretaría de Relaciones Esteriores e Interiores. Memorias. 12 vols. Mexico, 1823 — 1835,
1847.

These are the reports of the Finance Ministry and of the several ministries that had
jurisdiction over domestic economic affairs in the period of the study. The reports were
presented more or less on an annual basis, and contain valuable tables and appendices.
The Finance Ministry, in addition to its report cited above, was the source of the following
publications:

Balanza general del comercio marítimo por los puertos de la república mexicana. 1825 —
1828. 4 vols. Mexico, 1827 — 1831.

Informe presentado al exmo. señor presidente de los estados unidos mexicanos por el
contador mayor, gefe de la oficina de rezagos, Juan Antonio de Unzueta, en cumplimiento de la comisión que le confirió S. E. para que le manifestase el manejo y estado
que guardó la hacienda pública en los años de 1830, 1831 y 1832. Mexico, 1833.

Memoria sobre reformas del arancel mercantil que presenta el secretario de hacienda al
soberano congreso constituyente leída en sesión de 13 de enero de 1824. Mexico
[1824].

Suplemento del comercio marítimo que se hizo por algunos puertos en el año de 1825 y fue
omitido en la Balanza general del citado año. . . . [Mexico, 1828.]

(3) Separate agency reports

Banco de Avío. "Informe y cuentas . . . ," January 1, 1832, *Memoria de la secretaría de . . .*
relaciones interiores y exteriores. Appendix, 16 – 28. Mexico, 1832.

————. "Informe y cuentas . . . ," December 31, 1832, *Memoria de la secretaría de . . . rela-*
ciones interiores y exteriores. Appendix, 1 – 15. Mexico, 1833.

————. "Informe y cuentas . . . ," January 1, 1835, *Memoria de la secretaría de . . . rela-*
ciones interiores y exteriores. Appendix, 19 – 33. Mexico, 1835.

————. "Relación circunstanciada de las habilitaciones dadas por el Banco de Avío . . .
hasta el fin de julio de 1837," *Memoria del ministerio de lo interior.* Appendix 1.
Mexico, 1838.

————. *Informe y cuentas que el Banco de Avío presenta . . . redactado por el ciudadano*
José María Cosío y Pino, secretario de la junta directiva del mismo banco. Mexico,
1841.

These five reports constitute an invaluable supplement to the manuscript materials on
the Banco de Avío. They are especially useful for the early years when the officials
observed the legal requirement of presenting an annual accounting. The report for the
year ending December 31, 1833, was prepared but never published.

Dirección General de la Industria Nacional. *Memoria sobre el estado de la agricultura e*
industria. . . . *1843 – 1845.* 3 vols. Mexico, 1843 – 1846.

The most valuable printed source for understanding the progress and problems of
the textile and other industries in the years after 1837.

b. State authorities

Durango. *Memoria que el escmo. sr. gobernador del estado de Durango . . . presentó al*
honorable congreso el día 2 de agosto de 1831. Durango, 1831.

Durango. *Memoria en que el gobierno del estado de Durango da cuenta al H. congreso de la*
marcha de la administración pública en el año de 1847. . . . Victoria de Durango, 1848.

Guanajuato. *Memoria que presenta el gobernador . . . del estado de los negocios públicos*
. . . desde 10 de mayo de 1824 hasta 31 de diciembre 1825. [Guanajuato,] 1826.

Jalisco. *Memoria sobre el estado actual de la administración pública.* . . . Guadalajara, 1829.

Jalisco. *Memoria . . . del estado de Jalisco.* . . . Guadalajara, 1832.

Jalisco. *Informe sobre el estado actual de la administración pública del estado de Jalisco.*
. . . Guadalajara, 1835.

Mexico. Estado Libre de. *Memorias.* 7 vols. Mexico, Tlálpam and Toluca, 1826 – 1835.

Oaxaca. *Exposición que el vicegobernador en ejercicio del supremo poder egecutivo del*
estado hizo . . . el 2 de julio de 1831. Oaxaca, 1831.

Oaxaca. *Esposición que el tercer gobernador del estado hizo . . . el 2 de julio de 1832.*
Oaxaca, 1832.

Occidente. *Esposición sobre el estado actual del estado de Occidente.* Guadalajara, 1829.

Occidente. *Memoria presentada por el secretario del gobierno . . . del estado de Occidente.*
Guadalajara, 1829.

Puebla. *Memoria presentada al congreso*. [1826, 1827, 1830.] 3 vols. Puebla, 1826 — 1830.

Veracruz. *Memoria presentada por el gobierno del estado libre de Veracruz . . . en primero de enero de 1832*. Jalapa [1832].

These documents varied in value, but several provided interesting data on economic conditions in their respective states.

3. Other printed documents.

Alamán, Lucas. *Documentos diversos* (inéditos y muy raros) 3 vols. Colección de grandes autores mexicanos, Rafael Aguayo Spencer, comp. Mexico, 1945 — 1946.

This series contains all the reports presented by Alamán as minister of relaciones and as director-general of industry.

Barrio Lorenzot, Francisco del. *El trabajo en México durante la época colonial. Ordenanzas de gremios de la Nueva España*. . . . Mexico: Secretaría de Gobernación, 1920.

Bases de organización política de la república mexicana. Mexico, 1843.

Elhuyar, Fausto de. *Memoria sobre el influjo de la minería en la agricultura, industria, población, y civilización de la Nueva España*. . . . Madrid, 1825.

Estadística del estado libre y soberano de Veracruz. Cuaderno primero que comprende los departamentos de Orizava y Veracruz, y la memoria del Gobierno. Cuaderno segundo que comprende los departamentos de Acayucan y Jalapa. 2 vols. Jalapa, 1831.

Estatutos generales de la sociedad mexicana de industria agrícola y fabril . . . aprobados por el supremo gobierno con fecha 31 de octubre de 1828. Mexico, 1829.

Fonseca, Fabián de and Urrutia, Carlos de. *Historia general de real hacienda escrita . . . por orden del virrey, conde de Revillagigedo*. 6 vols. Mexico, 1845 — 1853.

Galván Rivera, Mariano. *Calendario manual y guía de forasteros para el año de 1832*. Mexico, 1832.

Great Britain. Parliament. *Parliamentary Papers*, vol. 39 (1842). "Return relating to the Trade of the United Kingdom with Mexico, and Number and Tonnage of Vessels employed; from the Year 1820 to the latest Account."

Guía de la hacienda de la república. 3 vols. Mexico, 1826 — 1828.

Humphreys, Robert A. ed. *British Consular Reports on the Trade and Politics of Latin America 1824 — 1826*. Camden Third Series, Vol. 53. London: Royal Historical Society, 1940.

Instrucciones que los virreyes de Nueva España dejaron a sus sucesores. Mexico, 1867.

La libertad del comercio en la Nueva España en la segunda decada del siglo XIX. Archivo Histórico de Hacienda, no. 1. Mexico, 1943.

México, Secretaría de Relaciones Exteriores. *Funcionarios de la secretaría de relaciones desde el año de 1821 a 1940*. Mexico, 1940.

Nota estadística remitida por el gobierno supremo del estado de Jalisco . . . año de 1826. Mexico, 1826.

Nota estadística remitida por la legislatura de Tabasco a la cámara del senado del soberano congreso. . . . N.p., 1826.

Present State of Mexico, The. London, 1825.

Proyecto de bases de organización para la república mexicana presentado a la honorable junta nacional legislativa por la comisión nombrada al efecto. Mexico, 1843.

Proyecto de constitución que presenta al soberano congreso constituyente la mayoría de su comisión especial. Voto particular de la minoría. Mexico, 1842.

Relaciones estadísticas de Nueva España de principios del siglo XIX. Archivo Histórico de Hacienda, no. 3. Mexico, 1944.

Revillagigedo, Conde de. *Instrucción reservada que el Conde de Revilla Gigedo dió a su sucesor en el mando Marqués de Branciforte sobre el gobierno de este continente en el tiempo que fué su virrey.* Mexico, 1831.

Rodríguez de S. Miguel, Juan. *La república mejicana en 1846 o sea directorio general de los supremos poderes y de las principales autoridades, corporaciones y oficinas de la nación.* Mexico, 1845.

Secretaría de la Economía Nacional. *Documentos para la historia económica de México.* 11 vols. Mimeographed. Mexico, 1933 — 1936.

Segura, Vicente. *Apuntes para la estadística del departamento de Orizava . . . en el año de 1826.* Jalapa, 1831.

Webster, Charles Kingsley, ed. *Britain and the Independence of Latin America 1812 — 1830. Select Documents from the Foreign Office Archives.* 2 vols. London: Oxford University Press, 1938.

C. Pamphlets: memorials, polemical tracts, projects

The importance of pamphlet literature in understanding the period can not be overestimated. The following items were found chiefly in the extensive collections belonging to the Biblioteca Nacional in Mexico City, and the Yale and Texas Universities.

Acta de la junta celebrada por los fabricantes de esta ciudad secundando los votos emitidos en 13 del actual por la de los fabricantes de México. Puebla, 1848.

Aldazoro, Santiago. *Exposición presentada a la cámara de diputados solicitando dispensa del pago de réditos por cinco años del capital que reconoce al Banco de Avío.* Mexico, 1841.

Algunas consideraciones económicas (sobre protección a la industria). Mexico, 1836.

A los habitantes del estado de Puebla. Su Congreso constituyente. Puebla, 1825.

Antuñano, Estevan de. *Acción productora de riqueza material. Emblema que representa el sistema industrial de México.* Puebla, 1844.

————. *Ampliación y corrección a los principales puntos del manifiesto sobre el algodón manufacturado y en greña.* Puebla, 1833.

————. *Breve memoria del estado que guarda la fábrica de hilados de algodón Constancia Mexicana y la industria de este ramo.* Puebla, 1837.

————. *De las clases productoras: su influencia sobre la riqueza, población, ilustración y espíritu público.* [Puebla, 1838.]

————. *Discurso analítico de algunos puntos de moral y economía política de Méjico con relación a su agricultura o sea pensamientos para un plan para animar la industria mejicana.* Puebla, 1834.

————. *Documentos para la historia de la industria algodonera de Méjico en lo fabril y en lo agrícola.* Puebla, 1843.

————. *Documentos para la historia de la industria moderna de México.* Mexico, 1845.

————. *Economía política en México.* [Puebla, 1841.]

————. *Economía política en México. Apuntes para la historia de la industria de algodones de México. Pensamientos patrióticos, sentimentales del que subscribe.* [Puebla, 1842.]

————. *Economía política en México. Documentos clásicos para la historia de la industria moderna.* Mexico, n.d.

————. *Economía política en México. Exposición respetuosa que el que subscribe dirige a las augustas cámaras de la nación.* [Puebla, 1839.]

———. *Economía política en México. Proposición. Mientras la generalidad del pueblo mexicano no se halle útil y honestamente ocupada, México no podrá ser bien regido por leyes muy benignas.* Puebla, 1839.

———. *Economía política. Refutación que el que subscribe hace, por notas, del artículo editorial del Monitor de Veracruz de fecha 25 de agosto, sobre importación de algodones extranjeros en rama.* Puebla, 1840.

———. *Insurrección industrial.* Puebla, 1846.

———. *Insurrección industrial. Economía política en México. Documentos para la historia de la industria moderna.* Puebla, 1846.

———. *Insurrección industrial: segunda época: año undécimo.* [Puebla, 1845.]

———. *Manifiesto sobre el algodón manufacturado y en greña.* Puebla, 1833.

———. *Memoria breve de la industria manufacturera desde el año de 1821 hasta el presente. . . .* [Puebla, 1835.]

———. *¡¡¡Mexicanos!!! El primer asunto de la patria. Insurrección para la independencia industrial fabril de México, Economía política en México. Documentos para la historia de la industria moderna de México.* [Puebla, 1845.]

———. *Opiniones demostrativas sobre el bloqueo de Francia a México por lo adverso y favorable, presente y futuro para la reputación, erario, e industria de México.* Puebla, 1838.

———. *Pensamientos para la regeneración industrial de México.* Puebla, 1837.

———. *Raciocinios para un plan para repeler noblemente la importación de algodones extranjeros, en cualquiera forma, por el desenvolvimiento violento de la industria nacional de la misma especie.* [Puebla, 1840.]

———. *Reflecsiones sobre el bloqueo y el erario de México.* Puebla, 1838.

———. *Teoría fundamental de la industria de algodones de México.* Puebla, 1840.

———. *Ventajas políticas, civiles, fabriles, y domésticas, que por dar ocupación también a las mujeres en las fábricas de maquinaria moderna que se está levantando en México, deben recibirse.* Puebla, 1837.

Antuñano, Estevan de, y Gumesindo Saviñón. *Esposición respetuosa que los que subscriben elevan a las soberanas cámaras de la unión sobre la prohibición de artefactos gordos de algodón estrangeros.* Puebla, 1835.

Apuntamientos sobre la necesidad de promover el cultivo del azúcar y otros frutos por medio de providencias que faciliten su extracción, y hagan necesarios y útiles en los mismos frutos los retornos del comercio exterior. Mexico, 1822.

Azcué y Zalvide, Pedro. *Contestación a los editores del Sol y del Registro o sea Observaciones sobre el Banco de Avío.* [Mexico, 1831.]

Bases para la formación de una junta protectora de la industria en la capital del estado de San Luis Potosí. San Luis Potosí, 1831.

Cancelada, Juan López. *Ruina a la Nueva España si se declara el comercio libre con los extrangeros.* Cadiz, 1811.

Certamen científico que el nacional y más antiguo colegio de S. Ildefonso de México dedica a su antiguo alumno el Ciudadano Guadalupe Victoria. Mexico, 1825.

Clamor de los artesanos o sea de los ciudadanos. [Guadalajara,] 1827.

Consideraciones sobre la situación política y social de la república mexicana en el año 1847. Mexico, 1848.

Contestación a la nota dirigida por la Junta de colonización e industria a la de industria de esta capital. Puebla, 1848.

Contestación que el supremo gobierno de Jalisco da al exmo. señor ministro de relaciones

sobre su comunicación fecha 6 de noviembre a serca del levantamiento de prohibiciones de los hilados y tegidos estrangeros de algodón. Guadalajara, 1849.

Corral, Juan José del. *Esposición acerca de los perjuicios que ha causado al erario de la
república y a su administación, el agiotaje sobre sus fondos y reflexiones sobre los
medios de remediar aquellos males.* Mexico, 1834.

Cuestión importantísima para la nación mexicana. [Mexico, 1839.]

Dirección de Colonización e Industria. *Documentos . . . sobre proyecto de levantar las
prohibiciones del arancel de aduanas marítimas.* Mexico, 1848.

Dirección General de Industria. *Representación dirigida al supremo gobierno . . . contes-
tando a lo que ha expuesto la junta de Puebla sobre proveer de algodón a las fábricas
de la república.* Mexico, 1843.

*Discurso pronunciado por el exmo. Sr. Gobernador al cerrarse las sesiones del honorable
congreso.* [Puebla, 1826.]

*Discusión habida en la sala de sesiones del honorable congreso de la Puebla sobre el
proyecto del Ciudadano José María Godoy y compañía.* N.p., 1829.

Economía interesante para la nación mexicana. [Guadalajara, 1826.]

*Ecsamen de la esposición dirigida al congreso por el general D. Mariano Arista pidiendo se
lleven a efecto las contratas que tiene celebradas para la introducción por el puerto de
Matamoros de efectos prohibidos.* Mexico, 1841.

Editores del Diario del Gobierno, Los. *Reflecsiones sobre la prohibición de hilazas y
mantas extranjeras de algodón.* Mexico, 1835.

Escritura de asociación y reglamento de la compañía de industria en Tlálpam. Mexico,
1837.

Escudero, José Agustín. *Respuesta que da un chihuahuense a la vigésima-nona pregunta de
las que en 15 de diciembre de 1830 circuló la dirección del banco de avío para fomento
de la industria nacional.* Mexico, 1831.

*Esposición dirigida al congreso de la nación por los fabricantes y cultivadores de algodón
leída en la cámara de diputados.* Mexico, 1841.

Estatutos de la sociedad económica de amantes del país de Chiapas. Puebla, 1821.

*Exposición con que la comisión nombrada para la reforma del arancel de las aduanas
marítimas y fronterizas dió cuenta al gobierno supremo del plan que siguió en el
cumplimiento de su encargo.* Mexico, 1845.

[Gálvez, Manuel]. *Examen de los fundamentos de la proposición del señor diputado D.
Manuel Alas publicada en el Siglo XIX . . . por el secretario de la Dirección General de
Industria.* Mexico, 1845.

*Gestiones de la junta de industria de Puebla con motivo del artículo que publica el Monitor
Republicano de 28 de noviembre sobre solicitudes para relajación de las leyes prohibitivas.* N.p., 1846.

[Godoy, Juan Ignacio]. *Explicación de los estados que la ciudad de Puebla remitió a México
para impugnar el proyecto del ciudadano Godoy.* Mexico, 1829.

———. *Exposición que se dirige no a la cámara sino en particular a cada uno de los señores
diputados presentando sólo hechos de los más notables, y pocos para no fastidiar.*
Mexico, 1829.

Gómez Pedraza, Manuel. *A los diputados del congreso de Puebla.* [Puebla, 1824.]

Horrorosa crueldad del obraje de Posadas. Mexico, 1826.

*Idea de la Sociedad Patriótica formada en este capital del estado de Puebla para fomento de
las artes. Año de 1831.* Puebla, 1831.

Informe dado por el establecimiento de minería a la comisión de industria del congreso general o sea Historia de las contribuciones impuestas y franquicias concedidas al cuerpo de mineros desde el año de 1521 hasta el de 1836, para deducir lo que más pueda fomentar los adelantos de tan importante ramo. Mexico, 1836.

Informe dirigido a S. M. por el consulado y comercio de esta plaza en 24 de julio sobre los perjuicios que se originarían de la concesión del comercio libre de los extrangeros con nuestras américas. Cadiz, 1811.

Iniciativa que el exma. junta departamental de México eleva al soberano congreso pidiendo no se aprueben los contratos celebrados por el general Arista para importar a la república la hilaza extrangera. Mexico, 1841.

Iniciativa que la h. legislatura del estado de Puebla dirige al congreso de la unión pidiendo se desheche la que le pasó el ministerio de hacienda el día 2 del actual sobre relajación de las leyes protectoras de la industria. Puebla, 1848.

Iniciativa que la legislatura de Querétaro dirige al augusto congreso sobre que no relajen las leyes prohibitivas que protegen la industria nacional. Querétaro, 1846.

Iniciativa que la legislatura de Querétaro dirije al congreso de la unión pidiendo que se reprueben las proposiciones que hizo el sr. diputado Azcue en la cámara de representantes en la sesión del 17 [sic] de agosto del presente año. Querétaro, 1831.

Intereses de la Puebla de los Angeles bien entendidos. [Puebla, 1821.]

Irazabel, Rafael de. Discurso primero que en apoyo del anterior dictamen . . . pronunció el día 5 de mayo de 1835. . . . [Mexico, 1836.]

[Jáuregui, José María]. Discurso en que se manifiesta que deben bajarse los réditos a proporción del quebranto que hayan sufrido en la insurrección los bienes y giros de los deudores. [Mexico,] 1820.

Landa, Carlos de. Sobre el sistema prohibitivo como contrario al interés nacional bien entendido o sea Refutación de las ideas del Siglo Diez y Nueve. Mexico, 1843.

Los males de la república y el modo de esterminarlos o sea Plan de expulsión contra coyotes y estrangeros. Guadalajara, 1831.

María Campos, Antonio de. Economía política de Méjico contestación a Don Carlos de Landa sobre comercio libre. Puebla, 1844.

Observaciones contra la libertad del comercio exterior, o sea Contestación al Diario del gobierno federal. Puebla, 1835.

Observaciones sobre la cuestión suscitada con motivo de la autorización concedida al General Arista para contratar la introducción de hilaza y otros efectos prohibidos en la república. Mexico, 1841.

Ortíz de la Torre, Manuel. Discurso de un diputado sobre la introducción de efectos estrangeros. Mexico, 1823.

Pacheco, J. R. Apéndice al Testamento del Año de 1839 (Contestación al Mosquito de 14. de febrero). Mexico, 1840.

———. El testamento del año de 1839. Mexico, 1840.

Piña y Cuevas, Manuel. Satisfacción al público del administrador de la aduana marítima de Matamoros. Matamoros, 1841.

El primer interés de Puebla. N.p., 1845.

Proyecto que para la organización de la compañía industrial promovida por el supremo gobierno presenta la comisión encargada de formarla. Mexico, 1830.

Quintana Roo, Andrés. Informe del apoderado de los acreedores a los fondos del establecimiento de minería. Mejico, 1834.

Quirós, José María. Ideas políticas económicas de gobierno. Memoria de instituto formada por . . . secretario de la junta gubernativa del consulado de Veracruz. Veracruz, 1821.

————. *Memoria de estatuto. Idea de la riqueza que daban a la masa circulante de Nueva España sus naturales producciones en los años de tranquilidad y su abatimiento en las presentes conmociones.* Veracruz, 1817.

————. *Memoria de instituto en que se manifiesta que el comercio marítimo . . . de España con las Américas ha contribuido entre diversas causas a la ruina de su población, agricultura, e industria.* Havana, 1814.

————. *Voz imperiosa de la verdad y desengaños políticos contra preocupaciones vulgares.* Mexico, 1810.

Representación al supremo gobierno de los empresarios de fábricas nacionales de hilados y tegidos de algodón. Mexico, 1840.

Representación de la junta de industria de Puebla y dictamen del exmo. consejo de gobierno del estado al exmo. sr. gobernador con motivo de las pretensiones para que se reformen las leyes que protejen la industria nacional. Puebla, 1846.

Representación de la sociedad de artesanos y comerciantes dirigida al soberano congreso de la unión. Guadalajara, 1828.

Representación del ayuntamiento de esta capital en defensa de la industria agrícola y fabril de la república. Mexico, 1841.

Representación del exmo. ayuntamiento de la capital de Puebla, al soberano congreso general. Puebla, 1836.

Representación dirigida al escmo. señor presidente de la república por la junta de industria de Puebla a fin de que se queme el algodón introducido clandestinamente. Puebla, 1843.

Representación que a favor del libre comercio dirigieron al excelentísimo señor Don Juan Ruiz de Apodoca . . . doscientos veinte y nueve vecinos de la ciudad de Veracruz. Havana, 1818.

Representación que el exmo. ayuntamiento de la capital del estado de Puebla, eleva a la augusta cámara del senado en favor de las leyes prohibitivas, protectoras de la industria agrícola y fabril. Puebla, 1848.

Representación que el exmo. ayuntamiento de la capital del estado de Puebla, eleva al soberano congreso general contra la iniciativa del exmo. señor ministro de hacienda sobre la introducción de hilazas y tegidos de algodón estrangero. Puebla, 1848.

Representación que el ilustre ayuntamiento de la ciudad de Cholula, eleva a la augusta cámara de senadores, en favor de las leyes prohibitivas, protectoras de la industria agrícola y fabril. Puebla, 1848.

Representación que la diputación provincial de Puebla hizo al soberano congreso en 12 de agosto de 1823. [Mexico, 1823.]

Representación, que los artesanos de algodón, y algunos ciudadanos de Puebla, dirigen al exmo. sr. presidente, a efecto, de que no se conceda a Santa Anna de Tamaulipas, el ser puerto de depósito. . . . Puebla, 1837.

[Solís, Diego]. *Específico y único remedio de la pobreza del imperio mexicano.* Guadalajara, 1822.

El tejedor poblano y su compadre, Plática familiar entre éstos y un aprendiz. Puebla, 1820.

Willie, Robert C. *México, noticia sobre su hacienda pública bajo el gobierno español y después de la independencia.* Mexico, 1845.

D. Periodical materials

The most useful collections were those of the Library of Congress, supplemented by the University of Texas Library, and the Hemeroteca Nacional, the special periodicals library of the Biblioteca Nacional, Mexico City.

1. Official gazettes (chronologically arranged)

Gaceta Imperial de México, 1821 — 1822.
Gaceta del Gobierno Imperial de México, Jan. 2 — Mar. 31, 1823.
Gaceta del Gobierno Supremo de México, Apr. 1, 1823 — May 31, 1825.
Gaceta Diaria de México, June 1, 1825 — Apr. 30, 1826.
Registro Oficial del Gobierno de los Estados Unidos Mexicanos, Jan. 22, 1830 — Jan. 10, 1833.
El Telégrafo, Periódico Oficial del Gobierno de los Estados Unidos Mexicanos, Jan. 11, 1833 — Feb. 9, 1835.
Diario del Gobierno de los Estados Unidos Mexicanos, 1835 — 1846.

These organs were of considerable value for their coverage of legislative debates, and for the texts of official orders, reports, and so on. After 1830, the gazette was used increasingly as a propaganda instrument by the party in power. The editorials, although they reflect the official view, do provide a key to the major issues of the day.

2. Newspapers

El Águila Mexicana (Mexico), 1823 — 1829.
El Amigo del Pueblo (Mexico), 1827 — 1828.
Los Amigos del Pueblo (Mexico), 1831 — 1832.
La Antorcha (Mexico), Apr. 1 — July 1, 1833.
    A proclerical paper.
El Astro Moreliano (Morelia), Apr. 2 — Mar. 29, 1830.
El Atleta (Mexico), Dec. 29, 1829 — May 8, 1830.
El Cardillo de los Agiotistas (Mexico), Apr. — May, 1837.
    The five issues of this paper were devoted to condemning the speculators in government debt.
Correo de la Federación (Mexico), 1828 — 1829.
    The voice of the Yorkino party and of Lorenzo de Zavala.
El Correo Semanario Político y Mercantil (Mexico), 1810.
    Contains useful data on cotton prices before the breakdown of authority.
El Cosmopolita (Mexico), 1835 — 1843.
    A leading federalist journal; conducted exposé of Banco de Avío "mismanagement" in 1837 — 38.
El Demócrata (Mexico), 1833 — 1834.
    Avid supporter of liberal reform attempt.
El Farol (Puebla), 1821 — 1822.
    Conservative, antirepublican paper.
El Federalista (Mexico), Jan. 5 — Feb. 2, 1831.
    Critical of industrial program.
El Fénix de la Libertad (Mexico), 1831 — 1834.
    Upholder of laissez-faire views, critical of government aid to manufacturing industry.
Gazetas de México. Compendio de Noticias de Nueva España. 1784 — 1809.
    Useful for statistics on domestic trade.
El Indicador de la Federación Mejicana (Mexico), 1833 — 1834.
    Liberal paper; Dr. José Mora a leading contributor.
El Iris (Mexico), 1837 — 1840.
La Lima (Mexico), 1834 — 1839.
    Conservative but independent journal.

El Mercurio Poblano (Puebla), 1843 — 1845.

El Mosquito Mexicano (Mexico), 1835 — 1836.

El Observador Mexicano (Mexico), June 6, 1827 — Jan. 2, 1828, Mar. 3 — Oct. 27, 1830.
Liberal paper; opposed to protective tariffs.

La Oposición (Mexico), Feb. 3 — May 27, 1835.
Liberal, federalist paper.

El Poblano (Puebla), Feb. 25 — May 13, 1827.

El Reformador (Toluca), 1833 — 1834.

El Siglo XIX (Mexico), 1845.

El Sol (Mexico), 1821 — 1832.
Useful for coverage of legislative debates.

El Zurriago. Periódico Científico, Literario e Industrial (Mexico), Aug. 27, 1839 — Jan. 25, 1840.

3. Other periodicals

Boletín del Instituto Nacional de Geografía y Estadística. Epoca 2. 9 vols. Mexico, 1852 — 1873.
Contains a number of valuable articles on population and economic conditions.

El Mosáico Mexicano. 7 vols. Mexico, 1840 — 1842.

Registro Trimestre o Colección de Memorias de Historia, Literatura, Ciencias y Artes. 2 vols. Mexico, 1832 — 1833.
The quarterly supplement of the official gazette.

Revista Económica y Comercial. Mexico, 1843.
An antiprohibitionist periodical published by Carlos Landa.

Semanario Artístico para la Educación y Progreso de los Artesanos. Nos. 1 — 78, Mexico, 1844 — 1846.
Published by the junta de fomento de artesanos en México, this weekly was intended to elevate the general and technical knowledge of its readers.

Semanario de la Industria Mexicana. Tomo 1, cuadernos 1 — 24; Tomo 2, cuadernos 1 — 11.
[Mexico, 1841 — 1842.]
Published by the manufacturers' association, the junta de fomento de la industria, this weekly was used as a medium to keep members informed and to exert pressure on the government. It contains statistics on textile factories and the texts of executive orders of interest to manufacturers.

E. Memoirs and travel accounts

Beaufoy, Mark. *Mexican Illustrations.* London: Carpenter and Son, 1828.

Becher, Carl Christian. *Mexiko in den ereignissvollen Jahren 1832 und 1833 . . . nebst mercantilischen und statistischen Notizen.* Hamburg: Perthes & Besser, 1834.

Beltrami, Giacomo Constantino. *Le Mexique.* 2 vols. Paris: Crevot, 1830.

Bocanegra, José María. *Memorias para la historia de México independiente.* 2 vols. Mexico: Impr. del gobierno federal, 1892 — 1897.

Bullock, W. *Six Months Residence and Travels in Mexico.* 2d. ed. 2 vols. London: John Murray, 1825.

Bustamante, Carlos. *Apuntes para la historia del gobierno del General D. Antonio López de Santa Anna, desde principios de octubre 1841 hasta 6 de diciembre de 1844.* Mexico: J. M. Lara, 1845.

———. *El gabinete mexicano durante el segundo período de la administración del exmo. Señor Presidente D. Anastasio Bustamante.* 2 vols. Mexico: J. M. Lara, 1842.

Byerle, John. *Le Mexique en 1823.* 2 vols. Paris, 1824.

Calderón de la Barca, Frances Erskine Inglis. *Life in Mexico during a Residence of Two Years in that Country.* 2 vols. 1843. Revised ed. Garden City, N.Y.: Doubleday, Anchor Book, 1970.

D'Orbigny, Alcide. *Voyage Pittoresque dans les Deux Amériques.* Paris, 1836.

Dos años en México o Memorias críticas sobre los principales sucesos de la República. . . . Escritos por un español. Valencia: Cabrerizo, 1832.
    An excellent and impartial review of the years 1829 – 1832.

Filisola, Vicente. *Memorias para la historia de la guerra de Tejas.* 2 vols. in 1, Mexico: I. Cumplido, 1848 – 1849.

[Folsom, George]. *Mexico in 1842.* New York: C. J. Folsom, 1842.

Gilliam, Albert. *Travels over the Tablelands and Cordilleras of Mexico during the years 1843 and 1844.* Philadelphia: J. W. Moore, 1846.

Hall, Basil. *Extracts from a Journal written on the Coasts of Chile, Peru, and Mexico in the years 1820, 1821, 1822.* 3d. ed. 2 vols. Edinburgh: A. Constable and Co., 1824.

Hardy, Robert William Hall. *Travels in the Interior of Mexico in 1825, 1826, 1827 and 1828.* London: H. Colburn and R. Bentley, 1829.

Humboldt, Alexander von. *Political Essay on the Kingdom of New Spain.* Translated by John Black. 4 vols. London: Longman, Hurst, Rees, Orme and Brown, 1811.
    The classic work of the European scientist and traveler; contains considerable data on the textile industry as of the turn of the century.

Löwenstern, Isidore. *Le Mexique, souvenirs d'un voyageur.* Paris: A. Bertrand, 1843.

Lyon, George Francis. *Journal of a Residence and Tour in the Republic of Mexico in the Year 1826.* 2 vols. London: J. Murray, 1828.

Mayer, Brantz. *Mexico As It Was and As It Is.* 3d. ed. Baltimore: W. Taylor & Co., 1846.
    Contains a sympathetic sketch of the textile industry.

———. *Mexico, Aztec, Spanish and Republican.* 2 vols. Hartford: S. Drake & Co., 1851.

Mexicanische Zustände aus den Jahren 1830 bis 1832 (Eduard Widenmann and Herman Hauff, eds. *Reisen und Länderbeschreibungen,* 10, 13). Stuttgart: J. G. Cotta, 1837.

Mühlenpfordt, Eduard. *Versuch einer getreuen Schilderung der Republik Mejico.* 2 vols. Hanover: C. F. Kius, 1844.

Niles, John Milton. *A View of South America and Mexico.* 2 vols. in 1. New York: H. Huntington, Jr., 1826.

Pacheco, J. R. *Lettres sur Le Mexique.* Bordeaux: C. Lawalle Neveu, 1833.

Payno, Manuel. "Un Viage a Veracruz en el invierno de 1843, carta 4ª, *"El Museo Mexicano"* 3 (1843).
    Important for its discussion of the Banco de Avío's origin.

[Perdreauville]. *Lettres sur Le Mexique . . . par un citoven de la Nouvelle-Orleans.* New Orleans, 1827.

[Poinsett, Joel. R.] *Notes on Mexico Made in the Autumn of 1822.* Philadelphia: H. C. Carey and I. Lea, 1824.

Prieto, Guillermo. *Memorias de mis tiempos 1828 a 1840.* Paris and Mexico: Vda de C. Bouret, 1906.

Richthofen, Emil K. H. *Die ausseren und inneren politischen Zustände der Republik Mexico.* Berlin: W. Hertz, 1859.
    Provides a review of industrial progress.

Rivero, Luis Manuel del. *Mégico en 1842*. Madrid: D. E. Aguado, 1844.

A Sketch of the Customs and Society of Mexico in a Series of Familiar Letters and a Journal of Travels in the Interior. London: Longman & Co., 1828.

Suárez y Navarro, Juan. *Historia de México y del General Antonio López de Santa Anna*. 2 vols. Mexico: I. Cumplido, 1850 – 1851.

Thompson, George Alexander. *Narrative of an Official Visit to Guatemala from Mexico*. London: J. Murray, 1829.

Thompson, Waddy. *Recollections of Mexico*. New York: Wiley and Putman, 1846.
Contains useful data on the textile industry.

Tudor, Henry. *Narrative of a Tour of North America; Comprising Mexico, the Mines of Real del Monte, the United States, and the British Colonies*. 2 vols. London: J. Duncan, 1834.

Ward, Henry George. *Mexico*. 2d. ed. 2 vols. London: Colburn, 1829.

Zavala, Lorenzo de. *Ensayo histórico de las revoluciones de Mégico desde 1808 hasta 1830*. 2 vols. Paris: P. Dupont, 1831 – 1832.
Valuable for reflecting the views of a leading political figure on the liberal side.

II. Secondary sources

Alamán, Lucas. *Historia de México*. 2d. ed. 5 vols. Mexico: V. Agüero y Comp., 1883 – 1885.
This work contains little on the author's personal efforts to promote industry.
Volume 1 does, however, contribute data on the industrial scene prior to 1810.

Alatriste, Oscar. "El capitalismo británico en los inicios del México independiente." *Estudios de Historia Moderna y Contemporánea de México* 6 (1977): 9 – 41.

Argüello Castañeda, Francisco. *Problemas económicas de algodón*. Mexico: Compañía Exportadora e Importadora Mexicana, 1946.

Arrangoiz, Francisco de Paula de. *Méjico desde 1808 hasta 1867*. 4 vols. Madrid: A. Perez Dubrull, 1871 – 1872.
The viewpoint in this work is that of the conservative party; it is essentially concerned with political history.

Aubry, Henry G. "Deliberate Industrialization." *Social Research* 16 (1949): 158 – 82.

Baines, Edward. *History of the Cotton Manufacture in Great Britain*. London: H. Fisher, R. Fisher and P. Jackson, 1835.

Bancroft, Hubert Howe. *History of Mexico*. 6 vols. San Francisco: A. L. Bancroft & Co., 1883 – 1888.
Still the most comprehensive work in English, but like most of the older general histories, its treatment of economic topics is sparse.

Baz, Gustavo and Gallo, Eduardo L. *History of the Mexican Railway*. Translated by G. F. Henderson. Mexico: Gallo & Co., 1876.

Bazant, Jan. "Estudio sobre la productividad de la industria algodonera mexicana en 1843 – 1845." In *La Industria nacional y el comercio exterior (1842 – 1851)*, pp. 29 – 85. Mexico: Banco Nacional de Comercio Exterior, 1962.

———. "Evolución de la industria textil poblana (1554 – 1845)." *Historia Mexicana* 13, no. 4 (April – June, 1964): 473 – 516.

———. "Industria algodonera poblana de 1803 – 1843 en números." *Historia Mexicana* 14, no. 1 (July – Sept. 1964): 131 – 43.

Bosch García, Carlos. *Problemas diplomáticos del México independiente*. Mexico: El Colegio de México, 1947.

Butterfield, Carlos. *United States and Mexican Mail Steamship Line, and Statistics of Mexico*. New York: J. A. H. Hasbrouck & Co., 1859.

Callcott, Wilfrid H. *Church and State in Mexico 1822 – 1857*. Durham, N.C.: Duke University Press, 1926.

———. *Santa Anna*. Norman: University of Oklahoma Press, 1936.

Chávez Orozco, Luis. *Historia de México (1808 – 1836)*. Mexico: Editorial Patria, 1947.

A highly readable account by a pioneer economic historian.

———. *Historia económica y social de México*. Mexico: Ediciones Botas, 1938.

An earlier presentation of many of the ideas offered in the work previously cited.

———. "Lucas Alamán Una Faceta." *Cuadernos Americanos* 10 (1943): 159 – 79.

Clark, Victor S. *History of Manufactures in the United States*. 2 vols. Washington, D.C.: Carnegie Institution, 1916 – 1928.

Cline, Howard F. "The Aurora Yucateca and the Spirit of Enterprise in Yucatan, 1821 – 1847." *Hispanic American Historical Review* 27 (1947): 30 – 46.

Cosío Villegas, Daniel. *Historia de la política aduanal*. La Cuestión Arancelaria en México, No. 3. Mexico: A Mijares, 1932.

A brief sketch based on an analysis of the general tariff laws.

———. "La riqueza legendaria de México." *El Trimestre Económico* 6 (1939): 58 – 83.

Cue Canovas, Agustín. *Historia social y económica de México. La Revolución de independencia y México independiente hasta 1854*. Mexico: Editoria América, 1947.

Delgado, Ricardo. *Las primeras tentativas de fundaciones bancarias en México*. Guadalajara: Hernández y Hernández, 1945.

A series of brief sketches on banking institutions from 1782 to 1865.

Díaz Dufoo, Carlos. *México y los capitales extrangeros*. Paris: La V^{da} de C. Bouret, 1918.

Diccionario universal de historia y de geografía. 10 vols. Mexico: Rafael and J. M. Andrade y F. Escalante, 1853 – 1856.

Dickens, Samuel N. "Cotton Regions of Mexico." *Economic Geography* 14 (1938): 363 – 71.

Estep, Raymond. "The Life of Lorenzo de Zavala," Ph.D. dissertation, University of Texas, 1942.

Fisher, Lillian. *The Background of the Revolution for Mexican Independence*. Boston: Christopher, 1934.

Flores Caballero, Romeo. *La contrarevolución en la independencia. Los españoles en la vida política, social y económica de México 1804 – 1838*. Mexico: El Colegio de México, 1969.

———. "Del libre cambio al proteccionismo," *Historia Mexicana* 19, no. 4 (Apr. – June 1970): 492 – 512.

Foster, Alice. "Orizava—a Community in the Sierra Madre Oriental." *Economic Geography* 1 (1925): 356 – 72.

Fox, John S. "Antonio de San José Muro, Political Economist of New Spain." *Hispanic American Historical Review* 26 (1941): 410 – 16.

García Cubas, Antonio. *Diccionario geográfico, histórico y biográfico de los Estados Unidos Mexicanos*. 5 vols. Mexico: Murguía, 1888 – 1891.

González Navarro, Moisés. *El pensamiento político de Lucas Alamán*. Mexico: El Colegio de México, 1952.

Harris, Helen W. "The Public Life of Juan Nepomuceno Almonte." Ph.D. dissertation, University of Texas, 1935.

Keremitsis, Dawn. *La industria textil mexicana en el siglo XIX*. Mexico: Secretaría de Educación Pública, 1973.

Lavallée, Felix. "Etudes historiques sur Le Mexique au point de vue politique et social d'après des documents originaux mexicaines." *Revue des Races Latines* (Paris), 1859.

Leduc, Alberto and Lara y Pardo, Luis. *Diccionario de geografía, historia y biografía mexicanas*. Mexico: V^da de C. Bouret, 1910.

Lerdo de Tejada, Miguel. *Comercio exterior de México desde la conquista hasta hoy*. Mexico: Rafael Rafael, 1853. Reprint. Mexico: Banco Nacional de Comercio Exterior, 1967.

————. *Cuadro sinóptico de la república mexicana en 1856*. Mexico: Ignacio Cumplido, 1856.

Lobato, Ernesto. *El crédito en México*. Mexico: Fondo de Cultura Económica, 1945.
Contains a chapter on the Banco de Avío.

McCaleb, Walter P. *Present and Past Banking in Mexico*. New York: Harper & Brothers, 1920.

Macedo, Pablo. *La evolución mercantil. Comunicaciones y obras públicas. La hacienda pública; tres monografías que dan idea de una parte de la evolución económica de México*. Mexico: J. Ballescá, 1905.

Mendizabel, Miguel Othon de. *Obras completas*. 6 vols. Mexico, 1946 – 1947.
A series of essays on a variety of subjects. Of special interest was the one entitled "Las artes textiles en México" which examines in detail the cloth industry from prehispanic to modern times.

Mora, José María Luis. *Méjico y sus revoluciones*. 3 vols. Paris: Rosa, 1836.
The unfinished magnum opus of the liberal theoretician. An advocate of laissez-faire and unrestricted trade, Mora was naturally critical of the efforts to foster industry.

————. *Obras sueltas*. 2 vols. Paris: Rosa, 1837.
Contains several papers of interest to the economic historian.

Naredo, José M. *Estudio geográfico, histórico y estadístico del cantón y de la ciudad de Orizaba*. 2 vols. Orizaba: Imprenta del Hospicio, 1898.

Ortiz de Ayala, Tadeo. *Resumen de la estadística del imperio mexicano*. Mexico: Herculana del Villar, 1822.

————. *México considerado como nación independiente y libre*. Bordeaux: C. Lawalle Sobrino, 1832.
A good discussion of the economic problems facing the country, and a plea for minimum restrictions on internal and external trade.

Otero, Mariano. *Ensayo sobre el verdadero estado de la cuestión social y política que se agita en la república mexicana*. Mexico: I. Cumplido, 1842.

Palavacini, Felix, et al. *México, historia de su evolución constructiva. . . .* 4 vols. Mexico: Editorial Libro, 1945.

Prieto, Guillermo. *Indicaciones sobre el origen, vicisitudes y estado de las rentas generales de la federación mexicana*. Mexico: I. Cumplido, 1850.
Useful for its analysis of tariff regulations.

Quintana, Miguel A. *Estevan de Antuñano fundador de la industria textil en Puebla*. 2 vols. Mexico: Secretaría de Hacienda y Crédito Público, 1957.

————. "Papel histórico de Puebla en el progreso industrial de la Nueva España y de México." *Revista de la Universidad de Puebla* 1 (1944): 35 – 61.

Ramírez, José F. *Noticias históricas y estadísticas de Durango*. Mexico: I. Cumplido, 1851.

Raso, Antonio de. "Notas estadísticas del departamento de Querétaro." *Boletín del Instituto Nacional de Geografía y Estadística* 3 (1852): 169 – 236.

Reed, W. B. "Foreign Relations of Mexico," *North American Review* 32 (1831): 317 – 43.

Riva Palacio, Vicente, ed. *México a través de los siglos*. 5 vols. Mexico: J. Ballescá, 1887 – 1889.

Rivera Cambas, Manuel. *Historia antigua y moderna de Jalapa y de las revoluciones del estado de Veracruz.* 5 vols. Mexico: I. Cumplido, 1869 – 1871.

Robles, Gonzalo. *La industrialización en Iberoamérica.* El Colegio de México, Centro de Estudios Sociales, Jornadas, 17. Mexico: El Colegio de México, 1944.

———. "Noticia sobre la industrialización de México," *El Trimestre Económico* 11 (1944): 256 – 83.

A rapid survey of industrial activities from pre-Aztec time to the present.

Rives, George Lockhart. *The United States and Mexico.* 2 vols. New York: Charles Scribner's Sons, 1913.

Roll, Erich. *A History of Economic Thought.* New York: Prentice-Hall, 1946.

Romero, Matías. *Geographical and Statistical Notes on Mexico.* New York: G. P. Putnam's Sons, 1898.

Ruiz y Sandoval, Alberto. *El algodón en México.* Mexico: Secretaría de Fomento, 1884.

Segura, Manuel de. "Apuntes estadísticos del distrito de Orizava formados el año de 1839." *Boletín del Instituto Nacional de Geografía y Estadística* 4 (1854): 3 – 70.

Septien y Villaseñor, José A. *Memoria estadística del estado de Querétaro.* Querétaro: González y Legarreta, 1875.

Sierra, Justo. *Evolución política del pueblo mexicano.* 2d ed. Mexico: La Casa de España, 1940.

———, ed. *Mexico: Its Social Evolution.* 2 vols. in 3. Mexico: J. Ballescá, 1900 – 1904.

A group of studies on various aspects of Mexican development translated into English. Some of the component parts were published separately, for example, Sierra's own contribution cited above, and Pablo Macedo's, also above. Of particular interest for the present study was the section by Carlos Díaz Dufoo entitled "Indus-

Silva Herzog, Jesús. "Las ideas económicas en México de 1821 a 1855." *Cuadernos Americanos* 13 (1947): 166 – 90.

———. *El pensamiento económico en México.* Mexico: Fondo de Cultura Económica, 1947.

Smith, Robert S. "José María Quirós: Balanza del Comercio Marítimo de Veracruz e Ideas Económicas." *El Trimestre Económico* 12 (1947): 680 – 711.

———. "Shipping in the Port of Veracruz 1790 – 1821." *Hispanic American Historical Review* 23 (1943): 6 – 20.

Sparks, Jared. "Gold and Silver in Mexico." *North American Review* 21 (1825): 429 – 43.

Turlington, Edgar. *Mexico and Her Foreign Creditors.* New York: Columbia University Press, 1930.

Valadés, José C. *Alamán estadista e historiador.* Mexico: José Porrua e Hijos, 1938.

Wythe, George. "The Rise of the Factory in Latin America." *Hispanic American Historical Review* 25 (1945): 295 – 314.

Zamacois, Niceto. *Historia de Méjico desde sus tiempos mas remotos hasta nuestros dias.* 23 vols. Barcelona: J. F. Parres, 1878 – 1888.

Essentially a political and military history of limited value for an economic study.

III. Bibliographic aids and archival guides

Bolton, Herbert E. *Guide to Materials for the History of the United States in the Principal Archives of Mexico.* Washington: Carnegie Institution, 1913.

Borah, Woodrow. "Archivo de la secretaría municipal de Puebla: Guía para la consulta de sus materiales." *Boletín del Archivo General de Mexico* 13 (1942): 207 – 39, 423 – 64.

Castañeda, Carlos E. and Dabbs, Jack Autry. *Guide to the Latin American Manuscripts in the University of Texas Library.* Cambridge: Harvard University Press, 1939.

Clagett, Helen L. *A Guide to the Law and Legal Literature of the Mexican States.* Washington: The Library of Congress, 1947.

Economic Literature of Latin America. A Tentative Bibliography. 2 vols. Cambridge: Harvard University Press, 1935 – 1936.

Guía del Archivo Histórico de Hacienda Siglos XVI a XIX. Mexico: Secretaría de Hacienda y Crédito Público, 1940 –. Loose-leaf.

Handbook of Latin American Studies. Vols. 1 – 13. Cambridge: Harvard University Press, 1936 – 1951.

Iguíñiz, Juan B. "La Biblioteca Nacional de México." *Revista de Historia de América,* no. 8 (April 1940), pp. 57 – 86.

Jones, Cecil K. *A Bibliography of Latin American Bibliographies.* 2d. ed. Washington: Library of Congress, 1942.

Ker, Annita Melville. *Mexican Government Publications. A Guide to the More Important Publications of the National Government of Mexico, 1821 – 1936.* Washington: Library of Congress, 1940.

Invaluable for the present study. Its description of the titles and locations of legislative and executive publications made it possible to trace rare items in the libraries of the United States and Mexico.

Millares Carlo, Agustín. "El Archivo de Notarías del Departamento del Distrito Federal (México, D.F.)." *Revista de Historia de América,* no. 17 (June 1944), pp. 69 – 118.

Still useful for its chronological index of the notaries whose papers comprise the historical section of the archive.

Rubio Mañé, J. I. "El Archivo General de la Nación." *Revista de Historia de América,* no. 9 (August 1940), pp. 63 – 189.

Secretaría de Hacienda y Crédito Público. *Bibliografía, 1821 – 1942.* Mexico, 1943.

Secretaría de la Economía Nacional. *Publicaciones oficiales.* Mexico, 1943.

Secretaría de Relaciones Exteriores. *Bibliografía de la secretaria. . . .* by Gabriel Saldivar. Mexico, 1943.

Spain and Spanish America in the Libraries of the University of California. 2 vols. Berkeley: University of California Press, 1928 – 1930.

Vance, John T., and Clagett, Helen. *A Guide to the Law and Legal Literature of Mexico.* Washington: The Library of Congress, 1945.

INDEX

Index

Munuera, Col., 69 n.26

Napoleonic Wars, 10, 40
Neri del Barrio, Felipe, 98, 117 n.3, 152
New Jersey, 55
Nuevo León, 55

Oaxaca, 4 n.13, 6 – 7, 27, 55; and foreign textile imports, 85, 87 n.17, n.19, 129
Obrador. See Handicraft industries
Obrajes. See Textile industry, pre-independence
Ojo de Agua factory, 160 n.55
Orizaba, 94 – 95, 146 n.2, 148 – 49, 152 n.27, 155 – 60
Otero, Mariano, 167

Pacheco, J. R., 88, 121, 124
Packenham, Richard, 152
Paper mills, 22 – 23, 26, 124; and Banco de Avío, 55, 65, 65 n.11, 68 n.22, 81, 88 – 89, 88 n.21, 95, 105, 108 – 10, 122
Pardo, Ramón, 91, 93 n.44, 94, 106 – 7, 107 n.35, 121, 124
Paredes, Mariano, 144
Parral, 59 n.37, n.38
Payno, Manuel, 45, 45 n.25
Payno y Bustamante, José Manuel, 45 n.26, 46
Peñasco, Count of, 52
Pennsylvania, 55
Peñon Blanco, 160 n.55
Pesado, José Joaquín, 100 – 101
Pizarro, Andrés, 117 n.3, n.6
Poder Conservador, 132
Political crises, 72 – 73, 93 – 94, 131 – 32, 134 – 35, 153
Pope Gregory XVI, 160
Portú, Manuel, 117 n.3
Potash, Robert A., 174 n.30
Prieto, Antonio, 91, 121, 124
Prohibitions, import, 24 – 25, 28, 30 – 32, 36 – 37, 140 – 41, 144. *See also* Tariff legislation
Promotor fiscal del Juzgado de Hacienda, 104, 110
Puebla, 23, 26 n.61, 44, 81, 127 – 28; as handicraft textile center, 4, 6 – 9; opposes foreign textile imports, 25 n.57, 32 – 36, 38, 85, 87 n.17, n.19, 133 n.32; site of new textile factories, 58 n.35, 59 n.37, n.42, 60 n.43, 146 n.1, 147 – 50, 153, 157 – 59

Puebla Glass Company, 118 n.9, 121, 124
Puebla Hospicio. *See Hospicio de Pobres de Puebla*
Puebla Industrial Company, 68
Puig, Francisco, 67, 70, 119, 121, 124

Querétaro, 3 – 4, 6, 22, 51 n.41, 133 n.32; and establishment of textile mills, 73, 108, 148, 157, 159, 160 n.55
Querétaro Industrial Company, 59 n.37, 71, 73, 83, 108, 124; relations with Banco de Avío, 66 – 68, 70 n.28, n.29, 83, 92, 121
Quirós, José María, 7

Randall, Robert, 169
Rayón, Ramón, 52, 64 – 65, 79, 90
Real Consulado (Merchant Guild), 53
Real de señoraje, 13
Registro Oficial, 54, 54 n.18
Registro Trimestre, 54 n.18
Relations Minister, 44 – 45, 47 – 48, 52, 72, 80 – 82, 92, 100 n.14
Religious holidays, 160, 160 n.60
Revenues, import, 14, 19, 24, 39, 131, 131 n.21. *See also* Customs revenues
Revillagigedo, Viceroy, 3, 54, 54 n.15
Reyes Heroles, Jesús, 167, 167 n.3
Roa, Victoriano: as Banco de Avío official, 53, 90, 97 – 100, 102; as borrower, 81, 81 n.41, 88, 94, 94 n.47, 106, 121; as factory owner, 78 – 81, 124, 146 n.1
Road building, 22
Rubio, Cayetano, 119, 121, 124, 142 n.84, 152, 152 n.33, 160 n.55
Ruiz, Luis, 129 n.11; and bank loan, 91, 94, 94 n.47, 105, 121, 124

Sáinz de Baranda, Pedro, 146, 146 n.4, 147 n.5
Sales tax. *See Alcabala*
Samudio, José Faustino, 115 n.62, 121, 124
San Andrés Tuxtla, 59 n.37, 60 n.43
San Angel, 22 – 23
San Blas, 10, 54, 144
Sánchez, Pascual, 63, 64, 69 n.26, 70 n.28, 121, 124
Sánchez Navarro, 171
Sánchez y Mora, José Mariano, 52, 108
San Juan de Ulúa, 16 n.22
San Luis Potosí, 51 n.41, 52, 59 n.37, 108, 171
San Miguel, 3, 6, 59, 59 n.37
San Miguel Industrial Company, 68 n.20